THE LOUVRE

THE

LOUVRE

BY

GERMAIN BAZIN

CONSERVATEUR-EN-CHEF
DU MUSÉE DU LOUVRE

LONDON
THAMES AND HUDSON

TRANSLATED FROM THE FRENCH BY M. I. MARTIN

© THAMES AND HUDSON 1957 — LONDON
SECOND EDITION 1959 · REVISED AND CORRECTED 1962
PRINTED IN GERMANY BY CARL SCHUNEMANN
THIS BOOK IS PUBLISHED IN FRANCE BY
EDITIONS AIMERY SOMOGY PARIS

CONTENTS

On the right, a detail from the *Reredos of the Paris 'Parlement'* (by a Flemish master working in Paris about 1460. Inventory: R. F. 2065).

The view of the Louvre in the background of this picture seems to be a faithful representation. The castle is quadrilateral in shape, flanked by double towers. The high roofs of the pavilion crown the main part of the building constructed by Charles V; the conical roof of the keep *(donjon)* appears behind the tower in the corner. On the left is the 'Corner Tower' of the enclosure of Charles V skirting the Seine; on the right, the Hôtel du Petit Bourbon.

THE LOUVRE

FOREWORD

THIS BOOK, an anthology of the most famous paintings in the Louvre, is intended as a work of reference. Also, the notes which accompany the hundred colour reproductions provide information on the history of the work concerned, the circumstances of its creation, and its life prior to its acquisition by the Louvre, rather than a subjective appreciation of the painting. The introductory essay briefly retraces the history of the collections of paintings assembled in the Louvre, in relation to that of the palace which now houses them. This history has never been written—at least, in its present form; the booklet published by the Musées Nationaux in 1930 (*Histoire des collections de peinture du Musée du Louvre,* with texts by Gaston Brière, Louis Hautecœur, Gabriel Rouchès and Madame Clotilde Brière-Misme) was divided up according to schools. The present work is an attempt to give a brief general history of the formation of the Louvre collection of paintings, from its origins to the present time; the impressionist collections have been omitted, however, since these have been dealt with in a separate work.

No effort has been spared to ensure that all the information in this book is accurate, to the best of the author's belief, though it would be presumptuous to claim that this has been achieved. The history of French art collections in general, of those of the Louvre in particular, has only been studied in a fragmentary fashion; most writings on the subject rely on the works of eminent cataloguers or historians such as Villot, Reiset, Engerand, or Bonnaffé. These men did a great deal to clear the ground, and were indeed remarkable for their time, but closer investigations have now revealed the gaps in their knowledge; and subsequent writings and catalogues have all too often repeated and even amplified their inaccuracies and errors of interpretation, their uncritical acceptance of legends and traditions.

9

I have myself, in previous writings, sometimes been too ready to accept unquestioningly the authority of the written word. For this short introduction, however, I have consulted with caution the published material, and in particular have benefited from the recent researches of Madame Christiane Aulanier, Mademoiselle Adeline Hulftegger, MM. Claude Ferraton and Jean Adhémar, and notes collected by the Service de Documentation of the Département des Peintures under the direction of Madame Jean Adhémar, the head of this department.

Scholars who may pick up this book will find that the usual historical apparatus of notes and references is missing; but it was felt that this would have discouraged the general reader, for whom the work is intended.

Now that the virgin soil of history has become buried beneath such an accumulation of exegeses, the seeker after truth has no option but to return to the sources. The history of the paintings in the Louvre can only be fully revealed if a team of research workers, freed from the constraints of routine museum work, can devote themselves to a methodical examination of the archives, setting aside everything that has hitherto been written on the subject, pending its verification. Meanwhile, perhaps those familiar with the galleries of the Louvre may learn from this brief and provisional synthesis something of the continuous effort which has built up this incomparable collection, in spite of changing tastes and fashions and the vicissitudes of peace and war; for more than four hundred years the various systems of government which France has experienced have all contributed to this effort, and have helped to bring about the creation of the most complete collection of works from all the great European Schools, from primitives to moderns, ever to be assembled under one roof.

GERMAIN BAZIN

THE COLLECTIONS OF THE FRENCH CROWN

MAKING HIS WAY down the Grande Galerie, the visitor to the Louvre is struck by the majestic air of two royal portraits. That of Francis I, by Titian, in the gallery, seems to be contemplating *La Gioconda*; at the far end Rigaud's Louis XIV surveys in royal fashion the long lines of masterpieces. Most of the pictures in this gallery owe their presence there to these two princes, who resembled each other in having a similar conception of the function of royalty. For both of them, the monarch was not only a political power, responsible for keeping at bay the enemies of the kingdom, for extending its frontiers, and for ensuring order and prosperity within it; it was his duty to be first in all things, a true *princeps*, the perfect example of the hero on which all his courtiers should try to model themselves, without ever hoping to equal him. A favoured lover, a victorious general, a protector of Arts and Letters—the king must be a man of universal attainments; Francis I was such a man; so, later, was Louis XIV. But this ideal was even more completely realized in Francis than in Louis; the latter belonged to that baroque world in which men organized their lives according to a conception which they formed of themselves, and he played the part of royalty as an actor of genius might have done. The men of the Renaissance, however, were still swayed by the vehement instincts of the preceding age; for all their refinement, they obeyed the impulses of the vital spark, and lived their life, not acted it. It is this conviction which gave its conquering drive to the civilizing process. Federico da Montefeltre, the most cultivated man of the Quattrocento, was a *condottiere*. His most redoubtable enemy, Francis I, was not to be content with merely vanquishing him in painting, as Louis XIV did later on the ceiling of his gallery at Versailles. The king's armour was no mere parade costume; he fought heroically at Marignan and Pavia, sword or lance in hand, rallying his men, scattering his enemies, always in the thick of the fighting and pursuing victory or death.

Francis I's 'modern' character, his 'Renaissance' spirit, is revealed in his high regard for painting. Thanks to the patient efforts of Florence, painting had become the major form of artistic expression during the years around 1500, even surpassing sculpture, which at one time had dictated its trend, but which, apart from Michelangelo, produced no new men of genius[1]. Perhaps the supremacy of painting was due to the fact that, more than any of the other arts, it was capable of imitating real appearances; on account of this power, Leonardo placed it in the forefront of all human activities. Francis I wished to adorn his palaces with masterpieces by Italian artists, the idealism of whose works so clearly proclaimed their liberation from the old mediaeval restrictions.

Francis was the first, in the whole of northern Europe as well as in France, who fully appreciated the value of the new aesthetics. Earlier kings had indeed owned collections of works of art, but these were simply a part of the royal treasure, the 'garde-robe'. At the beginning of the fifteenth century, however, France had possessed a most liberal patron of the arts in the person of the Duc de Berry. Entirely for the sake of the pleasure they gave him, he accumulated paintings, tapestries, illuminated manuscripts, Persian miniatures and antique intaglios, Oriental fabrics, coins and medals, in the various châteaux whose appearance has been recorded in the *Très Riches Heures* by the Limbourg brothers. He was indeed the type of person that Robert Estienne was to call a century later, in his Franco-Latin dictionary (1531), a 'curieux'–a word the latter translated as *'antiquarius'*, defining it as 'un homme curieux d'avoir ou savoir choses antiques'. But the Duc de Berry was also a true Maecenas, commissioning artists to produce illuminated manuscripts – those masterpieces of combined genius and patience. His brother Charles V also loved books, but more as a scholar than as a biblio-

---

[1] Except for Venice, which evolved along its own lines.

phile. Charles VI, Charles VII and the austere Louis XI enjoyed far less luxurious surroundings than the Dukes of Burgundy, who were, in their own fashion, Renaissance princes; the Kings of France at this period still lived in a mediaeval setting. There was indeed a *cabinet* of some kind at Amboise in the sixteenth century, but it contained a collection of arms and historical relics such as were popular with feudal overlords – and with well-to-do *bourgeois* as well, if we are to believe the description of Jacques Duché's Paris house written in the early fifteenth century by Guillebert de Metz.

Amboise witnessed the first manifestations of the new ultramontanism, after the return from the Naples expedition. But the famous statement of the wages paid to Italian workmen in 1497 and 1498 shows that Italy had influenced customs even more than taste; everything Italian was considered the height of fashion. Travellers' tales, exaggerated as usual, increased the general admiration for anything coming from the other side of the Alps. Anne of Beaujeu, the Regent, would have been overjoyed if Lorenzo de Medici could have been persuaded to give her his giraffe. The barons who took part in the first Italian expedition did not on the whole go further than this naïve delight; any Renaissance masterpiece entering France at this time usually did so through some noble Italian family. Mantegna's *Saint Sebastian*, for example (bought by the Louvre from the municipality of Aigueperse in 1910), must have been brought into the country in 1481, when the Comte de Montpensier married Clara di Gonzaga. A little later Fra Bartolommeo's *Mystical Marriage of Saint Catherine* (painted in 1511 – acquired by the Louvre in 1800) was given by the Signoria of Florence to Louis XII's ambassador Jacques Hurault, who presented it to the cathedral of Autun.

Louis XII displayed a more cultivated taste than his cousin. At Milan, so great was his enthusiasm for Leonardo's *Last Supper*, recently painted in Santa Maria delle Grazie, that he wanted to have it detached from the wall and transported to France. There is ample evidence to show the admiration which this painting aroused amongst the French; Cardinal d'Amboise had a copy of it made for

13

his château of Gaillon; the Louvre owns another fine replica which Henry II's favourite, the Constable Anne de Montmorency, had in his chapel in the château of Ecouen. In 1948 a huge ruined fresco inspired by the famous *Cenacolo* was discovered on the wall of the refectory in the monastery of the Franciscan friars at Blois, who had also owned Solario's *Virgin with the Cushion*, now in the Louvre. Francis I had a version of the picture woven in tapestry at Fontainebleau, and presented Pope Clement VII with a copy which is still in the Vatican.

The first work by Leonardo to be seen in France was a *Virgin with a Spindle*, bought by the Secretary of State, Florimond Robertet, and now lost. This picture created a sensation when it arrived at court, and may have prompted Louis XII's determination to bring Leonardo to France. He expressed this desire in the most pressing terms to the Florence Signoria in 1507. In that same year he made his triumphal entry into Milan, and it was Leonardo who organized the celebrations in his honour at the Castello Sforzesco. Louis XII continued to patronize the artist, who received a royal pension from him, and was his military engineer on the Venice expedition of 1509. It has sometimes been thought that the *Virgin of the Rocks* (which the Cardinal of Aragon's secretary does not mention as being in Leonardo's studio in 1517) may have been brought back from Milan by Louis XII.

Francis I was more successful than Louis XII, and managed to persuade Leonardo to come to France. After the victory of Marignan (14 September 1515) the King of France was once more a power to be reckoned with in Italy; Leonardo was discouraged by the lack of appreciation shown to him in his own country, and was glad to accept the protection of His Most Christian Majesty. In 1516 Francis I provided him with a pension, and installed him in a pleasant house at Cloux, near Amboise. Leonardo's hand was paralysed, and he could no longer do much painting; but he advised the king on questions of engineering and architecture, and devised festivals for his amusement. He had brought with him a few of his favourite works; on 10 October 1517 he showed three pictures to the Cardinal of Aragon, who came to visit him. The Cardinal's

14

secretary, Antonio de Beatis, has left an account of the occasion; the pictures were a *Saint John the Baptist*, the *Saint Anne*, and a portrait of a woman—which must certainly be *La Gioconda*. Perhaps Francis I bought these pictures (and possibly others, including the *Bacchus* and the *Belle Ferronière*) after Leonardo's death, on 2 May 1519, from his executor Francisco Melzi; in spite of all efforts, it has not yet been discovered how these pictures entered the royal collection. According to Père Dan, writing in 1642, *La Gioconda* was bought by the king for 4,000 gold crowns; perhaps it was purchased from Leonardo himself. In any case, Vasari mentions it as being at Fontainebleau in 1550, and Paolo Giovio, writing in 1529, describes the *Saint Anne* as belonging to the King of France. The Crown also owned another work by Leonardo—a *Leda*; some seventeenth-century prince must have objected to what he considered its indecency, and it was destroyed. A number of early copies, and particularly a drawing by Raphael at Windsor, give some idea of the masterpiece so regrettably lost.

Leonardo's paintings are the most valuable in the Louvre; they are also the *incunabula* of the gallery. However, in 1518, before Leonardo's death, Francis I summoned to France Andrea del Sarto, who was later to behave so badly to him. The king already owned a Madonna by this Florentine artist, and later acquired from him a *Holy Family* and the well known *Charity*. The French crown received various works of art from Italy as diplomatic gifts, including antiques presented by the Venetian Republic and, above all, two paintings by Raphael—the large *Holy Family* and the large *Saint Michael*. These two pictures, painted in 1517 and 1518, were presented by Lorenzo de' Medici, Duke of Urbino, acting on behalf of Pope Leo X; so the attractive legend of the king and the artist trying to outdo each other in generosity over these two works is without foundation.

The portrait of *Joan of Aragon*, on which Raphael and Giulio Romano are believed to have collaborated, was probably given to the king by Cardinal Bibiena. Other Italian paintings also crossed the Alps into France—works by Perugino, Sebastiano del Piombo (the *Visitation*), Fra Bartolommeo (the *Annunciation*), and even by Michelangelo, if we are to believe that he painted the *Leda* at Fontainebleau which has so often been ascribed to him. However, this picture is more probably an adaptation of the painting by Rosso in the National Gallery, London. The King was particularly attracted by Rome and Florence, with which he had diplomatic relations; he seems to have disregarded Venice, whose situation linked her with the Holy Roman Empire. Charles V owned a number of works by Titian, whom he created a Count Palatine; Francis I only possessed a single portrait of himself by that artist, done from a medal, without any contact between artist and sitter.

The early Renaissance had made its appearance in France in the Loire valley; the royal châteaux of Blois and Chambord had been the first to adapt Italianate features, broadly interpreted, to the traditional French style of architecture. Moving nearer to his capital, Francis I decided in 1528 to build himself a residence which would remind him of the beauties of Italy. He chose Fontainebleau, near the forest of Bière, which was well stocked with game. The building itself was carried out by a French mason, Gilles Lebreton, and there was nothing particularly novel about it; indeed, it was of a somewhat rustic character, and less advanced in style than Blois and Chambord. But there was nothing, even in Italy, to match its sumptuous interiors, decorated by Rosso and Primaticcio; the stucco work was in advance of what was being done in Rome, Parma, Mantua or Florence. Works of art continued to arrive from Italy; since the king could not obtain possession of the famous antique sculptures

On the right, the *Portrait of King Francis I*. (Inventory: INV. 3256. Canvas. Height: 0.96 m., Width: 0.74 m. [37¾″ × 29″].)

This portrait seems to have been in the royal collection ever since its completion. Père Dan (*Trésors et Merveilles de Fontainebleau* 1642) describes it as in the Pavilion of Paintings at Fontainebleau, where Henry IV had ordered the paintings of the Château to be placed, including those from the bath-rooms. In 1731 it was still at Fontainebleau. In 1784 it was in the *Direction des Bâtiments* at Versailles. It was exhibited in the historical museum of Versailles in 1837, and transferred to the Louvre in 1848. Père Dan attributed this painting to 'Jeannet', a pseudonym used by both Jean and François Clouet. This attribution has often been questioned; very little is known of Jean Clouet's paintings.

16

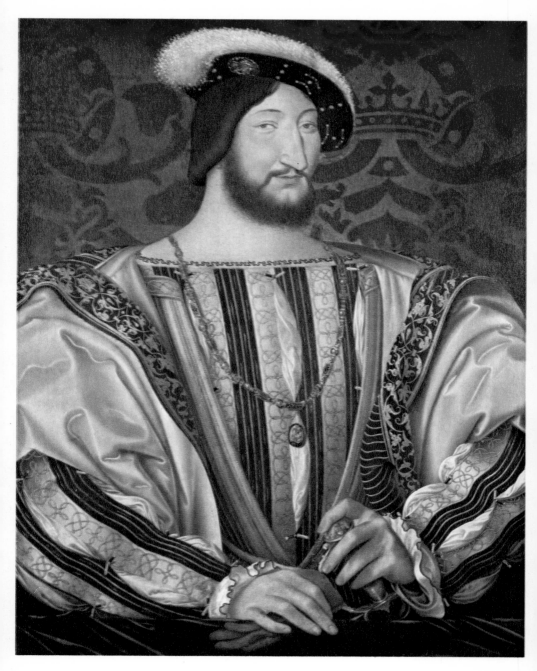

JEAN CLOUET · FRANCIS I

which had been discovered in Rome, he sent Primaticcio to have casts taken of them, and from these he had bronze replicas made to decorate his gardens. As for the Italian pictures brought by the king to this 'new Rome', they were not displayed in the galleries or the state apartments, or even in the private apartments, but oddly enough in the 'Chambres des Bains', installed between 1541 and 1542 beneath the Galerie des Réformés and only destroyed in the eighteenth century. There were baths there, and six retiring rooms where the pictures were arranged in decorative frames. When the king gave himself over to physical relaxation, therefore, he also sought refreshment of the mind, in looking at works by the great masters. Some pictures, however, were placed in the chapels; the *Visitation*, by Sebastiano del Piombo, in the lower chapel of Saint Saturnin, and Raphael's large *Holy Family* in the upper chapel.

The third stage of the Renaissance in France is marked by the reconstruction of the Louvre. On 2 August 1546 Francis I commissioned Pierre Lescot to erect a new building on the site of the old fortress built by Philippe Auguste, which Charles V had tried to embellish. Lescot's new wing was a correct and elegant application of Vitruvian principles – the first example of French classical architecture. The development of a French classicism out of antique basic principles was to take place under Henry II; to this monarch must go the credit for having carried out the project of Francis I, who died on 14 August 1547. The handsome façade which replaced the west wing of the old château was built in 1548. It was originally intended that this should be flanked by two simple galleries, but there was a change of plan, and a square château was envisaged, with four corner pavilions, exactly following the plan of the mediaeval fortress. French and Italian artists decorated the king's apartments in the Pavillon du Roi with fine wood-work, the remains of which were unfortunately removed to the Colonnade wing by Duban in 1850. In 1564 the Queen-mother, Catherine de Médicis, commissioned her favourite architect Philibert Delorme to build her a country residence a little way from the Louvre, just outside the city walls of Paris, on a spot known as the 'Tuileries'. In the following year she formed a plan for linking the Louvre and the Tuileries by means of a gallery, part of which would follow the line of Charles V's city wall along the river bank, and which would be connected with the Pavillon du Roi by a little gallery at right angles to it. In this she was following the example of what had been done in Florence in 1564 at the time of Francesco de Medici's marriage, when Vasari had joined the Uffizi and Pitti palaces by means of a gallery running across the Arno. Only the little gallery – later known as the Galerie d'Apollon – was undertaken by Catherine; the large one was carried out by Henry IV. Charles IX and Henry III continued the building of the Louvre as it had been envisaged by Francis I; but at some unknown date, probably before the death of Henry II, it was decided to embark on the 'grand dessein', an ambitious scheme which was to quadruple the area of the palace and link it with the Tuileries by means of two enormous wings, like the galleries with which Bramante had intended to join the Belvedere to the Vatican. The plan of the Louvre and the Tuileries – together with the Vatican and the Hermitage, the largest palace in the world – was already laid down, therefore, in the sixteenth century; three hundred years were needed to bring the colossus to completion. The slow progress of the work, constantly interrupted but always taken up afresh, is due to the fact that the Louvre was competing with the building of other royal palaces. Throughout its history it has been a dynastic work, to which each reign has brought its own contribution.

Did Henry II inherit his father's artistic tastes? It seems that in his day the naïve admiration for Italian masterpieces, presupposing a feeling of inferiority, was less exclusive than during the preceding reign. Assimilation of Renaissance principles brought about an awareness of a valid national art; the influence of Flemish and German artists, who had themselves profited by the example of Fontainebleau, came to counterbalance that of Italy. During this period, few foreign works of art seem to have been acquired by the royal collections. The new spirit of individualism, the problems of conscience set by protestantism and humanism, introduced a fashion for portraiture into France. Little pictures drawn or painted by

Jean Clouet or his son François, by Corneille de Lyon or by other artists whose names have not survived, accumulated in small rooms specially designed to contain them. Queen Catherine, who could 'esquicher et portraire elle-même' had several of these rooms in the private house she had built for her own use in Paris (later known as the Hôtel de Soissons), where the pictures were set in to the wood-work. It is this kind of presentation which I have tried to re-create in one of the rooms fitted up in the Louvre in 1953. In the *cabinet des émaux* in the Queen's house, there were thirty-two portraits displayed in company with thirty-nine Limoges enamels; the *cabinet des miroirs* contained eighty-three portraits and one hundred and nineteen Venetian mirrors.

It was probably not through indifference that Henry II left the masterpieces acquired by his father at Fontainebleau. Henry was very attached to Fontainebleau; no doubt he wished to respect his father's work in its entirety, and he undertook to complete it archi-tecturally. With its paintings by the great masters, its frescoes and stucco-work, its tapestries after designs by Giulio Romano (the car-toons for these were acquired by the crown in the time of Louis XVI, and are now in the Salon Carré), the casts after antique sculpture which adorn its parterres, and Benvenuto Cellini's famous Nymph, Fontainebleau was a kind of northern shrine of Italian art—a 'Rome of the North', as Vasari called it.

Under Henry IV, a measure of order was restored to the kingdom, after a shocking period of anarchy and civil war. This monarch followed an artistic policy which tended to renew the vitality of the French school, calling on foreign help where needed. What he chiefly required for his châteaux of Saint-Germain-en-Laye, Fontainebleau and the Louvre was not great works of art but good masons and decorators. He carried out a great deal of work on the Louvre; he completed the south wing of the Cour Carrée (begun by Henry II and Charles IX), finished the 'Petite Galerie', and made a definite advance in the progress of the 'grand dessein' by uniting the Louvre and the Tuileries, as Catherine de Médicis had planned. In 1595 the 'Grande Galerie' was begun by Jacques Audrouet du Cerceau and

Clément Métezeau; the building, running alongside the Seine for more than 480 yards, made rapid progress, and in 1606 the Dauphin was able to traverse the whole gallery from the Louvre to the Tuileries. In erecting this building, Henry IV was co-operating in the scheme to provide lodgings beneath the Grande Galerie for 'quantité de meilleurs ouvriers et plus suffisants maîtres que se pouvaient recouvrer tant de peinture, sculpture, orfèvrerie, orlogerie, insculpture en pierreries qu'aultres de plusieurs et excellens arts'. In these letters patent of 22 December 1602 lies the origin of the artists' lodgings and studios which continued to exist in the Louvre till the time of the First Empire. The king's intention, said Sauval, was to create 'a kind of nursery of craftsmen, trained by good masters, some of whom would later be dispersed throughout the kingdom, and who would be able to render great services to the country'. According to the same author, Henry IV also wanted to accommodate in the Louvre the greatest nobles in the kingdom, as well as the best artists, in order to establish an alliance between the aristocracy and the fine arts.

The Grande Galerie was simply a vast empty hall; the Petite Galerie, however, was full of portraits of past and present worthies, and formed a kind of historical museum, known as the 'Galerie des rois'. The kings were ranged along one side of it and the queens on the other, in between the windows; of this series, we still possess the solemn full-length portrait of *Marie de Médicis*, by Franz Pourbus the younger.

On the third floor of the Pavillon du Roi was the Grand Cabinet, where Henry IV gave audience; in it were kept all the various precious and rare objects and the souvenirs which the kings handed on to their successors. These formed a miscellaneous assembly of bronzes, goldsmiths' work, and curios, together with curiosities of natural history – the kind of collection which the Germans call a 'Wunderkammer'. Later, Louis XIII used to take refuge in this room during the hours of solitude which he loved; he was also fond of the *cabinet des armes* on the second floor of the same building.

As for the famous Italian masterpieces at Fontainebleau, it was observed that they were beginning to deteriorate in the unsuitable atmosphere of the Appartement des Bains on the ground floor, and they were moved to the first floor in the Pavillon du Fer à Cheval, which thus became known as the Pavillon des Peintures. But in order to preserve the décor of the Chambres des Bains as Francis I had created it, the original paintings were replaced by copies, of which some still exist at Fontainebleau—Michelin's copy of Raphael's large *Holy Family*, for example. It was decided to appoint a 'garde des tableaux' to look after these great paintings; and in 1608 Jean de Hoey of Utrecht, a painter of Dutch origin (a grandson on his mother's side of Lucas van Leyden) was put in charge of 'les peintures des vieux tableaux de Sa Majesté au château de Fontainebleau, tant pour rétablir ceux qui sont gastez, peints à l'huile sur bois ou sur toile, ensemble pour nettoyer les bordures des autres tableaux à fresque des chambres, salles, galeries, cabinets d'iceluy château'. When he died in 1615 he was succeeded by his son Claude, and Claude's son in his turn inherited the position from his father in 1660, and accompanied the collections when they were transferred to the Louvre. We are fairly well informed on the pictures which were at Fontainebleau in the seventeenth century, from two sources; in 1625 an Italian visitor to the château, Cassiano del Pozzo, left us an account of his visit, and in 1642 Père Dan described the Cabinet des Tableaux in his valuable work *Trésors et merveilles de Fontainebleau.*

Queen Marie de Médicis carried out various works in the interior of the Louvre, none of which has survived; she did not concern herself with the architectural progress of the building, being more interested in the erection of the Luxembourg palace for her own personal use. She summoned Rubens to decorate the latter palace for her; he may have been recommended by her sister, the Duchess of Mantua, as he had worked as official painter at that court, and possibly also by the Baron de Vicq, the Paris ambassador from the Low Countries, whose portrait by Rubens is in the Louvre. The Queen commissioned this artist to paint two galleries, one in honour of the late king, and one in her own honour. The latter was inaugurated on 11 May 1625, on the occasion of the marriage of

Louis XIII's sister, Henriette de France, and Charles I of England. In the last years of the *ancien régime*, when the palace became an appanage of the Comte de Provence, the twenty-one pictures were taken down and rolled up; they were exhibited there again in 1802, and in 1815 they were brought to the Louvre. They are one of the Museum's most splendid possessions. Unfortunately, the projected gallery in honour of Henry IV's exploits was never carried out, because of the Queen-mother's fall from favour; only sketches for it survive, and two unfinished paintings now in the Uffizi, Florence.

When Louis XIII began to reign in person, in 1624, he solemnly announced that he was going to resume work on the Louvre, which had been abandoned on the death of his father. The first stone of this new period of building activity was laid in the summer of 1624, and a medal was struck to mark the occasion. The architect was Pierre Lemercier. The quadrupling of the Cour Carrée, as planned in the time of Henry II, was now begun by extending Lescot's building for an equal distance beyond a pavilion with caryatids (the Pavillon de l'Horloge) which separated the old block from the new. Work continued on it throughout the reign, and Lemercier laid the foundations for the north-west corner pavilion of the north wing (bordering the Rue de Rivoli).

Louis XIII wanted to provide a worthy décor for the Grande Galerie, left undecorated during the preceding reign. Acting, no doubt, on the advice of Sublet des Noyers, the Surintendant des Bâtiments, he resolved to entrust this task to Poussin, who was then living in Rome, and whose reputation had crossed the frontiers into France. Monsieur de Chanteloup, who went to Rome for the special purpose of bringing Poussin back, managed to persuade him after much hesitation to accede to the royal request, and the artist arrived in Paris early in 1641. Gratified by the offer of a salary of 3,000 *livres*, received with honour and made director of all works carried out in the royal residences, Poussin prepared cartoons for paintings and

---

[1] Before his place was taken by Apollo, Hercules had been the symbol of royalty in Germany, Spain and Italy from the sixteenth century.

stucco work for a great decorative scheme representing the life of Hercules, who was accepted as a symbol of Louis XIII[1]. But in November 1642, driven to exasperation by Simon Vouet's scheming, and the airs of the Baron de Fouquière 'who only paints with his sword at his side', disgusted by court intrigues and at loggerheads with Lemercier over the distribution of the décor, Poussin fled to Rome, pleading anxiety on account of the health of 'his dearly-loved wife'. He left the work unfinished, promising to return; all that now remains of it are the drawings for the scheme, in the Cabinet des Dessins in the Louvre.

Louis XIII made a considerable contribution to the great work of building the Louvre, but he added little to the royal collections. The Queen, Anne of Austria, failed to take advantage of her connections with the Spanish court, and acquired no masterpieces by Velasquez —an artist unknown in France at that time, and not appreciated in that country till the eighteenth century. Among the portraits of her relations which the Queen kept in her Chambre des Bains, the best is that of the *Infanta Margarita*, now in the Grande Galerie; but this is only a studio work and not by Velasquez himself.

In the reign of Louis XIII it fell to Cardinal Richelieu to exercise the kingly privilege of patronage; and, with State funds, he amassed for his own benefit a collection which should have been assembled by the king. These works of art filled his Paris residence, the Palais Cardinal (now the Palais Royal), his château at Rueil, and the enormous château he built for himself in Poitou, near the town which bears his name. Before 1627, in which year most of the Gonzaga collection was sold to King Charles I of England, he secured for himself the fine series of paintings from Isabella d'Este's *Studiolo*, by Perugino, Mantegna and Lorenzo Costa. These were the gems of his collection in the château in Poitou; the Louvre acquired them when they were confiscated during the Revolution. It is not impossible that Richelieu arranged for this magnificent group of paintings to be offered to him by Vincenzo Gonzaga in 1624, when the latter was scheming with the French court to obtain the title of 'Altesse'. It emerges from the correspondence of the Duke's ambassador in Paris with his master that the Cardinal, 'grand curieux des peintures rares et qui en recherche partout', would be favourably influenced in the negotiations by the gift of a picture. Since the *Studiolo* was specifically excluded from the deal transacted with Charles I's representative in 1627, it may well be that by then Richelieu was already in possession of the pictures it had contained. In 1629 the Cardinal was in Piedmont, at Casal, to which he had just laid siege; there he bought Leonardo's *Saint Anne*, which must have ceased to belong to the Crown at some unknown date, probably as the result of a gift. In 1636 Richelieu bequeathed to the king the Palais Cardinal and all the treasures it contained—its pictures, its bronzes, and the famous chapel of goldsmiths' work. The king thus obtained a few additional masterpieces, notably a ceiling by Poussin (*Time Rescuing Truth from Discord and Envy*), later installed in the Grand Cabinet du Roi in the Louvre, Veronese's *Pilgrim at Emmaus*, and Leonardo's *Saint Anne;* also some works by contemporary Italian masters, particularly the Carracci.

During the second half of the seventeenth century in France, the passion for collecting and for dealing in curios was intensified; there was keen competition to obtain masterpieces, and speculation played its part. 'Pictures are as good as gold bars', wrote the Baron de Coulanges to Madame de Sévigné, in August 1675. 'There never was a better investment. You can sell them whenever you like, at twice

On the right, the *Portrait of Louis XIV, King of France.* (Inventory: INV. 7492. Canvas. Height: 2.79 m., Width: 1.90 m. [110″×94¾″]. Signed: Hyacinthe Rigaud et Sévin.)

The details of the circumstances surrounding the painting of this portrait in 1701 and 1702, originally intended for the Court of Spain, are well known. But the king was so pleased with this work which portrayed him with all the outward symbols of monarchial power, that he kept it for Versailles and had another sent to Madrid. Louis XIV was 63 years old when he sat for this painting.

It is probable that only the face of the king was painted from life. This canvas was later inlaid in a larger one, and finished in the studio with the help of Sévin de la Pennaye, who usually assisted Rigaud with the elaboration of costumes and accessories. He has, moreover, signed his name 'Sévin' on a book-mark, on the reverse of which Rigaud affixed his signature.

24

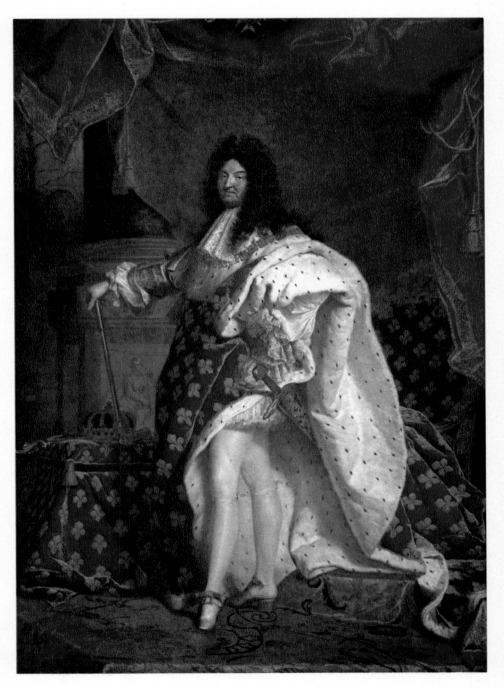

HYACINTHE RIGAUD · Louis XIV

what you gave for them.' According to J. Spon, in 1673, Paris possessed eighty-five important collections; in 1691, Blégny mentions one hundred and thirty-four 'fameux curieux parisiens' in his *Livre commode des adresses de Paris*. One of these 'curieux', Loménie de Brienne, wrote his memoirs, which provide a little account of collecting in that period.

The most ardent 'curieux' of all was undoubtedly Mazarin. Loménie de Brienne, who was the Cardinal's secretary, relates how, just before his death in 1661, he wandered about like a ghost amongst his collection, grieving: 'All must be left–how I have struggled to possess these things! ... Where I am going, I will never see them again!' He trafficked unceasingly in works of art, buying and, after selecting what he wanted out of the material reaching him from Italy, selling it again–even organizing public sales in a house specially rented for the purpose: the Hôtel d'Estrées. His collections included countless numbers of curios, as well as masterpieces of painting and sculpture; they were housed in his apartments in the Louvre and in the two fine galleries, upper and lower, which formed the famous 'Galerie Mazarine'. These are now part of the Bibliothèque Nationale; they were built round the Hôtel Tubeuf, which Mazarin had bought and which he commissioned Mansart to alter. When the Cardinal fled, driven away by the Fronde, his collections and library were sold by auction; and a decree of the Parlement in December 1651 even arranged that the sum promised as a reward to whoever handed over Mazarin, alive or dead, should be provided out of the proceeds of his sales.

However, the interests of the Cardinal (who lived in style, even during his exile) were secretly safeguarded in Paris by his secretary Colbert; a certain number of items from his collection were saved and restored to him.

In 1650 Mazarin, having got wind of the breaking-up of Charles I's collection in England, commissioned Everhard Jabach (who was travelling to that country) to buy some works for him. Cromwell's government did indeed commit the great error of selling the king's collection–the finest to have been assembled in the first half of the seventeenth century. Charles' first acquisition had been the purchase in 1627 of most of the masterpieces in the Gonzaga collection at Mantua. This group of paintings and sculpture must have been the richest Renaissance collection in existence; it had been amassed by the uninterrupted efforts of a family who had patronized the arts and letters for more than a hundred years, from the end of the fifteenth century. Luigi and his wife Barbara of Brandenburg employed Mantegna, who also worked for Francesco, husband of Isabella d'Este, a princess always anxious to possess fine paintings. Guglielmo, the protector of Palestrina, had added to the collection; finally Vincenzo I (1587–1612), patron of Rubens and of Monteverde (and who had *Orfeo* staged on 24 February 1617 in the Accademia dei Invaghati) had a gallery built to house these works, and added a number of treasures such as Caravaggio's *Death of the Virgin*. But their love of festivities, horses and works of art finally brought ruin to this extravagant family. The last duke of the Italian branch, Vincenzo II,[1] whose biographer describes him as 'a worm of a man, rather than a prince', only reigned a few months – but long enough to sell this collection, the finest in Italy, to Charles I of England, through the intermediary of the merchant Daniel Nys.

All Europe benefited from Charles I's sale, but the best part of his collection came to France, thanks to the financier Everhard Jabach and to Cardinal Mazarin who shared the spoils when it was dispersed between 1649 and 1653. The sales were carried on in a friendly fashion, by negotiation; Jabach bought without counting the cost; the more parsimonious Mazarin bargained at great length in order to obtain a reduced price and often saw the coveted object removed from his grasp, sometimes by Jabach himself. But the Cardinal lost nothing by waiting, because he was able to acquire a part of Jabach's collection later, on advantageous terms, when the latter was temporarily short of money.

Everhard Jabach was a native of Cologne, and belonged to a well-to-do bourgeois family whose name is connected with a famous work

[1] He was succeeded by a prince of the French branch, Charles I of Nevers.

by Albrecht Dürer. He was naturalized in 1647. He was a banker, and director of the Compagnie des Indes Orientales; in 1667 he received in addition a contract for providing leather equipment for the royal army. His good fortune deserted him at one point, and he had to sell his pictures – a proceeding which benefited Mazarin, the Duc de Richelieu and the king. However, matters subsequently improved and he was able to form a second collection. Le Brun painted a portrait of him, showing him with his family; it was in the Museum at Berlin, and was burnt in 1945. In opposition to the aristocratic collectors such as Loménie de Brienne, the Marquis de Hauterive, or the Duc de Richelieu, Jabach represents the type of financier-collector frequently encountered in the eighteenth century.

When Mazarin died, for the first time since Henry IV the king refused to be satisfied with reigning; he decided to govern. Henceforth, he was to lead both in politics and as art patron; after the lapse of a century, he took up the tradition of Francis I, who had made patronage a kingly right and duty. Assisted by Colbert, who had learnt a great deal from his apprenticeship with the Cardinal, Louis established this principle as an institution of the monarchy.

The king began with a master-stroke, and acquired some of Mazarin's pictures. He had refused to accept the Cardinal's offer, a few days before his death, of his whole fortune; but he accepted a legacy of some pictures and eighteen large diamonds. Furthermore, he bought from Mazarin's heirs the most famous paintings and statues. In this way the Louvre acquired some of its greatest treasures: *Balthasar Castiglione* (Charles I), *Saint George* and *Saint Michael*, by Raphael, Titian's *Venus of the Pardo*, which had been given by Philip IV to Charles I when the latter visited Madrid in 1623, Correggio's *Allegory of the Vices* and *Antiope* (Charles I), and the *Marriage of Saint Catherine* by the same artist (Cardinal Barberini), the *Deluge* by Antonio Carracci (Charles I), and a curious picture of the German Renaissance – a *History of David* in the form of a table top by Hans Sebald Beham.

Not much is known of the transactions which took place with Jabach. We only know that on 31 March 1671 Colbert obtained from him 5,542 drawings and 101 pictures for 220,000 *livres* — which prompted Loménie de Brienne to remark that Colbert had behaved to Jabach 'not like a Christian, but like a Moor'. The inventory of the drawings bought by Jabach still exists, but not that of the paintings. Recent researches carried out by Mademoiselle Adeline Hulftegger seem to indicate that, except for a few items, they were not of great importance, and that the most celebrated canvases had already become the king's property by 1671, either by donation or by transfer. In any case, the Crown obtained possession by these means of some magnificent works: the *Man with the Glove*, the *Entombment* (Charles I), the *Pilgrims at Emmaus*, the so-called *Allegory of Alfonso of Avalos*, the *Woman at her Toilet* by Titian, Giorgione's *Concert Champêtre*, Gentileschi's *Holy Family* (Charles I), Caravaggio's *Death of the Virgin* (Charles I), Claude's *Capture of the Pass at Susa* and *Siege of La Rochelle* (from Brienne), Domenichino's *Saint Cecilia*, several works by Veronese including *Susanna Bathing* and *Esther*, Correggio's *Allegory of the Vices*, thus reunited with its companion piece the *Allegory of the Virtues*, acquired through Mazarin, Leonardo's *Saint John the Baptist* which, according to a tradition no longer accepted, Louis XIII had exchanged for Holbein's *Erasmus* (in fact, this exchange was made with the Duc de Liancourt); the surviving documents incline Mademoiselle Hulftegger to the belief that the *Erasmus* came into Louis XIV's possession through Jabach with all the other Louvre Holbeins, bought in England and originally in the Arundel collection — *Archbishop Warham, Nicolas Kratzer, Sir Henry Wyatt* and *Anne of Cleves*.

Since the Renaissance, the gift of works of art was considered one of the best diplomatic means of acquiring a sovereign's good graces. The most splendid present Louis XIV ever received was Veronese's *Feast in the House of Simon*, given to him in 1665, together with a Titian, by the Republic of Venice. Courtiers also availed themselves of this elegant method of paying their respects — a method so greatly appreciated by the king. In 1693, Le Nôtre offered him three Poussins, two Claudes and his Albanis; Louis XIV did not wish to be indebted to his landscape gardener, and granted him a pension of 6,000 *livres*. Knowing the king's taste for contemporary Italian paintings, the princes of the Roman families sent him some of these. In 1665 Prince Pamfili gave Bernini (summoned to Paris to work on the Louvre) eight pictures to take to the king, including some Albanis, *Hunting Scene* and *Fishing Scene* by Annibale Carracci, a magnificent Titian, the *Virgin with SS. Maurice, Stephen and Ambrose*, the *Fortune Teller* by Caravaggio. From Monsignor Orsini the king received the superb *Battle Scene* by Salvator Rosa, and various Italian prelates gave him other less important Seicento works.

An important event in the history of the collections of the Crown under Louis XIV took place in 1665 – the purchase from the Duc de Richelieu (the Cardinal's nephew) of thirteen Poussins, two Claudes (one of them the very fine *Ulysses restoring Chryseis to her Father*), and various Italian pictures, including the beautiful *Virgin with a Rabbit*, one of Titian's best-preserved paintings. According to Loménie de Brienne, this last painting was the stake in a game of tennis, in which the king defeated the duke; recent researches by M. Claude Ferraton, who has discovered the receipt for the sale, neither prove nor disprove the legend. Among the Poussins acquired on this occasion were the *Diogenes*, the *Four Seasons*, the flamboyant *Bacchante and Lute Player*, *Eliezer and Rebecca*, which so exercised the Académie, the *Ecstasy of Saint Paul*, and the *Philistines Struck by the Plague*, a brilliant Mantegnesque work.

A great number of paintings by contemporary French artists were bought at this time. Louis XIV had thirty-two Poussins, eleven Claudes, twenty-six Le Bruns, seventeen Mignards, without taking into account the decorative work of the last two painters. French taste was 'classic' in character and definitely preferred French and Italian painting; the Hapsburgs, on the other hand, as a result of their position in Europe, were equally in favour of the Northern and of the Italian schools. Being in possession of Spain, they naturally owned works by Spanish masters as well, so that at the end of the seventeenth century the collections of Vienna and Madrid were more representative than that of Versailles of all the great European schools of painting. The situation changed during the eighteenth and nineteenth centuries, but the Louvre has always preserved something of this spirit of exclusiveness which presided over the formation of the royal collections.

During the reign of Louis XIV, however, the Crown acquired a certain number of Northern pictures. We have already mentioned the Holbeins purchased from Jabach. At that time the Flemish artist most appreciated in France was Van Dyck, much esteemed as a court painter; the *Mercure galant* mentions no less than fourteen of his works in the collection stored in the Louvre which the king visited in 1681. The conviction that drawing was more important than colour, and noble subjects superior to *genre* (a prejudice imposed by the 'Poussinist' spirit of the Académie) led to a belief that Rubens' work was vulgar, with its 'fat, well-fed, pot-bellied gods', its brilliant presentation of 'beauty out-of-doors', its pigment applied like cosmetics, and its 'licentious' character. During the second half of the reign, however, under the influence of Mignard, Jouvenet, Largillière and Roger de Piles, Rubens came back into favour, with the result that Poussins were less sought after. The Duc de Richelieu, who had sold his Poussins to the king, later bought Rubens' work instead. In spite of the remark attributed to Louis XIV by Voltaire (no doubt apocryphal),[1] the royal collections began to acquire Flemish works. The *Mercure galant* of 1681 mentions Rubens' *Virgin of the Holy Innocents*, which Mademoiselle Hulftegger thinks may have been bought as early as 1671 from M. de la Feuille, together with *Queen Thomirys and Cyrus*; and in 1685 the king did not hesitate to buy the *Kermesse* — one of the artist's most 'popular' works — from the Marquis de Hauterive. Finally, the 1683 inventory mentions the *Portrait of Rembrandt as an old Man*, possibly bought in 1671 from M. de la Feuille.

By now, a special organization and administration had become necessary to look after the very extensive collections. Le Brun was

---

[1] 'Otez-moi ces magots-là', Louis is supposed to have exclaimed, on seeing some Teniers which had been hung in his apartments (Voltaire, *Mélange d'histoires anecdotiques sur Louis XIV*).

30

put in charge of it, and thus added the title 'Garde des tableaux et dessins du roi' to those he already held – 'Premier Peintre' and 'Directeur de la Manufacture des Meubles de la Couronne' (the Gobelins). He took up his new duties in 1671, and held the post till his death in 1690. In 1683 he drew up a detailed inventory of the royal collections, which mentioned 426 pictures. The inventory compiled in 1709–1710 by Bailly, Garde des tableaux de Versailles et des Maisons royales, listed 2,376 items, of which 369 were Italian, 179 by northern artists and 930 French, the balance being made up of copies, decorative works and sketches.

In the time of Le Brun, the king's paintings were housed in the Louvre, in the wing built by Le Vau after the fire of 1661 round the present court which contains the antiquities of Assos and Maeander. The surplus was in the neighbouring Hôtel de Gramont. An article in the *Mercure galant*, December 1681, gives an account of a visit 'which His Majesty paid on 5 December 1681 to the Louvre, to see his collection of paintings.' The writer, full of admiration, announced that 'there is no longer any need to travel to see the rarest treasures'. The pictures covered the entire walls, reaching to above the cornice; there were even three layers of them, one behind the other, which could be inspected by a system of hinged screens (the picture stores in modern museums employ the same principle). In the Hôtel de Gramont, for safety's sake, 'the oldest and most precious are kept shut up in flat gilded cupboards'. The chronicler relates that on that occasion the king chose fifteen new pictures to be transferred to Versailles; he now no longer lived in the Louvre, which was simply a storehouse.

In 1690, after Le Brun's death, the position of Garde des tableaux was given to Mignard. When the latter died in 1695, the duties were divided between two officials, one responsible for the Louvre, the other for Versailles and the royal residences (Marly, Fontainebleau, and the Luxembourg). The painter Houasse, Garde des tableaux of the Louvre, only admitted to ninety paintings in the inventory made when he took up his duties; during the eighteenth century, the collection in the Louvre became a collection of drawings only.

At Versailles, the most valuable paintings were earmarked for the 'Cabinet des raretés', which had the best light for their display; but the majority were used to adorn the palace. A mixture of schools was evidently found pleasing, contemporary French paintings being shown in the company of works by Italian artists. In the Salon de Mars, for example, Veronese's *Pilgrims at Emmaus* was hung as a pendant to Le Brun's *Alexander in the Tent of Darius*; Voltaire, comparing them, preferred the French picture to the Venetian one. The Surintendance had magnificent frames made for the king's pictures; the finest examples are perhaps those which still surround two pictures by Annibale Carracci – *Hunting Scene* and *Fishing Scene*.

When the king visited the Louvre in 1685, it was already seven years since he had abandoned it for Versailles. From that time, all his efforts were directed to the creation of his own personal legend; but he had already contributed more than any other monarch to the great dynastic task of rebuilding the Louvre, and it had witnessed the fifteen best years of his reign – its most brilliant and most carefree period.

When Louis XIV had returned to Paris in 1652, he carried out a considerable amount of redecoration in the royal apartments; some of the woodwork still survives, but was removed to the Colonnade wing in the nineteenth century. The Queen-mother, Anne of Austria, had an apartment fitted up for herself in 1655, on the ground floor of the Petite Galerie, with a 'modern' décor consisting of stuccoes by Michel Anguier and paintings by the Italian Romanelli. In 1659 Mazarin put his favourite architect Le Vau to work on the north wing of the Cour Carrée; so that nothing might be allowed to interrupt the building programme, a royal ordinance was actually issued forbidding private persons to 'entreprendre aucun nouveau bâtiment'. On 6 February 1661, however, fire broke out in the Petite Galerie, and though the Queen-mother's summer apartment was saved, the first floor was gutted. The gallery was rebuilt by Le Vau, who added a wing on the left side to house the library; Le Brun undertook its decoration, planning a painted schema in honour of Apollo (Louis XIV's symbol) which was never finished.

Colbert, Surintendant des Bâtiments in 1663, wanted to give a new impetus to the building of the Louvre; he had the Tuileries completed and enlarged by Le Vau, and wished to provide the palace with a triumphal entry on the east side. He threw this project open to competition, and consulted a great many architects, including Bernini; the latter came to Paris in 1665, and left it overwhelmed with honours, but misunderstood. Finally, the part known as the 'Colonnade' was entrusted to Claude Perrault; he based his work on a synthesis of various earlier schemes, and the deliberations of a council of which he had himself been a member, in the company of Le Vau and Le Brun. Building was begun in 1667, and the plans had to be modified to take into account the doubling of the south wing of the Cour Carrée. In 1670 the main fabric of the Colonnade was completed; but work on the Louvre slowed down in favour of that being carried out at Versailles, and finally came to a halt in 1678.

THE BEGINNINGS OF THE MUSEUM

AT THE BEGINNING OF THE 18TH CENTURY, a small number of noblemen and financiers continued in the tradition of the great collectors of the previous century. The Regent had no less than 478 pictures on show in his Palais Royal gallery, including works by the great Renaissance masters; in 1704 Baron Crozat de Thiers installed his collection of 19,000 drawings and 400 pictures in his house in the Rue de Richelieu. However, collectors had lost the taste for the grand manner in art; the great 'machines' of earlier centuries, darkened during the passage of years, did not suit the small apartments, with their light-coloured woodwork and cheerful mirrors, which were now the homes of a society grown weary of the uncomfortable ostentation of the 'grand siècle'. Pier-glasses were needed now instead, and door-panel designs by living artists in fresh clear colours, representing 'sujets galants' which required no mental effort on the part of the beholder. The bourgeois influence brought into favour the work of the minor Dutch and Flemish artists, the size and subjects of whose paintings were more in keeping with the spirit of the time. Rembrandt was admired, but Gerard Dou was worshipped, and became one of the most popular masters of the century. Finally, the mania for objects – knick-knacks and curios, pieces of furniture, *chinoiseries* – dealt a severe blow to painting.

Amsterdam and Paris became the two great picture-markets of Europe. The Dutch had outstripped the French in their organization of the commercial side of collecting; Gersaint, Watteau's dealer, had been to Holland and studied the Dutch method of auctioning works of art, which he then introduced into France. There were a number of experts in Paris during the eighteenth century – Gersaint, Mariette, Rémy, Glomy, Lebrun (the husband of Marie-Antoinette's portrait painter, Madame Louise Vigée). Printed catalogues were carefully prepared by experts for the important sales; more than 2,000 of these survive from the eighteenth century, of which about half were for Holland and the remainder for Paris. Towards the end of the *ancien régime* sales became more frequent; works of art constantly changed hands, and at this period Paris collectors sold more than they bought. It seems strange to find Rémy, in his preface to the catalogue of the Tallard sale (1756), deploring the fact that so many masterpieces were leaving France. 'Already', he states, 'our all-too-frequent losses have given us sufficent warning that foreigners have been enriching themselves enormously at our expense, and that if we do not take care they will soon have despoiled us completely of all those fine pictures which were the glory of our country, and which were brought here from Italy at so much cost.' Later, Bachaumont, in his *Mémoires secrets,* voices his regrets that a foreigner should have been the only one to benefit from the sale of a famous collection: 'The Empress of Russia,' he said, 'has carried off all the pictures formerly belonging to the Comte de Thiers, the well-known connoisseur, who had a fine collection of this kind of work. Monsieur de Marigny [the Directeur des Bâtiments] has had to suffer the disappointment of seeing these treasures go abroad, for want of funds with which to acquire them on the king's behalf.' The countries which had produced all the great modern schools of painting – Italy, France, Belgium and the Netherlands – were emptied of their masterpieces for the benefit of England, Germany, Austria and Russia. Frederick the Great, the Electors of Saxony, Augustus the Strong and Augustus II, Catherine the Great (whose Paris agent was Diderot) and Baron Stroganoff all became the owners of paintings by the great masters sold by French collectors; across the Channel, the English aristocracy became enamoured of French classical painting, and bought all the finest works of Poussin, Claude and Gaspard Dughet both in Italy and in France.

The Crown did not derive as much benefit as it might have done from the ample products of French talent during that period. The regimentation of the fine arts introduced under Louis XIV had resulted in the formation of an official art, which always lagged

35

behind the innovators. From this there developed a rift between the State and the most vital manifestations of contemporary art, which went on widening until the nineteenth century, when the gulf became unbridgeable. In the eighteenth century, the royal administration gave its commissions to the most facile, not to the most gifted. Watteau and his disciples were left out, and, later, Fragonard; Chardin had better success amongst the citizens than he had at court. Up to 1869, the date of the La Caze gift, the Louvre only owned one Watteau – *The Embarkation for Cythera,* his Académie diploma piece. The collections where French art of this period was best represented, therefore, were not those of the King of France, but those formed by the foreign princes and sovereigns already mentioned – with the addition of Queen Louise of Sweden, sister of Frederick the Great, whose adviser was her Ambassador in Paris, Charles Gustave Tessin.

The only important acquisition of earlier works during the reign of Louis XV was from the estate of Amédée de Savoie, Prince de Carignan, in 1742. The painter Hyacinthe Rigaud, who usually advised Augustus of Saxony, King of Poland, bought approximately twenty pictures for the King of France on this occasion, including masterpieces by northern artists: Rubens' *Tournament* and his *Lot Fleeing from Sodom* and *The Angel Leaving Tobias,* by Rembrandt. He also rescued a Raphael, the *Madonna with the Veil,* and Solario's *Virgin with the Cushion,* bought by Marie de Médicis in 1619 from the Franciscans at Blois, and at one time owned by Mazarin. Finally, somewhat surprisingly in view of their lack of popularity at court, Rigaud also bought some Seicento pictures, by Annibale Carracci, Castiglione, Guido Reni and Carlo Maratti. However, the sale of the magnificent Crozat collection was allowed to pass without anything being saved from it, thus provoking the lamentations of Bachaumont already mentioned above.

The eighteenth century witnessed the growth of historical studies in France. Research work was methodically carried out by the Benedictines on the history of France, and in 1729–1733 was published the *Monuments de la Monarchie française,* by Dom Bernard de

Montfaucon. This movement had been initiated in the seventeenth century, however, by a few 'curieux'. One of these, François Roger de Gaignières, had travelled round Europe visiting a vast number of monasteries and castles, and had assembled an extraordinary collection 'of nearly 27,000 prints of all kinds by famous Engravers, maps or Plans of Towns, Battles, Carrousels, Burials, Autographs of several Kings, Queens, Princes, Princesses, Portraits in miniature, all kinds of coloured glass such as is found here and there in old churches; *item* all sorts of ancient fashions of dress worn in France since the reign of Saint Louis till our own day, together with a great quantity of odds and ends, maps, pictures and other things'.[1] Gaignières was one of the tutors of the Duke of Burgundy, and had formed this historical museum to assist in the education of the prince, with the aid of money from the latter and from Madame de Maintenon. In 1711 he made it over to the king, at the same time requesting various payments for himself and his heirs. In 1716, a year after his death, all the documents were transferred to the Bibliothèque Royale[2]; but in the following year the various objects were sold, and all the pictures except one – the portrait of *King John the Good of France*, which was also handed over to the Bibliothèque Royale. This was inherited by the Bibliothèque Nationale, and was exchanged with the Louvre for some miniatures in 1925. Very fortunately, the genealogist Clérambault saved a great many of the little portraits, inserting them in the bundles of documents in the archives of the Cabinet des Titres Nobiliaires. They now form the main part of the collection of Renaissance portraits in Versailles and the Louvre.

Louis XVI's reign, on the other hand, was one of the greatest periods in the history of the Louvre. France was shaking off her lethargy, and was aware of the need for regeneration. No age was

[1] *Séjour de Paris, c'est-à-dire Instructions fidèles pour les Voyageurs de Condition*, by S. J. C. Nemeitz, Leyden, 1727. Revised edition by Alfred Franklin, *La Vie de Paris sous la Régence*, Paris, 1897.
[2] In 1784 some of the documents were stolen from the Bibliothèque du Roi, and eventually found their way into the Bodleian Library, Oxford.

ever more fertile in the desire to carry out various schemes, in projects for reform of different kinds, than this feverish period. In the development of museums, as well as in many other fields, revolutionary France made use of principles laid down during the *ancien régime*.

Under Louis XV, much indignation was expressed at the situation in which the change of taste at court had left the king's collection of paintings. Louis XIV had lived a public life, and access to the royal apartments was easily obtainable in his day. The life of Louis XV, however, was more intimate, more secret, and it was not possible to admire 'the most valuable works of the great European masters in His Majesty's collection, buried in the badly-lit little rooms into which they are now crowded, hidden in the town of Versailles [a reference to the Direction des Bâtiments], unknown to foreigners or of no interest to them because of their inaccessibility'. Courtiers borrowed pictures from the king; between 1715 and 1736 the Duc d'Antin exhibited in the gallery of his Paris house some of the finest gems from the royal collection – Raphael's *Balthasar Castiglione*, Annibale Carracci's *Hunting Scene* and *Fishing Scene*, and three works by Titian: the *Venus of the Pardo*, the *Virgin with the Rabbit*, and a *Portrait of a Man*. As early as 1744, an anonymous note to the Directeur des Bâtiments[1] deplored this dispersal, and demanded that these masterpieces be exhibited in the Galerie des Ambassadeurs, in the Tuileries. A new attack was launched in 1747, this time in a printed pamphlet by Lafont de Saint Yenne: *Réflexions sur quelques causes de l'état de la peinture en France*, from which we have just quoted a passage. In his view, masterpieces of painting had an exemplary value; by studying them, artists should rescue story painting from the decadence into which it had fallen (it was coming back into favour with the newly-developing neo-classical taste). Lafont de Saint Yenne recommended the building of a special gallery. Two years later, in 1749, he again took up the idea in a new pamphlet, in which he reported an imagin-

[1] Paul Lacroix attributed it to Bachaumont.

ary conversation between '*l'Ombre du grand Colbert, le Louvre et la Ville de Paris*', in the manner of Lucian's *Dialogues*.

At that time, the Grande Galerie was in no condition to receive the pictures. It was in a very dilapidated state, and, ever since 1754, its whole length had been filled with the extraordinary collection of plans of the fortresses of the kingdom, of which the first elements had been installed there in 1697. However, public opinion was not disregarded. In 1750 Jacques Bailly, who had succeeded his father Nicolas Bailly as Garde des Tableaux at Versailles, was ordered by the Marquis de Marigny, Directeur des Bâtiments, to put in order the Queen of Spain's apartments in the Luxembourg, with a view to exhibiting a selection of the paintings belonging to the crown. This provisional museum was opened on 14 October; it could be visited on Wednesday and Saturday every week, in the morning from October to April and in the afternoon from April to October, except on public holidays.

There one could see 110 paintings and a collection of drawings which, as a precautionary measure, were exhibited in rotation. Attention was now paid to the study of methods for restoring old pictures which had already been injured by time – particularly the processes of renewing the canvas, or transferring the painting to a new support. Strollers in the Luxembourg could marvel to behold Andrea del Sarto's *Charity*, transferred to canvas by Picault, exhibited alongside its former wooden support. The choice was eclectic: Raphael, Leonardo, Veronese, Correggio, Titian, Rembrandt, Rubens, Van Dyck, Poussin, Claude, Clouet, Pourbus, Le Brun, Annibale Carracci, Rigaud, Le Valentin, Van Berchem . . .

The number of editions of the catalogue proves how successful this venture was with the public. But in 1778 the Luxembourg palace was given in appanage to the Comte de Provence, and the exhibition had to be closed in 1779. It is interesting to observe that the paintings of the Galerie Médicis were not included in the donation; it was intended to exhibit these in the Louvre, and they were taken down, rolled up, and removed to the Dépôt of the Surintendance at Versailles.

The exhibition in the Luxembourg was only of a temporary character. In 1765 Diderot, in Volume IX of the *Encyclopédie,* transformed the vague project of Lafont de Sainte Yenne into a veritable museological programme making rational use of the accommodation in the Louvre. The ground floor was to contain the sculptures, brought in from the gardens where they were slowly deteriorating; the paintings were to be housed in the 'Galerie du bord de l'eau' (the Grande Galerie). On the north (no doubt in a gallery yet to be built) were to go the plans of the fortresses of the kingdom; elsewhere, the natural history exhibits and the Coins and Medals. At the same time, the Académies were to be installed in a more logical fashion in the Louvre, and the Académiciens were to be provided with accommodation there.

The idea of making the collection of the Crown (hitherto the privilege of the court) contribute to the advancement of the arts and sciences is linked with the Encyclopaedic movement in France – and also in England. The Comte d'Angiviller, appointed Directeur des Bâtiments in 1774, worked methodically for the formation of the 'Museum' in the Grande Galerie of the Louvre. He resumed the policy of regular acquisitions, abandoned since Louis XIV; but in a truly 'museological' spirit he directed his purchases to filling the gaps in the royal collections, so that he could present the public with a more complete picture of the Schools of painting. During the last years of the *ancien régime* considerable efforts were made. As a result of the neo-classical reaction and a return to favour of

On the right, a detail of the *Plan for furnishing the 'Grande Galerie' containing the Paintings of the Central Museum of the Louvre.* (Inventory: R. F. 2050. Canvas. Height: 0.34 m., Width: 0.42 m. [13^1/$_2$"×16^1/$_2$"]. Hippolyte Destailleur sale, 19 May 1896, No. 670; Jacques Doucet sale, 6 June 1912, No. 184, at which it was acquired by Maurice Fenaille who then donated it to the Louvre.)

Sketch (with variations) of the large painting exhibited in the Salon of 1796 under the number 392 and with the title *Plan for lighting the gallery of the museum through the arches and for dividing it without obstructing the view of the length of the gallery.* This painting, which was once in the palace of Tsarskoye Selo, was later sold by the Soviet Government. The décor conceived by Hubert Robert was partially executed during the reign of Napoleon, when the great double arches were constructed, but was completed only in our time.

HUBERT ROBERT · THE 'GRANDE GALERIE'

history painting, Seicento Italian works were again bought: Guido Reni, Procaccini, Crespi, Solimena, Fetti, and so on. In 1786 the English miniaturist Richard Cosway offered to the king the four enormous tapestry cartoons by Giulio Romano, illustrating *Fructus Belli* and the *History of Scipio*; after various misadventures these works were restored in 1952 and in 1953 took their place in the Salon Carré. They are painted in tempera on paper, and are comparable with two other great series of Renaissance cartoons – Mantegna's *Triumph of Caesar* at Hampton Court, and Raphael's *Acts of the Apostles* in the Victoria and Albert Museum, London.

The seventeenth-century French collections were intelligently completed by the purchase of works which the academic taste of Louis XIV's court had despised: the *Forge*, by Le Nain, the *Last Supper* by Philippe de Champaigne, the *Life of Saint Bruno* series by Le Sueur, bought from the Carthusians in 1776, and the *Chamber of the Muses* and the *Cabinet d'Amour*, also by Le Sueur, removed from the Hôtel Lambert the same year.

But d'Angiviller's attention was turned chiefly to the Northern Schools, which were the most poorly represented in the royal collections, and he maintained a team of agents in the Low Countries. Most of the work of these Schools now in the Louvre was acquired during this period. In particular, except for the La Caze bequest, the gallery of Dutch painting in the Museum was assembled almost entirely in the reign of Louis XVI. Rembrandt's *Portrait of the Artist with a Gold Chain* and his *Pilgrims at Emmaus* were acquired at this time, to name but two out of a host of trophies; and the purchases made at the Comte de Vaudreuil's sale in 1784 included Ruisdael's *Ray of Sunlight*, Rembrandt's *Hendrickje Stoffels* and his two *Philosophers*[1], the *Evangelists* by Jordaens, and *Hélène Fourment and her Children*, by Rubens. *Charles I*, by Van Dyck, was brought from the Comtesse du Barry in 1775. D'Angiviller had agents throughout Europe who warned him whenever a good opportunity of obtaining pictures presented itself. He tried to obtain

[1] Of which one is a school work.

some of the pictures put up for sale by the Belgian religious communities, dissolved by the Emperor Joseph II of Austria. But the latter adopted tactics for which he has never been reproached– though the French governments during the Revolution and the Empire were severely criticized for behaving in a similar fashion; he simply took possession of the best pieces from the suppressed convents to enrich his gallery in Vienna, thus somewhat limiting the choice of other collectors. In spite of everything, however, d'Angiviller managed to acquire Rubens' *Adoration of the Magi*, from the Annunciades of Brussels, and the *Martyrdom of Saint Liévin* by the same artist, painted for the Jesuits of Ghent. This latter picture returned to Belgium later; it was included in the works allotted to the Brussels Museum in 1803.

The administration did not neglect the Cabinet des Dessins. True, it failed to purchase *en bloc* the collection of drawings assembled by the connoisseur and scholar Mariette, as would have been desirable; but at the entreaties of Cochin (the keeper of drawings) a selection of more than 1,300 items was bought at the sale for 52,000 *livres*. Unfortunately, the choice of drawings was dictated by a somewhat academic taste, and the finest works left France.

In a memorandum submitted to the king in 1783, requesting 150,000 *livres* for the purchase of Dutch paintings in England, d'Angiviller pointed out that the acquisition of these would 'contribute materially to establishing the superiority of the King's gallery, and be of service to the State because of the many foreigners who come to share their enjoyment'. The Surintendant, looking ahead, was already thinking of the tourist traffic! Admittedly the paintings in question were only by Van der Werf and even lesser artists, which goes to show how popular these minor genre painters were, when Vermeer was still unknown. The last purchases made at the end of the *ancien régime* were mainly of works by Wouvermann, Karel du Jardin, Teniers, Metsu, Terborch *(Lady Entertaining a Soldier)* and Cuyp.

Purchases from living artists were less fortunate, because they were influenced by contemporary taste. It would take too long to examine in detail all the causes of the 'return to virtue' which took place at the end of the eighteenth century. In any case, the administration which had been blamed in the time of Louis XV for its indifference to the public welfare became so attentive to the latter in the reign of Louis XVI that it extended its concern to the moral education of the people. The Comte d'Angiviller became the apostle of this movement; according to M. Hautecœur, he 'displayed a zeal on behalf of virtue which was all the more creditable in view of the fact that none of his offices was due to it'. During this period, far too many Greuzes, Viens and Vernets, too many paintings inspired by ancient history and the history of France 'calculated to re-awaken patriotic virtues and feelings', found their way into the national collections.

Concurrently with the enlargement of the collection, d'Angiviller undertook the restoration of works which had been damaged by the passage of time or the activities of man, and also gave his attention to the framing of the pictures. The magnificent carved frames which had been fashionable since Louis XIV's time were not to his taste; he preferred something simpler, with a cartouche containing the name of the artist and the subject depicted. With an excessive concern for museological consistency, he used this same type of frame for all schools of painting. When the Museum opened, Alexandre Lenoir, the Conservateur of the Dépôt des Grands Augustins, summed up the former Director's activities quite fairly when he said of the pictures exhibited: 'd'Angiviller had frames made for them which set them off well, without adding anything to their value.'

In 1784 the painter Hubert Robert was made keeper of the future Museum gallery, and given the task of having it fitted out. The Premier Peintre, Pierre, second-in-command to the Directeur des Bâtiments, devoted much labour to this project.

During this period, work on the palace made little progress. The Louvre was no longer used as a royal residence; from the end of the seventeenth century, it was invaded by archives, offices and the various Académies who took up their quarters there in a rough and ready fashion. From 1725 on, the Académie de Peinture gave exhibitions at irregular intervals of work by its members. These took place in the large room between the Grande Galerie and the Petite Galerie, known as the Salon, which gave its name to all future manifestations of this nature. The enormous unfinished palace also served as a place of refuge for various protégés of the king: members of the court, and artists who behaved with all the less restraint since they were not in their own homes. In the midst of all this chaos, the Surintendance still tried to complete the building. Beginning in 1754, Gabriel changed the appearance of the Cour Carrée by replacing the attic and its sloping roof with a flat-roofed storey; the former was in any case unfinished. The west wing, however, was allowed to retain the high-roofed attic, in order to leave Lescot's design undisturbed. Finally, all the buildings which prevented a clear view of the Colonnade were demolished, and for the first time Parisians were able to see the whole arrangement of the façade at once.

Under the directorship of d'Angiviller, various schemes and projects were again undertaken, this time for the completion of the proposed 'Museum' in the Grande Galerie. To provide a more convenient approach to it, Soufflot planned a new monumental staircase, the building of which was begun by Brébion in 1781; it led up to the Salon Carré. The problem of lighting and decorating the Grande Galerie, which had been cleared of the plans of fortresses in 1777, occupied several years. Finally, overhead lighting was decided upon; this was judged best for paintings, and a number of sale rooms and private galleries in Paris already employed it. As an experiment, the Salon Carré was provided with it in 1789. During this period, the Galerie was provided with parquet flooring, the timber of the roof was replaced by brick, precautions were taken against the spread of fire by the insertion of fire-resisting walls in the framework of the building and by installing a lightning-conductor – a sensational innovation at the time. Finally, the question of décor was considered; to accompany the masterpieces, sculptors were commissioned to provide statues of great men.

44

All Paris eagerly awaited the opening of the Museum. In 1787, referring to the old gallery of plans, the Abbé Thierry said in his *Guide des amateurs et étrangers à Paris*: 'It is intended to turn this gallery into a Museum which will house the pictures belonging to the king, now exhibited in the store-rooms in the Louvre and in the Surintendance at Versailles. Let us hope that we shall see the completion of this glorious project, which may well immortalize Monsieur le Comte de la Billarderie d'Angiviller, who conceived it.' The financial difficulties of the last years of the *ancien régime* deprived d'Angiviller of the honour of opening the Louvre Museum; but his name will always be coupled with this great institution.

THE MUSÉE NAPOLÉON

THE PERIOD in which the long-awaited Museum took shape can hardly be called a propitious one. The treasury was bankrupt; on all sides, enemies were threatening the frontiers, and ragged troops, levied in their thousands, were holding at bay the old armies of Europe. Internally, France was a nation wild with enthusiasm and hatreds – civil war, the terror, and executioners with more work than they could handle. Yet during all this, governments which rose and fell like meteors worked devotedly to bring the museum into being.

The project formed during the *ancien régime* was to be far outstripped by the nationalization of most of the works of art still in France: the art treasures of the Crown, the property of churches, and the confiscated possessions of *émigrés* accumulated in the dépôts prepared for their reception. In 1790 a 'commission conservatrice des monuments' (which, incidentally, did not fulfil its object) undertook the enormous task of making an inventory of all the art treasures in France. In Paris, the sculpture and pictures from the national monuments – in particular the churches – were sent to the Couvent des Petits Augustins (now the Ecole des Beaux-Arts); manuscripts were sent to other religious houses; the collections of the Crown, from Versailles and other royal residences, were removed to the Louvre. Confiscated *émigré* property was deposited in the Hôtel de Nesles; the Museum Commission was authorised to select from amongst it whatever seemed likely to be of interest for the art gallery which was being formed. To give some idea of the scale on which the 'National Monuments' were ransacked, it may be pointed out that Jan van Eyck's *Madonna of Chancellor Rolin* was taken from the cathedral of Autun; Fra Bartolommeo's large *Mystical Marriage of Saint Catherine*, one of the first Italian paintings to enter France, was later seized from the same church.

As for the property of the *émigrés*, part of it was sold, either for the benefit of the State or for the repayment of creditors – since most of the great families of France were riddled with debt at the end of the *ancien régime*. The Museum Commission secured a number of masterpieces before the goods were put up for sale; from the Duc de Richelieu's collection the Louvre obtained the *Allegories* by Mantegna, Costa and Perugino from Isabella d'Este's *Studiolo* at Mantua. These were taken from the Château of Richelieu in Poitou, and were joined by Michelangelo's *Slaves*, found in a house in Paris belonging to the Duke. The famous gilded gallery of the house in Toulouse which is now the Banque de France was stripped of pictures by Poussin, Guido Reni, Pietro da Cortona, Carlo Maratta, Guercino, and Alessandro Veronese; and when this gallery was restored in 1870–1876 these paintings (two of which are now abroad) were replaced by copies. The statement of objects chosen for the museum reveals that the majority were works by minor Dutch and Flemish masters, which were very popular at the end of the eighteenth century. Although it is not easy to determine how much of the material in the house of the Directeur Général des Bâtiments was his own property, and how much of it belonged to the Crown, it seems that the Comte d'Angiviller, who did so much to help in the formation of the museum, also contributed in spite of himself to the enrichment of its collection. *Saint Matthew and the Angel* – for example – one of Rembrandt's finest works – had formerly been his property.

Shaken by political upheavals, various directorships and commissions successively carried on the task of preparing the Museum, to which the painter David lent both the support and the turmoil of his passionate enthusiasm, and of his whole personality. On 27 July 1793 the 'Muséum Central des Arts' was created by decree; on 10 August in the same year the Grande Galerie of the Louvre was officially opened. It was rather dark, being lit from the side; the pictures were placed between the windows, and along the centre were tables on which were arranged bronzes, busts, objets d'art, clocks, and other curiosities: 'precious spoils taken from our tyrants, or from other enemies of our country.' The inauguration was only a symbolic one, as the gallery had to be closed again immediately for essential repairs; it was re-opened on 18 November. Out of the ten days in the *decade* which had now replaced the week, five were reserved for copyists, three for the public, and two for cleaning. On 26 April the gallery had to be closed again for more extensive repairs, undertaken by the architect Reymond. The public was not admitted again till 7 April 1799, and then only to a part of the gallery; the rest was not ready till 14 July 1801. The Galerie d'Apollon was used for exhibiting drawings. The Museum was so successful that, as the police records tell us, the centre of prostitution shifted from the Tuileries to the gallery entrance.

Works continued to flow in from the four points of the compass. In 1794 the Convention decided to requisition works of art in the Low Countries, which had recently been delivered from the Austrian yoke; in this way Paris acquired the splendid Rubens paintings from Antwerp.

The greatest contributor to the Museum, however, was Bonaparte, whose victorious standards were advancing through Italy, the classic land of art. There, works of art were requisitioned under the terms of armistices and treaties, or accepted in lieu of war taxes; a commission of specialists made the selection. The armistices agreed upon with the Dukes of Piacenza and Modena (9 and 27 May 1796), and the truce signed with the Pope at Bologna (8 June 1796) which was followed by the Treaty of Tolentino (19 February 1797) resulted in the handing over of art treasures from the galleries of Parma,

On the right, the *Portrait of General Bonaparte*. (Inventory: R. F. 1942–18. Canvas. Height: 0.81 m., Width: 0.64 m. [31^1/$_2$″×25^1/$_4$″]. Vivant-Denon sale of 1826; Duke of Bassano collection; Seligman collection; entered the Louvre with the Carlos de Beistegui legacy, 1953.)

This sketch, in which only the face is slightly elaborated, is all that was executed in 1797 of a large historical painting, 86^5/$_8$″×118″, which was to depict the General, on the Plateau de Rivoli, the Alps in the background, with the treaty of Campo-Formio in his hand, followed by his Staff Officer, while his orderly held his horse by the bridle.

Bonaparte came to the Louvre, where David had his studio, preceded by two orderlies who carried his uniform; this he donned and posed for three hours, the only occasion he ever sat for a painter.

JACQUES-LOUIS DAVID · GENERAL BONAPARTE

Modena, Milan, Cremona, Bologna, Perugia, and Rome; requisitioning of works of art from the States of Venice and Rome followed in 1798, and from Florence and Turin in 1800. On 9 and 10 Thermidor in the Year VI (26 and 27 July 1798), the arrival of the first consignment was celebrated in Paris. It was a regular 'victory parade' of the armies of Italy. The captured treasures were brought by water, and unloaded near the Jardin des Plantes; there they were hoisted on to wagons, and taken across Paris, accompanied by the various corporate bodies: the wagons drew up in a circle around the statue of Liberty in the Champ de Mars. Roman antique sculpture could be seen alongside carts loaded with collections of medals, natural history specimens, books, and crates full of pictures; together with these were dromedaries, bears from Berne, and other 'curiosities'. The antiques were preceded by a standard bearing the words:

'La Grèce les céda, Rome les a perdus;
    Leur sort changea deux fois, il ne changera plus'

(Greece gave them up, Rome has lost them; twice their fortune has changed, but it will change no more.) But appearances were deceptive, and the victory was to prove indeed a Pyrrhic one.

The Louvre certainly deserved the title of 'Musée Napoléon' which Cambacérès bestowed upon it in 1803, and which the Emperor did not dispute. Europe, brought into subjection by his victories, gave up yet more trophies. Napoleon had inherited the old Revolutionary hatred of the German and Austrian states, looked upon as strongholds of absolutism, and he did not spare them. In 1806 and 1807 Berlin, Custrin, Potsdam, Cassel, Schwerin, Vienna, and the Duchy of Brunswick contributed an important consignment of works by northern artists; Napoleon was able to hang Altdorfer's *Battle of Alexander and Darius* in his study at Saint-Cloud. After 1810, defeats brought about a slowing-down of this influx; nevertheless, a convoy of packing-cases full of Spanish works was halted at Bayonne, in 1814, by the collapse of the Empire.

Not content with the masterpieces which poured in from the whole of France, and later from all Europe, the Museum continued to make purchases. On 17 February 1793, one of the most critical periods of the Convention, *The King Drinks*, by Jordaens, and Rembrandt's *Carpenter's Family* were bought at the Comte de Choiseul-Praslin's sale. In 1801 the Museum bought Pieter de Hooch's *Card Players*.

As for Denon, the Director of the Museum under the Empire, he never missed an opportunity of filling some gap in the collections by the purchase of a rare work. His taste can be recognised in such acquisitions as *The Banker and his Wife* by Matsys (1806) and Bourdon's *Self-Portrait* (1807). Italy was hardly touched by the awakening interest in primitive painters, prejudiced as she was in favour of classical art; but in Germany and France works by the early masters of the various schools of painting were eagerly sought after. In 1811, Denon carried out a special mission to Italy in order to acquire them; some pictures he bought, others he appropriated from among the possessions of the suppressed monasteries; he organised exchanges between the Louvre and the Brera. From this expedition the Louvre still retains a number of major works, including Giotto's *Saint Francis receiving the Stigmata*, Cimabue's *Madonna with Angels*, Fra Angelico's *Coronation of the Virgin*, the *Visitation* by Ghirlandaio, and Gentile da Fabriano's *Presentation in the Temple*. In exchange for works by Rubens, Rembrandt, Van Dyck and Jordaens, the Louvre received from the Brera four pictures, including Carpaccio's *Saint Stephen Preaching*, and Boltraffio's *Casio Madonna*.

Individuals also contributed to the treasures of the Museum; voluntary gifts are recorded in this period. On 22 Frimaire of the Year VII (11 December 1798), Citizen Clauzel, Adjutant-General of the Army of Italy (later a Marshal of the Empire) offered to the Directory Gerard Dou's *Dropsical Woman*, which had been given to him by Charles Emmanuel IV of Savoy.

The pictures occupied the old quarters of the former Académie—the Salon Carré and the Grande Galerie; furthermore, their continually increasing numbers made any definitive classification impossible. In the Salon, the administration, 'anxious to increase the pleasure of the public, and to provide artists with objects of study', arranged temporary exhibitions of the most recently acquired works. The last of these consisted of 123 pictures collected by Denon in the course of his 1811 mission; it opened on 25 July 1814, after the fall of the Empire, and during enemy occupation.

The Emperor added little to the fabric of the Louvre, but he had at least the merit of having finished off the Cour Carrée, and of bringing a little nearer to realisation the 'Grand Dessein' (later to be completed by Napoleon III) by initiating the junction of the Louvre and the Tuileries on the north side by a building starting from the Tuileries. The building operations were chiefly concerned with the fitting up of the Museum. To house the antiques, Reymond made use of the apartment formerly belonging to Anne of Austria (under the Galerie d'Apollon); this section of the Museum was opened on 18 Brumaire in the Year IX (9 November 1800). Between 1806 and 1817, Percier and Fontaine extended it to the south wing of the Cour Carrée; in 1812 the Salle des Cariatides was opened, containing the Borghese collection. The red and white marble of this *antiquarium* was based on the décor designed by Simonetti for Clement XIV in the Vatican Belvedere, and was intended to create an atmosphere reminiscent of the architecture of ancient Rome. As for the Grande Galerie, Percier and Fontaine undertook to redecorate it, making use of schemes devised during the *ancien régime*, and recorded by Hubert Robert in a picture exhibited in the Salon of 1796. Part of the Galerie was provided with overhead lighting; great transverse arches supported on double columns were built, to divide this immense perspective into bays. Actually, the complete project was only finished in our own day; it was inaugurated in 1947.

The magnificent Musée Napoléon was one of the glories of the Empire. People came from all over Europe to visit it; particularly from England, as is proved by the publication of several catalogues in English. The rooms were thronged with copyists. In fact, the Louvre was to play a major rôle in the destiny of French painting. Previously, the education of an artist had been in the hands of a master; henceforth, from Delacroix to Matisse, by way of Courbet and Renoir, it was the great masters in the Museum who supervised artistic education.

Requisition, selection, distribution, installation, removals, reinstallation, classification, restoration, inventories, exhibitions, catalogues, for thousands upon thousands of works—this veritable museological orgy was presided over by Baron Vivant-Denon, appointed Director General of the museum by Napoleon. The Baron combined an extremely acute mind with reckless bravery, and was the epitome of all the blue-blooded qualities of a nobleman of the *ancien régime*. He had been a courtier of Louis XV, and during the Revolution he managed to find favour with the *farouche* David. He won over Napoleon by his courage during the Egyptian campaign, in which he was a member of the scientific expedition, and he displayed the same courage when he had to face the enemy again in 1815. A curious print, showing him working on a staircase in the middle of mountains of books, objets d'art, statues and scientific instruments, expresses in a picturesque manner the formidable task which he assumed so cheerfully. In 1814 he was complimented by the King of Prussia himself on the organisation of the Museum. It is amazing that he was able to accomplish so much with so few collaborators; to assist him, he only had Lavallée, Secretary General, Dufourny, Keeper of Paintings, and Ennius Quirinus Visconti, Keeper of Antiques. The latter was none other than the Keeper of Antiques in the Capitol; he was a keen supporter of Revolutionary ideas, and had been Minister of the Interior and Consul of the Roman Republic in 1798. When the Roman antiques came to the Louvre, he followed them.

The activities of the Revolution and the Empire were not confined to the Louvre, which was by no means the only depository of captured treasures. On several occasions after the year VIII (1798–99), distributions finally involving more than a thousand pictures were carried out, benefiting twenty-two museums in the various *Départements* of the Empire. In this way the provincial museums of art were originated.

In Paris itself, the gallery of the Luxembourg Palace, now known as the Palais du Sénat, had been re-opened in 1802. The paintings by Rubens had been re-installed and could now be seen there, as well as works by Philippe de Champaigne, Vernet's series of the

Ports of France, continued by Hue, and works by living artists, notably David. Thus the idea of making the Luxembourg the 'noviciate' of the Louvre came into being; it was taken up again by Louis XVIII's administration.

A decree of 24 November 1793 had instituted a 'Musée spécial de l'École Française' at Versailles, in order to appease the municipality, who resisted with all their strength the transfer of the royal pictures to the Louvre. A number of paintings considered unworthy to appear in the company of the great masters—*bambochades*, erotic paintings of the eighteenth century, and so on—had thus been relegated to Versailles, together with the diploma pieces of late *académiciens*. This museum played a secondary rôle, and did not last long; as early as 1800 it was stripped and its pictures allotted to various official residences. By the end of the Empire, it was nothing but a memory.

The Musée des Monuments Français formed in the Dépôt des Petits Augustins is not really connected with our subject, since it contained hardly any paintings; nevertheless, as an institution devoted to mediaeval and Renaissance art, it deserves to be mentioned amongst the great museological undertakings of the Revolution.

All this transferring of works of art from one place to another by the Revolutionary government and the Empire has called forth much severe criticism. The indignation of historians is perhaps based on the 'nationalist' ideas of our own time, which were less applicable in the past. After all, it was not long after Napoleon had transported so many European works of art to the Louvre that Lord Elgin also removed the marble reliefs from the Parthenon. The Emperor of Austria acted in the same fashion as Napoleon without incurring the reproaches of history; when Francis II fell back on Vienna in 1815, he conveniently forgot to restore to their countries of origin the Treasure of the Golden Fleece, from Brussels, and the regalia of the Holy Roman Empire, from Frankfort and Nuremberg, to prevent them from falling into the hands of the French armies. And what of the depredations of Gustavus Adolphus' armies, in Germany and the rest of Europe, during the Thirty Years' War?

These deportations of works of art gave rise to much controversy in Paris. In 1796, a petition of protest was addressed to the Directory. The neo-classical aesthetician Quatremère de Quincy, who initiated it, published it under the title 'Letter concerning the harm done to science by the removal of works of art from Italy'. The petition was signed by a number of distinguished artists: the painter Valenciennes, the architects Percier and Fontaine, and the painters Moreau le Jeune, Louis David, Vien, Girodet, Vincent and Clérisseau. Feelings ran high on both sides, and a counter-petition was addressed to the government in the same year, supporting the opposite point of view. Among the signatories were the painters Gérard, Regnault, J. B. Isabey, and the Conservateur of the Dépôt des Petits Augustins. In order to appreciate the intentions of the governments responsible for these deportations, one should try to understand their attitude of mind. The concentration in Paris of some of the greatest European works of art is the outcome of museological policy which was itself closely bound up with the general political aims of the Revolution and the Empire. The Convention and the Directory were convinced that they were liberating the world from tyranny and absolutism; they dreamed of a Europe united under the democratic principles which were the real achievement of the Revolution. The men of this period were imbued with certain political, social and philosophical ideals which they believed would benefit humanity, and which should be extended to include all nations. It therefore seemed natural to concentrate the vital forces of the nation and of Europe in Paris, which would thus set an example of progress to the world. The great achievements in the arts and sciences, born of the patronage of princes and of the Church, had been in some degree 'contaminated by absolutism and obscurantism'; henceforth, they had to be collected together in Paris, in order to contribute to the progress of the human race. This idea is clearly expressed in the letter written on 11 Ventose of the Year V (28 February 1797) by the Minister of Justice, Merlin de Douai, to Bonaparte, General of the Army of Italy, to persuade him to bring to Paris 'the type used by the pontifical press of the Propaganda'. 'You know to what use this type was formerly put, and you will understand that to send it to Paris, the richest storehouse of human knowledge, is to put into the hands of the government a most powerful means of propagating philosophical principles, the achievements of science and the discoveries of engineering, and of hastening the growth of reason and happiness to which humanity is entitled.' In Paris were to be built up the archives of civilization, making it possible for French scholars to revise the history of politics, the arts, and science, in a spirit of liberation of the nations. This explains the removal of the archives of Simancas from Spain, and of the dossier of the Galileo trial from the pontifical archives.

The name 'Muséum Central des Arts' given to the Louvre by the Convention bears the stamp of this principle, which Napoleon continued to apply on a still larger scale. In fact, he wanted the capital of his thirty *Départements* to contain, like ancient Rome, the richest store of treasures in the Empire. But his solicitude also extended to other towns. The revolutionary principles propagated by his armies led to the formation throughout Europe of large museums which allowed the public to enjoy the advantages of collections which had previously been reserved for the privileged – the courts of nobles or of church dignitaries. In the Kingdom of Italy, under the influence of the Viceroy, Eugène de Beauharnais, the museological rationalization of the new State was particularly active. A decree of 1 September 1803 had created Academies of the Fine Arts at Milan and Bologna; and another on 12 February 1807 extended this measure to Venice, after that town had been annexed to the Kingdom by the Treaty of Pressburg (26 December 1805). Picture galleries were to be attached to these Academies[1]. Two of the largest galleries in Italy – the Accademia in Venice and the Brera in Milan – originated in this manner; they were made up of pictures belonging to the municipalities, supplemented out of the depots in which were stored works taken from the suppressed

---

[1] The galleries of Genoa, Mantua and Bologna also owe their origin to dépôts of the Revolutionary and Imperial period, later transformed into museums.

religious houses. The present wealth of the Brera gallery is explained by the fact that, as Milan was the capital of the kingdom, its gallery was therefore to be the finest and most complete in Italy. In order to build up its collection, the Viceroy's administration sent commissioners to Bologna and Venice, through Emilia and the Veneto, to select works from the dépôts formed there, and these commissioners were no more welcome to the local authorities than those of Bonaparte had previously been. The Veneto was the richest area in the kingdom, artistically speaking; it was particularly affected by these requisitions, which explains the relative inferiority of the Accademia when compared with the Brera, at least as far as Quattrocento painting is concerned. The Brera was the 'Muséum Central' – in fact, a 'Musée Napoléon' built up by 'pillaging' other Italian towns, and still remaining intact. Eugène de Beauharnais, full of concern for the success of his museum, bestowed fabulous gifts on it; the gallery owes some of its greatest treasures to his generosity – the *Madonna of Urbino*, by Piero della Francesca, Bellini's *Pietà*, and Raphael's *Sposalizio*. The other 'Napoleonides', installed on thrones created for them throughout Europe, also undertook the formation of museums in their kingdoms. Louis Napoleon, king of Holland, founded in 1808 what is now the Rijksmuseum, Amsterdam; Jérôme Bonaparte, king of Westphalia, employed Grandjean de Montigny to continue the building of the *'Fridericianum Museum'*, at Cassel, begun by Simon Louis de Ry for the Landgrave of Hesse. Finally, amid all the disturbances of war, King Joseph decided to create a picture gallery in the Prado, Madrid, by a decree of 20 December 1809, making use of the pictures belonging to the crown of Spain and those from the suppressed religious houses; fifteen hundred paintings were assembled in this manner. With a view to benefiting his subjects, this monarch, whose remarkable administrative gifts would have been better employed during a more peaceful period, devoted more attention to the enrichment of this museum than to that of the Louvre; Ferdinand VII was carrying on Joseph's project when he opened the museum of the Prado on 19 November 1819.

In the *Départements* which were under the direct administration of the Republic and later of the Empire, fifteen museums were created by the decree of 1 September 1801, signed by the First Consul. These new museums were to benefit by the redistribution of works of art carried out at the expense either of the Louvre or of the various dépôts set up locally as a result of the confiscations. Three museums created in towns which are now outside France —Brussels, Geneva, Mainz—thus found themselves in possession of pictures from the Louvre, some of which had even belonged to the French Crown; for example the *Martyrdom of Saint Liévin*, by Rubens, which had been bought by Louis XVI, was allotted to Brussels.

In addition to the official activities, the movement created by the Revolutionary spirit caused the formation of museums throughout Europe, either on the decision of the local authorities (Antwerp, Bologna) or through private initiative (Bergamo). And in 1815, when works of art were given back to the towns from which they had been taken, in the majority of cases they did not return to their former owners but were sent to the museum. In this way the Venice Accademia obtained from the Austrian government a great many pictures which had been taken from churches. When the paintings from Parma returned to that city from the Louvre, they were not restored to the churches and convents from whence they had come; in 1816 they went to make up a picture gallery round the former ducal *Quadreria*, founded in 1752 by Don Felippe di Borbone.

To understand this policy, one should avoid trying to compare it with the example recently given by the Nazis, in deporting works of art from the occupied countries of Europe. The justifications appeared to be the same: the creation of European unity and the superiority of the victorious nation. But the aims were fundamentally different. The French Revolution introduced into Europe the fertile germ of democratic liberties, and it is precisely as a result of the development of the principles it laid down that we are now able to criticise its policy of artistic centralization. These high ideals cannot be compared with those of National-Socialism, based on the suppression of liberty in favour of one party and of a racial dogma, and which, in order to carry out this policy of oppression, invented something never before seen in Europe or the civilized world: concentration camps, wholesale deportation, and the gas chamber; so that a new word had to be coined to fit this crime without precedent in the history of our civilization—*genocide*. A single example will illustrate these facts: Spain detested the French, and witnessed the halting of Napoleon's advance, yet it was King Joseph's government which did away with the Inquisition.

This concentration of works of art is now foreign to our habits of thinking; but it did not seem particularly scandalous to the enemies of France who occupied the country in 1814, since they did not interfere with the Musée Napoléon (which was then known as the Musée Royal). In 1814, only works not on exhibition were given back, and many of the pictures which had been requisitioned in Prussia without treaty.

Amongst the allies, certain individuals – and those not the least important – were in favour of the Museum; Baron Humboldt, for example, Minister of Prussia, and a personal friend of Denon. The King of Prussia and the Emperor of Austria, when they visited the Louvre, congratulated Denon on his well-kept galleries. The clauses in past treaties which had enriched its collections were not annulled by the Treaty of Paris; no doubt the various sovereigns who wished to help their 'cousin' in his task of restoring monarchical principles did not wish to deprive him of the works of art in the Museum, which was part of the Civil List of the king of France, and an important element of royal prestige. Thus Louis XVIII was able to say later to the Chambre des Représentants: 'The masterpieces of art henceforth belong to us by rights more stable than those of victory.'

Then came Waterloo. The allies were exasperated at having to kill Revolutionary France a second time, and gave her no quarter. Napoleon's valiant escapade cost his Museum its life, as it cost France several of her territorial possessions: the Saar, Landau, Savoy and the Val d'Aosta. The Museum was not in fact very vigorously defended. Talleyrand made an attempt, but did not persist; diplomatic agreement with the allies threatened to present such difficulties that it was judged best not to introduce additional ones on a subject considered to be of only secondary importance. 'Laissez faire' was the order of the day. This attitude clearly emerges from Denon's correspondence with Vaublanc, Minister of the Interior, with the Duc de Richelieu, Minister of the King's Household, and with the Comte de Pradel, all of whom appear to have been ready to leave the responsibility for any actions to their underlings, and were evidently prepared to disown them later, in whatever direction they had operated, on the pretext that they had been acting without orders.

Under the threat of bayonets, therefore, Denon and Lavallée had to resist unaided the claims of the foreign commissioners, in conditions which were intolerable to such punctilious officials. The first commissioners to present themselves – those of Prussia – were so insolent that their sovereign disowned them. On the other hand, Denon readily acknowledged the urbanity of the Austrian commissioners. The last to arrive were those from the Italian states; at their head paraded the sculptor Canova, who insisted on being addressed as 'Monsieur l'Ambassadeur', which won for him the nickname of 'Monsieur l'Emballeur' (i. e. 'the humbug') from the caustic Talleyrand. It was these last that Denon, with Humboldt's support, resisted most firmly, clinging doggedly to the clauses of the treaties.

In November 1815 Lavallée was able to furnish a statement of the works which had been reclaimed; it contained 5,233 items. However, most of the pictures which had been sent to the provinces, some of which were taken outside France, remained where they were. Denon was able to keep for the Louvre about a hundred canvases and eight hundred drawings. The Florentine commissioners were particularly courteous; by an agreement duly drawn up, they abandoned twenty-nine pictures, and so Denon was able to keep the primitives which he had collected during his mission of 1811, since at that time the Florentines did not appreciate these painters. Thus Cimabue, Giotto, and Fra Angelico remained at the Louvre. The largest painting to be abandoned was left behind by the Austrian commissioner Rosa, representing Venice. Veronese's *Marriage at Cana* had been transported from Venice to Paris with great difficulty; this enormous picture had had to be cut in half, and it was not possible to perform the same operation to facilitate its return, because of the way in which it had been put together. Rosa appreciated all these obstacles, and preferred to leave the picture in the Louvre, taking in exchange for it a painting of a similar subject by Le Brun, *Mary Magdalen at the feet of the Pharisee*, to put in its place in the refectory of San Giorgio.

These successes were due to Denon's own personal qualities. The greatest compliment he ever received was paid to him by an enemy. Ribbentrop, the Intendant General of the Prussian Armies, had been particularly hostile to him, even going so far as to threaten him with arrest and internment in the fortress of Graudentz; but on leaving Paris he wrote Denon a letter which contained the following passage: 'My gratitude for the pleasant moments passed in your company is joined by that of the whole civilized world, which owes to you the preservation of its great works of art.'

Louis XVIII's government was to prove less generous than the enemy. Denon, who recalled too vividly a glorious past, was not on good terms with the court. In October 1815, weary and aged (he was 62), he requested 'permission to retire from his labours'. His Majesty accepted his resignation, and expressed satisfaction 'with his zealous efforts to save for France some of the masterpieces which she had now lost'. Lavallée, a less skilful courtier than Denon, was not so well treated. He was reproached with ill-timed zeal at the time when the allies were reclaiming their art treasures; and the administration, which at the critical moment had turned a deaf ear to all his appeals, now accused him of not having consulted it. Full of indignation, Lavallée made a sharp reply to his accusers. In November 1816 he was dismissed.

THE CIVIL LIST MUSEUM

DURING THE CONVENTION, the Louvre was a democratic institution. Throughout the nineteenth century, till the end of the Second Empire, the museum was attached to the sovereign's civil list and, except for the short interlude of the Second Republic, was a monarchical institution. From the time of the Renaissance, the protection of the arts and the formation of collections had been princely privileges. None of the sovereigns who reigned in France during the nineteenth century – Napoleon III least of all – neglected this powerful means of increasing prestige, and during this period the Louvre was to benefit from a conception which identified the interests of the museum with those of the monarch.

Immediately after the allies had reclaimed their art treasures, the poor stripped Louvre seemed a veritable symbol of defeat. An attempt was made to re-stock it; Lavallée, alone now that Denon had resigned, wanted to build up the gallery of paintings again by recalling the works which had been distributed to the provinces by his administration, but he encountered the stubborn resistance of Vaublanc, the Minister of the Interior. Louis XVIII's administration made matters even worse by sending another 300 pictures and 120 objets d'art to various museums and churches. However, the king confirmed certain of the artistic gains made during the Revolution; he gave orders that works seized from *émigrés* should remain museum property, except for those which were not on view.

The walls of the Grande Galerie were then covered by bringing in the pictures which had been installed in the Luxembourg in 1802: Vernet's series of *Ports*, Le Sueur's *Life of Saint Bruno*, and above all the *History of Marie de Médicis* by Rubens, now removed for the second time from the palace for which it had been designed (and where, in any case, it was not in its original position).

61

The gaps left in the Louvre by the departure of the antiquities and of the paintings by the great masters were in fact destined to be filled in a manner of which contemporaries could have had not the slightest inkling.

Having created Egyptology, France took the initiative in Assyriology, and was to play a leading rôle in the discovery of early civilization. Works of art were to pour into the Museum in their thousands; moreover, the neo-classical taste which extolled the superiority of Graeco-Roman antiquity made up for the loss of the Vatican sculptures with fine collections of vases, bronzes, and a few original Greek statues. Finally, the increasing interest in the Middle Ages and the Renaissance, due to the Romantic movement, was to initiate the formation of collections of objets d'art of those periods.

A second factor, of which contemporaries were beginning to be aware, was to bring into the Louvre so many masterpieces of painting that the walls could scarcely hold them. The museum was to benefit from the fact that during the nineteenth century France had the good fortune to give birth to a school of painting so rich in talents that only the Italian Renaissance, it has been said, could be compared with it.

Fortunately for contemporary art, the Restoration proved liberal compared with the July monarchy of Louis Philippe. Most of the hundred and eleven pictures which Louis XVIII's administration bought for a total of 668,256 francs are modern works. Louis XVIII, and later Charles X, did not wish to appear less favourable to artists than Napoleon had done. The picture by Heim, showing Charles X distributing the awards to the Salon prize-winners of 1824, is evidence of his intention to support them. In the Salons, mentions and medals went to the boldest of the innovators; the state bought Delacroix' *Dante and Virgil* (Salon of 1822) and his *Massacres of Scio* (Salon of 1824). From the regicide David, who was a voluntary exile in Brussels, and who had declined the king's invitation to return to Paris, Louis XVIII bought *Leonidas at Thermopylae* and the *Rape of the Sabines* in 1819 for 100,000 francs, a considerable sum in those days. His administration also bought Prud'hon's *Christ on the Cross* and his *Assumption*. Under Charles X, the Comte de Forbin bought Géricault's *Raft of the Méduse*, depicting an event which had been considered a scandal for the royal government; the same Director was also responsible for acquiring David's *Madame Récamier*.

All these works were installed in the 'Galerie royale du Luxembourg'; contemporary masterpieces bought by the state had to spend some time there before joining the Immortals in the Louvre. The Luxembourg gallery was opened on 24 April 1818 for the work of living artists. The recruiting of paintings for this museum did not depend on the Conservateurs of the Louvre, but on other officials of the Administration des Beaux-Arts; these made most of their purchases at the Salons, and their choice was unfortunately guided by that of the juries and followed the official taste of the time.

The museum of Versailles was dedicated by Louis Philippe 'to the glory of great men of all periods', including the revolutionaries, and absorbed most of the funds spent on the fine arts by the July monarchy. Building work on the Louvre was abandoned; but the collections continued to grow as a result of archaeological researches, and even through the generosity of the king, who liked to take his little daily walk there, in true bourgeois fashion.

Archaeology made rapid strides during this reign, but the activities of the Département des Peintures seemed to slow down; however, a few important items were added to the collection. It seems a pity that more purchases were not made, when prices were so advantageous; Chardin's *Self-Portrait* was bought in 1839, together with that of his wife, for 196 francs. Simone Martini's *Christ carrying the Cross*, which would fetch several hundred thousand dollars today, had been bought in 1834 for 200 francs; Paolo Uccello's *Portraits of Artists* was acquired for 1,467 francs, and the Museum also purchased Mabuse's fine *Carondelet Diptych*. One must not omit to mention the modern works, by Ingres, Delacroix and others, purchased during the reign of the bourgeois king by an Administration des Beaux-Arts which was fortunately eclectic in its tastes.

Louis Philippe gave the Louvre a truly royal present, which it only kept for a few years. Taking up an idea formerly suggested by Denon, the king entrusted to Baron Taylor – a strange and ambitious character who had made a name for himself by purchasing and transporting the obelisk of Luxor – the sum of a million francs from his personal fortune, with instructions to go to Spain and form a collection of pictures from that country. The moment was propitious; the Carlist war was at its height – the Jesuits and nine hundred religious houses had been suppressed. Baron Taylor, who knew Spain well, brought back for 1,327,000 francs a collection of 412 Spanish pictures, 15 by northern artists, and 26 by Italian masters. The collection was lent to the Louvre by the king, and opened on 7 January 1838 on the first floor of the Colonnade wing. Of course, it contained a good many second-rate paintings, because of the conditions under which it was assembled – Taylor had chiefly aimed at quantity; but there were also a great number of magnificent pictures. These Spanish works were joined by another collection left to the king by a Scottish admirer, F. Hall Standish; this brought in an additional 220 pictures, mostly Spanish, but not of such high quality.

These two collections were claimed by Louis Philippe with his personal goods after the revolution of 1848. The Republic did not come to any arrangement for compensation with the Orleans family; the Spanish museum was given up between 1850 and 1851, after the death of the king, and sold in London in 1853 for the sum of 940,000 francs. Louis Philippe's gallery is one of the Louvre's lost opportunities; one does not dare to think of what the museum would have been if this collection had been retained. Some idea can be gained from the fact that it is the source of most of the Spanish pictures now dispersed in the galleries of Europe and America! ... Although it was on exhibition for such a short time, contemporary painting reflected its influence; the early work of Courbet and Millet show traces of it, and Manet, young as he was at the time, was deeply impressed; this early contact determined his definite leaning towards Spanish art. Several canvases returned to France later: the four Zurbarans in the museum of Grenoble, and El Greco's *Christ on the Cross* in the Louvre, bought from Prades in 1908.

Until 1848, most of the Galerie des Peintures was only on show for half the year. In accordance with a custom which originated during the *ancien régime*, the annual Salon was held in the 'Salon' of the Louvre, and occupied part of the Grande Galerie. During the three months of the exhibition, and for a similar length of time while it was being installed, the public was therefore deprived of a large proportion of the pictures in the collection. Under the July monarchy there were many protests at this state of affairs, which did not even benefit the Salon, since the Louvre was a very inconvenient place for it. The Museum was finally relieved of this encumbrance during the Second Republic.

The July Monarchy may appear to have ended with a favourable balance, but one must not forget that it left the arts in a somewhat adverse situation. Millions of francs swallowed up by the history paintings at Versailles, the misguided restorations at Fontainebleau, the 804,000 francs generously granted to Horace Vernet for covering acres of canvas, the hundreds of pompous history pieces bought at the various Salons which now make hideous France's provincial museums, the vast decorative works carried out in public buildings or in the Paris churches – the period is irrevocably branded with these errors.

One cannot lay all the blame for this situation on the personality of Louis Philippe alone. The fault is mainly due to the fact that an increasing influence was exercised over the fine arts by an incompetent administration, which looked for inspiration to the aesthetic dogmas propagated by the Institut, and to the rise of the middle classes, who gradually took the place of the aristocratic patrons.

Till the time of Louis Philippe, the king had been accepted as a sort of regent of the arts. It was in his reign that for the first time a conflict arose between the royal patronage and the administration; at the 1832 session of the Chamber, the deputies disputed the king's claim to govern the artists on his own. Nevertheless, authority over the arts remained almost entirely vested in the civil list, on which the Louvre depended, so the king was able to exercise a considerable influence. But the administration of the Beaux-Arts also had large sums at its disposal (sometimes the Parlement voted it special funds, as in the case of the archaeological excavations of Botta). Aided by the Ecole des Beaux-Arts and the Institut, which became more and more actively concerned, this administration helped to increase the discord between official circles and living artists, forcing the latter to take up a revolutionary attitude which was to have dire consequences later.

The short-lived Republic of 1848 played an important part in the fortunes of the Louvre. It was this government which initiated the completion of the palace, finally achieved under Napoleon III. The young republic, born in enthusiasm, was determined not to be outdone by the monarchy in anything concerning the arts. Having decided to complete the 'grand dessein', the government wished to dedicate the 'palais du peuple' to the arts and the sciences (thus, in fact, adopting Diderot's project), by housing the enlarged museum in it, together with the Bibliothèque Nationale, and allotting rooms for industrial exhibitions. It is a pity that this programme was not followed up by Napoleon III and by the Third Republic, which turned the Louvre over to offices.

The sum of money granted by the Assembly was not sufficient to allow the architect Duban to do more than restore – on the pretext of re-establishing their original condition – the outer façades of the Galerie d'Apollon and the Grande Galerie, and put in order the dilapidated rooms in the Museum. The Salon Carré and the Salle des Sept Cheminées were provided with ceilings, heavily ornamented but not unpleasing; the Galerie d'Apollon acquired a ceiling painted by Delacroix – one of his finest works: *Apollo overcoming the Python*. Unfortunately, the original décor was altered to some extent by Duban.

Meanwhile, the Département des Peintures was completely re-classified and reorganised by its *conservateur* Villot, who was an amateur painter, a friend of Delacroix, and a man of discerning tastes. He was attached to the Museum administration in various capacities from

1848 to 1874; his painter's studio could be seen for many years in the Louvre, above the Egyptian staircase. On this occasion he compiled the remarkable catalogues which are still the basis of any study of the history of the Département des Peintures. His re-classification remained for the most part unchanged till 1914; it gave evidence of a scientific approach. Pictures were arranged chronologically, and works by the same artist were grouped together. The Salle des Sept Cheminées was devoted to paintings of the Empire period; in the Grande Galerie, works of earlier schools were displayed in order, grouped according to their country of origin. In the Salon Carré were assembled the greatest masterpieces of all schools, on the model of the *Tribuna* of the Uffizi, Florence. On 5 June 1851 the Prince President inaugurated the new installations, accompanied by Monsieur de Nieuwerkerke, a sculptor and a man of good family, who had been appointed Directeur des Musées in 1849. During the Empire he was the Surintendant des Beaux-Arts, and the salon he held in the Louvre was to be one of the most famous in Paris. His predecessor as Directeur des Musées de la République had been the painter Jeanron. The tradition established during the *ancien régime* of putting an artist in charge of works of art was to remain in force for a long time.

The republican Jeanron was director only for a very short time, but in spite of his brief term of office (28 February 1848–25 December 1849) he made a deep impression on the Museum.

The *Conservateurs* did not devote their time entirely to classification and restoration; they also continued to purchase works of art. During Jeanron's directorship, the Louvre bought seven pictures for 11,820 francs, four of them by Géricault; during that of Nieuwerkerke, ten pictures were bought for 135,464 francs, among which were a Hobbema, a Perugino, a Rubens, a Memling and three Géricaults.

The annual sum allocated to the Museum for new acquisitions was 50,000 francs, raised to 100,000 francs in 1852. Villot was already complaining of its inadequacy in his own time; but in that fortunate epoch the Parlement did not consider the affairs of the Museum to be beneath its notice, and voted supplementary funds to enable the Louvre to deal with exceptional circumstances. Thus, the museum was granted 100,000 francs so that it could be properly represented at the sale of the King of the Netherlands' gallery in August 1850, when it acquired Perugino's *Madonna with two Saints and two Angels* for 53,302 francs; the *Portrait of Baron du Vicq* by Rubens for 15,984 francs, and Memling's *Saint John and Saint Mary Magdalen* for 11,728 francs. In the same way the Chambres voted a sum of 23,400 francs to allow the Louvre to buy two pictures by Géricault, the *Wounded Cuirassier* and the *Officer of the Chasseurs*, at the sale of the effects of the late King Louis Philippe, on 29 April 1851.

During the reign of Napoleon III, the Louvre was again to enjoy a brilliant period. A monarchy unsupported by traditional legitimacy is all the more in need of a dazzling façade to gain acceptance. One knows how Napoleon III tried to live down his revolutionary origins by constantly affirming that he was successor of the kings of France. It was in this spirit that he resumed work on the 'grand dessein' – the plan for the completion of the Louvre.

He made his intention clear immediately upon his accession, and had a space cleared for the masons by Baron Haussman, who gained experience for his later undertakings by cleaning up the approaches, where the neighbouring buildings had become entangled with the older parts of the palace. The first stone of the new building programme was laid on 25 July 1852, under the direction of the architect Louis-Tullius Joachim Visconti, son of the Conservateur des Antiques in the Louvre. He united the Louvre with the Tuileries on the north, and built a second wing parallel to the Grande Galerie, running about half its length, making a similar addition to its northern counterpart. A number of new courts were thus created. He altered the west outer façade of the Cour Carrée in order to adapt it to the style of his own buildings, and finally provided the Grande Galerie with overhead sources of light. The main structure of this colossal scheme was completed on 14 August 1857. Unfortunately, Napoleon III was not satisfied with what had been done; on the whole, the work had been carried out with due respect for the past, but it was not rich enough for his taste, and so did not sufficiently advertise the prosperity of the

Empire and the magnificence of his reign. He therefore had the whole of it modified between 1861 and 1865 by Hector Lefuel, who covered the Palace with an exuberance of decorative sculpture, and destroyed all traces of the old palace in the west part by demolishing that side of the Grande Galerie, thus reducing it by a half—an extraordinary act of vandalism. At the same time, he endowed the palace with those enormous staircases which for nineteenth-century Europe seem to have been the perfect symbol of power, splendour, and a high level of culture. One finds it hard to believe that these gigantic enterprises were completed in so short a time. Even with the advantages of modern machinery, giving a hundred times greater capacity of work, we are far from matching such records today.

Political intentions underlay everything which Napoleon III undertook concerning the museum. One of his first acts was to found the 'Musée des Souverains', affirming the monarchical principle, as renewed by successive dynasties. This museum was installed on the first floor of the Colonnade wing, where Duban had moved the panelling taken from the apartments in the Pavillon du Roi.

At the beginning of the century, the Museum had received, not undeservedly, the title of 'Musée Napoléon'. The Emperor also cherished the ambition of attaching his name to some great museological creation. The opportunity soon presented itself; the Campana collection in Rome was offered for sale. The Marquis Campana was one of the collecting maniacs so often encountered in the nineteenth century. He spent nearly ten million on acquiring throughout Italy objets d'art of all kind—vases, bronzes, antique terra cottas, majolica, furniture, and mediaeval and Renaissance paintings. Having thus spent his entire fortune, he deposited his whole collection with the Roman pawnbroker's office, of which he was himself the director, and borrowed against this pledge in order to be able to buy more—with the result that his borrowings soon came to four million more than the amount of his surety. He was condemned to the galleys, but saved himself by giving up his works of art. The pontifical government considered reserving for itself the right to buy back the collection in order to complete its own; but it gave up this plan before

69

long. The existence of this immense museum for sale aroused covetous feelings throughout Europe; Russia had already acquired several pieces, and the British Museum had begun negotiations. But, thanks to Napoleon III's initiative, France triumphed. Léon Renier, a member of the Institut, assisted by the painter Sébastien Cornu, a pupil of Ingres, was sent to Rome to discuss the purchase. A special fund of 4,260,000 francs was voted as an emergency measure for the acquisition, the transport and the installation of the collections; they were bought for 4,360,440 francs, and were exhibited from 1 May to 1 October 1864 in the Palais de l'Industrie of the Exposition Universelle of 1855. This museum received the name of 'Musée Napoléon III'.

The collection could not be transferred to the Louvre in its entirety; in any case some of the antiques were archaeological finds of little value. The objects regarded as 'inutiles' for the Louvre collections were shared out between the departmental museums. The collection of paintings consisted of 646 items, mainly from Cardinal Fesch's collection, which had been broken up in 1843, and from the religious houses of central Italy; it was made up chiefly of fourteenth and fifteenth century works which are highly appreciated today, but at that time were considered to be chiefly of historical interest. In that period the Louvre was regarded as a museum of masterpieces, and the conservateurs of the Département des Peintures gave little heed to items of documentary value. For this reason Baron Reiset only reserved ninety-seven paintings for the Louvre, when he was given the task of distributing the collection, though when the Académie des Beaux-Arts was consulted it increased the number to 313. The discarded canvases were divided up between sixty-seven provincial museums.

This dispersal aroused vehement protests in the literary and artistic circles of the time, in which Ingres and Delacroix took part. The press took up the affair, and the critics were divided in two camps–for or against the transfer of the collection to the Louvre. Supporters of the autonomy of the Musée Napoléon wanted the collection to become a 'Musée d'études pratiques', or a museum for encouraging industrial art; it was to be a source of models in all genres of applied or decorative arts, on the lines of the Victoria and Albert Museum, London (established in 1852) which aroused a great deal of interest in France.

Emile Galichon, one of the most ardent supporters of this scheme, argued that the entry of the Campana collection into the Louvre would not be in keeping with the original intention of that Museum 'which should confine itself exclusively to pure works of art'.

The 313 pictures which remained in the Louvre were installed in the rooms in the Colonnade, while the antique objets d'art were arranged in the old Salle des Gardes, which had become the Salle des Etats during the Restoration, and which in 1869 was to house the La Caze collection. A painting by Giraud, bought by the Louvre, shows how the room looked before the Campana collection had made way for the La Caze paintings. On 15 August 1863, the feast of the Emperor's patron saint, he opened the museum which bore his name.

Reiset was extremely unwilling to admit the pictures retained by the Académie. He seems to have had nothing but scorn for the Campana collection; perhaps a traditionally classical taste prevented him from appreciating those works by the Italian primitives whose great value had been understood by Delacroix, and yet he himself gave to the Louvre an unsigned work by a primitive artist – this time French: the *Martyrdom of Saint Denis,* attributed to Malouel (1863). When the Empire fell, Reiset lost no time in breaking up the collection. On 8 July 1872 the Minister of Public Instruction made a general distribution of pictures among the provincial museums; the Campana collection lost 141 items, and another 38 during the succeeding years.

It is not so much the actual distribution, but the way in which it was carried out, which is open to criticism. Given the importance of the collection, it was reasonable that Paris should not be the only town to benefit from it; but it would have been better to have divided it into a few large groups of items and kept these groups together in the museums of some of the more important towns, rather than scatter it far and wide. Polyptychs were dismembered, and the separate pieces sent to the four corners of France; series were broken up, *cassoni* were pulled apart, and the distribution was moreover made with so little method that it is now difficult to trace some of the works. In our own time Monsieur Vergnet Ruiz, Inspector-General of Provincial Museums, has applied himself to the task of regrouping, by means of exchanges, a part of the collection in order to form a museum of primitive Italian painting at Avignon – a work demanding much patience, and on which he has spent nearly ten years.

The Louvre, which was poor in Italian works of the fourteenth and fifteenth centuries, kept for itself from the collection a few paintings by Tura, Crivelli, Vivarini, Signorelli, Sano di Pietro, Lorenzo Veneziano, and two great masterpieces, Leonardo's *Annunciation* and Uccello's *Battle Scene*.

The Département des Peintures was further enriched, just before the fall of the Empire, by what was undoubtedly the most splendid gift it ever received. In 1869, Doctor Louis La Caze died, bequeathing his collection to the Louvre; it contained no less than 802 paintings, of which 302, in accordance with the wishes of the donor himself, were distributed amongst the provinces. This prodigious assembly of works of art, containing masterpieces of all the schools of painting, was built up by its owner's taste and flair, rather than his wealth. Doctor La Caze, who lived only for medicine and painting, lived in a house in the rue du Cherche-Midi, completely bare of furniture, among heaps of pictures which had even overflowed into the stables and coach-houses. Some of the greatest masterpieces in the Louvre are there because of his generosity; the quality of his collection can be judged by the following items: Ribera's *Boy with a Club Foot*, the *Portrait of an Old Woman* and the *Gipsy Girl* by Frans Hals, the *Reading Lesson* by Terborch, Rembrandt's *Man with a Stick* and *Bathsheba*, the *Benedicite* by Nicolas Maes, *Philopomene recognised by an Old Woman*, and sketches for the ceiling of the Jesuit Church at Antwerp, by Rubens, all of which are amongst the museum's most valuable possessions. The collection of French works, however, was of capital importance, and included paintings by Le Nain, Largillière, Chardin, two of Fragonard's finest works, and, finally, eight Watteaus – an unprecedented windfall for the Louvre; because of Louis XV's lack of perception, Watteau would have remained almost unknown in France if it had not been for La Caze.

Numerous purchases were made during the same period, with the evident intention of filling gaps in the collection. Works by Chardin were bought, the *Water-Mill* by Hobbema, the *Lace-Maker* (the Louvre's only Vermeer), and Rembrandt's *Flayed Ox*. An attempt was made to re-stock the Spanish gallery, so inopportunely lost in 1848. Several pictures from Marshal Soult's famous collection were bought in 1852, 1858 and 1867: Herrera's *Saint Basil*, Murillo's *Immaculate Conception*, his *Miracle of Saint James* (the *Cuisine des Anges*) and his *Birth of the Virgin, Christ in the Tomb*, at that time attributed to Ribera, and Zurbaran's two great panels the *History of Saint Bonaventure* and *Saint Apollonia*. Murillo's *Immaculate Conception*, which came from the Hospital of the Venerable Fathers in Seville, cost an enormous sum (586,000 francs plus expenses, which brought it up to 615,000 francs) at the Soult sale in 1852. More than a century later it left the Louvre; in 1941 it was exchanged with the Prado for Velasquez' *Queen Marianna*, since the gallery possessed no authentic work by this artist.

The work of restoring the paintings was being actively carried on at this time; some of the pictures were in poor condition due to their age, and the colours were hidden under darkening layers of varnish. This work sometimes aroused hostile criticism which was echoed in the press — particularly in 1860, when violent disapproval was expressed at the restoration of certain Italian paintings in the Grande Galerie (Raphael's *Saint Michael,* Cima da Conegliano's *Madonna,* and Palma Vecchio's *Adoration of the Shepherds*) and of Rubens' *Galerie Médicis*. Villot was attacked personally; he was then transferred from the conservancy to the administrative branch. Since the *Galerie Médicis* had been painted by Rubens, it had suffered many vicissitudes. To those already mentioned must be added its stay in the Gobelins from 1828 to 1838; with incredible lack of thought, the paintings themselves had been used as cartoons, and remained rolled up on the looms for years. Villot therefore decided to restore them. The restoration carried out in 1952, before they were installed in their present quarters, revealed the injustice of the attacks on Villot nearly a century earlier; except for three or four whose deterioration was due to other causes than restoration, these pictures are in a remarkably good state of preservation.

During the war of 1870, the Louvre was used as an arsenal and a clothing store. When Paris was threatened, two hundred and ninety pictures were evacuated to Brest. When the Empire fell, the Director General, the Comte de Nieuwerkerke, resigned, and the administration was carried on by a Conservatoire of artists, among whom were Courbet, Daumier and Braquemond. The burning of the Tuileries by the Commune destroyed the only old portion of the western end of the Palace; but the fire was prevented from spreading to the Grande Galerie by the action of a battalion of Chasseurs, under Commandant de Bernardy de Sigoyer.

THE MUSÉE NATIONAL

UNDER THE MONARCHICAL RÉGIMES of the 19th century, an institution which made the national collections dependent on the sovereign had not always been regarded with a friendly eye. This mistrust, already visible in the time of Louis Philippe, became more marked over the question of the Campana collection. Certain pamphleteers had protested at the acquisition by the Louvre – a civil list Museum – of a collection which had not been bought with funds from that source, but with money specially voted by Parlement. They claimed that the State ought to possess a museum distinct from the Louvre, and tried to create discord between the Ministry of State and that of the Imperial Household. When the allies were reclaiming works of art in 1815, had not Louis XVIII tried to persuade the sovereigns concerned that the collections in the Louvre, whose upkeep was provided for out of his civil list, were the property of the Crown?

Under the Republic, this ambiguous situation was to come to an end. The Museum became the property of the Nation, a state of affairs which had both advantages and drawbacks. The Museum no longer benefited from the personal interest of Princes; it became simply one of many State institutions, of even less importance, if anything, than the rest. Its fortunes were no longer in the hands of a man for whom it was an important source of prestige; they depended on a 'disinterested' administration, itself dependent on a government and a Parlement for whom the arts had little importance as a political factor.

On the other hand, once the Museum had become national property, it considerably stimulated private initiative. Gifts from individuals had already been received under the Second Empire – objets d'art from Sauvageot and paintings from La Caze; during the following period these were no longer exceptional, but became the usual method of extending the collections; the Louvre came to depend more on the generosity of private persons than on that of the State. Art lovers interested in the future of the Museum eventually pooled their endeavours and formed themselves into a society—the *Société des Amis du Louvre*, founded in 1897—which has been responsible for the acquisition by the Département des Peintures of some splendid works, such as the Avignon *Pietà*.

During the early years of the Republic, the Museum was in a very precarious position. The general Budget of the State only allotted 162,000 francs for the acquisition of new items—a sum which would not have been sufficient to purchase even one major work. The position changed in 1895, when a law was passed instituting the Réunion des Musées Nationaux; this organisation possessed a distinct civil and moral individuality, had its own funds, and was governed by an assembly known as the Conseil des Musées Nationaux. The latter body was divided into two parts in 1941; the administrative council, concerned with financial allocations, and the artistic council, whose rôle was to examine proposed acquisitions suggested by the various heads of departments, who had previously had to submit them to the *Comité des Conservateurs*. With a view to ensuring that the *Conseil Artistique* should be representative of the taste of all the various elements of society, and that as much control as possible should be exercised over the *Conservateurs*, this body includes today members of the Institut, officials of the Council of State, of the Cour des Comptes, and of the Ministry of Finance, honorary keepers of the museums, and a certain number of connoisseurs.

The funds of the National Museums were henceforth supplemented by a budgetary allowance, in addition to their own income from various sources: entrance money, sale of the Crown diamonds (1887), sale of Madame Thiers' necklace (1924), and legacies of money.

During the period between 1890 and 1914 Paris was at its height as an international art market. Works of art poured into the French capital from all over the world; opportunities for increasing the collections were therefore frequent. But the Louvre was faced with competition from rich private collectors, from France and elsewhere, and from more recently founded foreign museums which spent considerable sums on stocking their galleries. At that time there was bitter rivalry between museums throughout the world; this is less the case today, since a spirit of international solidarity has developed in the profession. As an example of the desperate struggles to acquire masterpieces, one may cite the case of the *Adoration of the Magi,* by Hugo van der Goes; this was being sold at Montforte de Lemos, in Spain, in 1910, having been discovered in a mysterious way. Paul Leprieur, Conservateur des Peintures, was notified of this by Salomon Reinach, and went with all possible speed to Montforte, only to find that others were there before him— Sir W. Armstrong, Director of the Museum at Dublin, M. Hulin de Loo, Director of the Brussels Museum, and an envoy of Dr. Bode, Director of the Berlin Museum. It was the last who carried off the picture, for 1,180,000 gold francs—an enormous sum at that time.

The resources of the museum were not sufficient to allow it to fill all the gaps in the collection of earlier paintings, as would have been desirable, and to enable it to take advantage of the fact that works of art were changing hands with great frequency between 1880 and 1930. However, a number of important acquisitions were made of works by the Primitives: the *Resurrection of Lazarus,* by Geertgen tot Sint Jans, the *Braque Triptych* by Rogier van der Weyden, bought in 1913 for 800,000 francs, and the Avignon *Pietà,* bought by the Amis du Louvre from the Hospice of Villeneuve-les-Avignon for 100,000 francs; after the exhibition of French Primitives in 1904, Dürer's *Self-Portrait* was also bought in 1922, for 300,000. Particular efforts were made to obtain works of schools which were inadequately represented in the Louvre; some good English pictures were thus acquired for the collection.

Such was the reputation of the Louvre that it even enjoyed the patronage of foreign benefactors. It owes Patinir's *Saint Jerome,* a valuable addition to the Dutch collection, to the English dealer Lord Duveen. In 1927, the Louvre tried in vain to purchase at the Warneck sale a rare work by Adriaen Brouwer (a landscape) which went for 380,000 francs; with the greatest courtesy Colonel Friedsam, President of the Metropolitan Museum, New York, bought it in order to offer it to the Louvre. In 1948 Mr. Percy Moore Turner, an Englishman, presented the museum with several pictures, including Georges de La Tour's *Saint Joseph;* the Louvre also received a Constable from him in 1952. The most striking demonstration of sympathy with the museum ever given by a foreigner is the gift made to it by Carlos de Beistegui, a Mexican citizen who collected rare pictures for nearly fifty years; he intended that they should eventually go to the Louvre, and sometimes acted on the advice of the *Conservateur* in buying pictures beyond the reach of the latter. His collection entered the Louvre in 1953, after the death of its owner. As well as superb portraits by Ingres and David—including the latter's *Napoleon with the Treaty of Campo Formio*—it includes one of Goya's great masterpieces, the *Countess del Carpio,* and admirable pictures by Largillière, Fragonard, Rubens and Van Dyck, together with two valuable French Primitives. The money left to the Louvre by the American-born Princesse de Polignac-Singer for the acquisition of masterpieces of painting and sculpture should also be considered as a piece of foreign generosity. Thanks to this legacy, the Louvre has been able to resume the position in the international market which it had occupied before the 1914–1918 war; among the works which I have been able to obtain for the Museum through the money thus available must be mentioned the three panels of the polyptych painted by Sassetta at Borgo San Sepolcro, which I had discovered at Bordeaux in 1952.

However, the principal additions to the treasures of the gallery were paintings of the modern French school. Under Villot, paintings of the Imperial school were already being shown in the Louvre, in the Salle des Sept Cheminées; but the canvases of Ingres and Delacroix still waited in the Luxembourg. They were transferred at the beginning of the Third Republic; Napoleon III's Salle des Etats was allotted to them, and provided with a massive ceiling decoration in stucco which was removed in 1949–1950, when the large Venetian room was organised. The inauguration took place on 27 October 1886; Ingres' *Roger delivering Angelica* and his *Apotheosis of Homer* were exhibited there, together with Delacroix' great canvases, the *Massacres of Scio, Liberty guiding the People*, the *Women of Algiers*, the *Jewish Wedding*, and the *Entry of the Crusaders into Constantinople* – the last item having been removed from the Galerie des Batailles at Versailles.

A revolutionary spirit inspires all the art of the century. Each group, each artist asserts the right to independence; the powers of innovation of men of genius outstripped the comprehension of society, who laughed at masterpieces which were subsequently to be worshipped. With infallible sureness, the Académie des Beaux-Arts (the chief influence in the Salons) turned public taste in the wrong direction. Ingres and Delacroix, cherished by the Institut and provided with State commissions, enjoyed an official position. Matters were very different for the lesser romantic masters – for the Barbizon landscape painters, for Daumier, Courbet and Millet. Except for a few purchases at the Salons, by which Millet and Courbet benefited, works by these artists were not bought by the State until they had become dear – in other words, till after the artists were dead – owing to the unfortunate eclectic policy which was pursued. After 1880, successive *Conservateurs* made praiseworthy efforts to redeem the errors of the Beaux-Arts administration; they would have achieved little, however, without the help of donors. Courbet's *Burial at Ornans* was given to the Museum in 1883 by the artist's sister, Mlle. Juliette Courbet; in 1889 a group of art-lovers banded together to purchase the same artist's *Deer Covert* at the Secrétan sale; in 1890 Madame Pommery offered Millet's *Gleaners*, acquired at the same sale, to the Louvre. Two men in particular devoted themselves to the rehabilitation of romantic painting. Thomy-Thierry, a man of refined taste, living quietly in retirement, devoted his fortune to acquiring a collection of 121 pictures by Corot, Rousseau, Dupré, Delacroix, Diaz, Millet, Daubigny, Decamps, Meissonier, Troyon and Isabey, which he bequeathed to the Louvre in 1902. Chauchard, founder of the Magasins du Louvre, bequeathed 140 pictures by the same artists to the museum in 1910; but his collection had a slightly different character; it was created less to satisfy his personal taste than to fulfil a desire for luxurious surroundings which was quite natural in the case of a successful and important business man who wished to live in a setting worthy of his fortune. He therefore spent large sums on the formation of a collection which was on the whole not so fine as that of Thomy-Thierry; the price of 553,000 francs which he gave for Millet's *Angelus* at the Secrétan sale is still famous in the annals of art dealing.

The minor romantic artists entered the Louvre without having to pass through a penitential period in the Luxembourg. Théodore Rousseau, constantly rejected from the Salon by hostile juries, condemned to obscurity and poverty by the obstinate lack of understanding of mediocre academicians, now has approximately twenty pictures in the Louvre. During his lifetime, his works had no market value; in 1912 the museum gave 287,000 francs for his famous *Avenue of Chestnuts* at the Landolfo-Carcano sale.

The State itself made sacrifices in order to obtain for the Louvre some great nineteenth-century paintings which joined works purchased in the Salons on the walls of the museum. With the help of national subscription and a contribution from the Amis du Louvre, Courbet's *The Artist's Studio* was bought in 1919 for 900,000 francs. Two years later, Delacroix' *Sardanapalus* was acquired from Baron Vitta for 800,000 francs.

In spite of the scandal they caused, the Impressionists did not have to wait so long at the door of the museum. They entered the Luxembourg as part of the Caillebotte legacy, of which, unfortunately, only a portion was accepted.

The last gift which we must record in this book is that which Moreau-Nélaton presented to the Louvre in 1906. It is symbolic of the continuity of French painting; Moreau-Nélaton, who was the biographer of Corot, Millet, Daubigny and Manet, had collected works by Manet, Monet, Sisley and Pissarro as well as those by Corot, Delacroix and Daumier. His bequest was housed in the Musée des Arts Décoratifs till 1934, when it was transferred to the Louvre and joined Caillebotte's Impressionists, brought from the Luxembourg in 1929.

With Caillebotte and Moreau-Nélaton begins the great contest of generosity which was to endow the Louvre with the finest collection of Impressionists to be found in any museum. However, this is not the place for describing the episodes of this sensational retribution for official hostility; this book stops short in the years around 1850, and the dramatic story of the Impressionists forms the subject of another volume which I have written for this series, dedicated to the gallery of the Jeu de Paume.

In 1815, after the dissolution of the Musée Napoléon, Vivant-Denon wrote: 'Such an assembly – this comparison of the achievements of the human mind through the centuries, this tribunal where talent was constantly being judged by talent – in a word, this light which sprang perpetually from the inter-reaction of merits of all kinds has just been extinguished, and will never shine again.' Denon, in his mood of despair, was an unreliable prophet; but how could he have foreseen that in the nineteenth and twentieth centuries the Louvre was to fulfil even more exactly the universal mission of the short-lived Musée Napoléon?

The collections of paintings in the enormous palace of the Louvre have been reorganised a great many times during the past century and a half. The Grande Galerie has always remained its backbone; but it benefited considerably from the buildings erected during the Second Empire by Visconti and Lefuel. In 1929 M. Henri Verne, Director of National Museums, decided to rearrange on a more rational basis the multiple collections which had been accumulating in the Louvre since the founding of the Museum. This project entered upon a period of great activity, as far as the Département des Peintures was concerned, when René Huyghe was appointed head of this department. Under his directorship (1937–1952) the Grande Galerie in particular was completely redesigned. The alterations of Percier and Fontaine during the First Empire, and Lefuel under the Second Empire, had made it into a hall more than 300 yards long, its walls painted in Pompeian red, and divided into only four bays by the great transverse arches which had been envisaged as long ago as the revolutionary period. This style of décor lent itself admirably to nineteenth-century taste, and during that century the walls were hung with pictures arranged 'en tapisserie' covering them from top to bottom. The fundamental change of aesthetic attitude in our own time required that selected works should be arranged in a single line, and the gallery was therefore redesigned; subdivisions were introduced by means of marble projections with niches containing antique sculpture. These projecting features included pilasters supporting an entablature which had the effect of diminishing the apparent height of the walls. Except for minor details, this impressive scheme of decoration followed the project exhibited by Hubert Robert at the Salon of 1796 (a sketch for this project is in the Louvre, p. 40). M. Huyghe had intended the walls to be covered with velvet, but this part of the plan was unfortunately discarded by the architectural commission. After a century and a half, therefore, the décor of the Grande Galerie was at last completed; the gallery was inaugurated in 1949 and the paintings of the Italian schools were displayed in it. M. Huyghe was also responsible for the splendid rearrangement of the great monumental works of the nineteenth-century French school in the enormous rooms which had formerly housed, for three-quarters of a century, nearly all the seventeenth- and eighteenth-century French paintings, exhibited in rows one above the other. The same *Conservateur* must also be credited with having re-grouped the unique collection of large Venetian paintings in the former Salle des Etats; Veronese's *Marriage at Cana* is hung at one end of the room, where it can be viewed from a sufficient distance; the Salon Carré was not large enough to allow of this. The northern schools were to be placed between the Grande Galerie and the Pavillon de Flore, and the French school was to be arranged in order in the rooms round the Cour Carrée.

When I was put in charge of the Département des Peintures in 1953, and a new allocation of funds became available for further improvements, I felt that the most urgent requirement was the exhibiting of works by northern artists, and the admission into the Louvre of the French paintings which the City of Paris had very hospitably sheltered for some years in the Petit Palais. New rooms were envisaged round the Cour Carrée and in the Pavillon de Flore,

82

but their immediate construction proved impossible, and I was therefore obliged to modify the original plan, in order to give these masterpieces the benefit of the rooms on the first floor—which, whatever happens, will always be the *piano nobile* of the Louvre. The general current of ideas, sanctioned by numerous post-war books on painting, made it possible to classify a picture gallery otherwise than strictly in accordance with national schools. I therefore determined to exhibit the paintings in such a manner as to show the evolution of styles—as far as this was possible with the accommodation at my disposal—rather than the evolution of individual schools.

The Grande Galerie, up to the Gioconda tribune, is devoted to the growth and maturity of Italian classicism. From the tribune to the far end of the Louvre one can trace more completely than anywhere else in the world the extraordinary flowering of painting in seventeenth-century Europe, in all its varied aspects. The part played by Caravaggio's artistic vision is made clear by a comparison with its development in France and Spain. Proceeding along the gallery, the visitor is reminded in turn of the work of Caravaggio, Guercino, Valentin, the Neapolitan school, Ribera, Zurbaran, Georges de La Tour and the Le Nain brothers. The Grande Galerie ends, however, in the apotheosis of French classicism with the work of Claude and Poussin—both 'Roman' artists. On the far wall, Rigaud's *Louis XIV* views this long perspective of masterpieces, many of them there as a result of his patronage.

The triumph of Baroque is represented by Van Dyck, Jordaens and Rubens, whose works are displayed in a room leading into the Galerie Médicis. Thanks to alterations carried out in the latter room, I have been able to display the Rubens series from the Luxembourg in its original order, in spite of the somewhat cramped quarters. This Golden Age of painting ends with the Dutch school. The visitor should then be introduced to the eighteenth century, presented in the same spirit, with French, English, Italian and Spanish paintings; but unfortunately the Pavillon de Flore is still occupied by the Ministry of Finance, and the eighteenth-century pictures have had to be exhibited some distance away, in the Colonnade wing.

The little rooms built in 1900 on either side of the Galerie Médicis have been modernised, and the paintings are now very well lit. With the assistance of the architect Jean-Charles Moreux, the décor of each of these rooms has been designed as a setting for the paintings it was to contain. The series of rooms on the south side show the development of Franco-Flemish and Flemish art, flourishing in northern Europe in the fifteenth century. The northern rooms are divided into two series; four of them contain gems of seventeenth-century Dutch and Flemish art, and four exhibit what may be called the 'humanist' aspect of northern European painting in the sixteenth century—mostly in portraits.

In order to preserve from further damage the Giulio Romano tapestry cartoons which were deteriorating in the Orangerie at Fontainebleau, I found it necessary to install them in the Salon Carré, and this naturally led to the exhibition in the same room of Italian, French and Flemish Mannerist paintings of the sixteenth century. This arrangement was to be ratified three years later by the exhibition 'The Triumph of Mannerism' at Amsterdam, organised on an international basis. The almost impossible problem presented by three rooms which were lit from both sides, between the Grande Galerie and the Pavillon Mollien, was solved very ingeniously by Jean-Charles Moreux; velvet-covered easels were provided, whose position is determined by the requirements of the pictures they support. These rooms were divided into two galleries; one provided accommodation for the fine collection of paintings bequeathed by Carlos de Beistegui; and, to accompany them (since they are almost all portraits), a magnificent selection of French nineteenth-century portraits, from David to Courbet, has been hung in the other gallery.

Concurrently with all this work on the building, another task has been carried on for the past twenty years, concerned with the presentation of the paintings themselves. Patiently and methodically, the dark varnish with which they were covered in the nineteenth century has been removed—or, rather, lightened, leaving in every case a layer of older varnish, in accordance with the prudence and moderation practised by the French school of restorers. Moreover, a very great effort has been made to provide the pictures with old frames which would give them a worthy setting. As a result of this effort, sustained with perseverance for twenty years, and assisted by gifts such as those of Jules Strauss or of Dalbret, the Louvre picture gallery now possesses more antique frames than any other museum. In some parts of it—the Salle des Sept Mètres, the Grande Galerie and the small rooms, for example—the framing has been entirely overhauled.

The work now being carried out will provide improved storage quarters and the installation of a complete circuit of French paintings, from the origins to the Impressionists, round the four sides of the Cour Carrée. The exceedingly rich collection of French paintings will in fact allow the Louvre to exhibit the works of the French school both independently and in conjunction with the other European schools of painting.

The Louvre collection of paintings will then be in a position to fulfil the double purpose made possible by its exceptional richness: it will express the idea of the universal, and will at the same time glorify French achievements.

THE PLATES

CIMABUE (CENNI DI PEPO), active 1240–1302   *Italian School*
MADONNA WITH ANGELS   Panel

Inventory: INV. 254   Height 4.24 m. (167")
                                                       Width 2.76 m. (108⅝")

This enormous altarpiece was formerly in the church of San Francesco
at Pisa. In 1811 Baron Vivant-Denon, the director of the Musée Napoléon,
undertook an expedition in search of Italian primitives for his museum, and
selected this painting from amongst the property of the suppressed religious
houses of Tuscany. It was in the Louvre in 1813, but was not on exhibition
till the following year; the Florentine commission of 1815, charged with
reclaiming the paintings which had been taken from Tuscany, left it in the
possession of the museum.

This work is related to two other large thirteenth-century altarpieces:
the Madonna of the Uffizi in Florence, and the Rucellai Madonna in Santa
Maria Novella. Vasari states that all three were painted by Cimabue, but
modern criticism does not accept this attribution in each case. The Uffizi
Madonna is universally accepted as the work of Cimabue, but the Madonna
in Santa Maria Novella is usually attributed to Duccio. With regard to the
Louvre Madonna, opinions vary; many critics regard it as a late work by
Cimabue, attributing it to his last years to account for the fact that it
displays a greater preoccupation with form than the other two paintings.
Others, however, consider it to belong to a later period than Cimabue; but
Luisa Marcucci (1956) believes it to be an early work by the master. It has
been pointed out, moreover, that the twenty-six medallions on the frame,
depicting Christ, the Apostles, angels and saints, seem to be in a more
advanced style than the picture itself.

Cimabue's *œuvre* remains in fact very conjectural, for want of documents
relating to the surviving works, which would provide a starting point for
definite attributions. Vasari recounts that the Louvre Madonna won
tremendous acclaim for the artist, who was generously rewarded for it by
the Pisans.

Cimabue was rediscovered in modern times; when Vivant-Denon chose
this picture for the Louvre it was among the paintings confiscated from the
supressed religious houses stored in the Campo Santo, Pisa, and was priced
at 5 francs.

It is in remarkably good condition for so old a work. The gold background is covered with an incised pattern.

SIMONE MARTINI, 1284–1344   *Italian School*
CHRIST ON THE WAY TO CALVARY   Panel

Inventory: INV. 670 bis   Height 0.25 m. (9⁷/₈")
                             Width 0.55 m. (21³/₄")

This little panel was part of a larger composition which was divided up in 1826 at Dijon. Four of the pieces (the *Annunciation*, on two panels, the *Deposition*, and the *Crucifixion*) passed into the Van Ertborn collection, which was bequeathed to the Antwerp museum in 1840; the *Entombment* went to the Berlin museum in 1901. The Louvre panel was bought from M. L. Saint Denis in 1834, for 200 francs. The *Deposition* and the *Crucifixion* are signed on the frame: 'Symon Pinxit'. The picture is painted on a canvas mounted on wood and covered with a coat of fine plaster.

This polyptych of the Passion was one of the little portable altars which accompanied prelates on their travels and formed part of the furnishing of their 'chapel'. A prelate is represented, kneeling, in the *Deposition* panel; formerly, when it was thought that the painting was executed at Avignon, he was believed to be Bishop Jacopo Stefaneschi. The Louvre panel, however, has the Orsini arms on the back, and the polyptych must have been commissioned by a member of that family.

The distinctly gothic character of the work, and the fact that it was found in France in the nineteenth century, led G. de Nicola (1906) to attribute it to the last period of Simone's career – the Avignon period, between 1339 and 1344. The latest biographer, however, (M. Paccagnini – 1955) believes on stylistic grounds that the picture was painted in Italy before that date. The iconography of the polyptych, especially the panel with the *Way to Calvary*, has connections with Duccio. As it was sold at Dijon in 1826, Salomon Reinach (1927) believed that it must have been in the Chartreuse of Champmol, the 'Saint-Denis' of the Dukes of Burgundy. Some support is lent to this theory by the fact that the *Way to Calvary* was imitated in a painting on vellum (bought by the Louvre in 1952) attributed to the school of Avignon by M. René Huyghe, but which according to Dr. Otto Pächt may be a miniature from the *Grandes Heures* of the Duc de Berry, painted by Jacquemart de Hesdin.

Another piece of evidence, as yet unpublished, also supports Salomon Reinach's hypothesis; it consists of a painting, probably dating from the sixteenth century, in the church of Ranc-les-Saint-Amour in the Jura, which was examined by the Louvre in 1939. It is a literal copy of Simone's *Way to Calvary*, interpreted in a later style.

In the sixteenth century this portrait was in the possession of the family of Gouffier, Francis I's tutor, at the château of Oiron, where it was purchased in the seventeenth century by Roger de Gaignières. In 1717, when the greater part of Gaignières' legacy to the king was sold by order of the Crown, this painting was retained for the Bibliothèque Royale. In 1925 the Bibliothèque Nationale handed it over to the Louvre in exchange for some miniatures belonging to the latter.

This picture is the earliest example we possess of a true portrait by a northern artist. Portraiture was very much in vogue at the court of the Valois. We know that in Charles V's apartments in the Hôtel Saint Pol there was a quadriptych consisting of portraits 'done from life' of King John the Good, the Emperor Charles IV, Edward III of England, and Charles V when he was Duke of Normandy. We also know, from a entry in Charles V's inventory, that the painter Gérard d'Orléans had painted 'a picture on wood in four parts'; it is therefore possible that the two are identical, and that the Louvre painting is the last surviving panel. Moreover, Gérard d'Orléans was King John's painter and *valet de chambre*, shared his captivity in England (1356–1359), and accompanied him to Avignon in 1362. To judge by the apparent age of the king (1319–1364), the portrait was probably painted towards the end of his life. He is portrayed with a remarkable degree of naturalism; this interest in the delineation of character, even to the point of accentuating the individual features, is quite common in portraits in the miniatures during the reigns of John the Good and Charles V.

This picture, regarded simply as a historical document, has never been restored; large pieces of the ground and of the picture surface have become detached from the support, but the work has the merit of being entirely free of re-touching. In order to preserve it, however, and to prevent further crumbling, the gaps have been filled with mastic and the colour simply matched up; in this way the new additions can be clearly seen, and at the same time a unified surface has been restored to the painting.

·Jehan rey de .aux

FRANCO-FLEMISH SCHOOL, c. 1400
PIETÀ   Panel

Inventory: M. I. 692   Tondo
                                              Diameter 0.64 m. (25¹/₄")

Bought from M. Jules Pujol of Toulouse in 1864, for 3.000 francs.

On the back of the painting are the arms of France and Burgundy, a fact which suggests that it may have been commissioned by one of the Dukes of Burgundy of the period indicated by the style of the work – either Philip the Bold (d. 1404) or John the Fearless (d. 1419). Moreover, the painting really depicts the *Blessed Trinity*, beneath whose patronage was placed the Charterhouse of Champmol at Dijon, built and richly embellished by the Dukes in order to house their tombs.

The elegance of the draughtsmanship is reminiscent of Paris, but the softness and fluidity of the modelling and the brilliance of the colours are Flemish in origin. Historians have hitherto dwelt mainly on these characteristics; it is surprising that they have not also pointed out other elements which denote Italian influence. The figure of Christ, for example, derives from Duccio; the flowing contours also recall the Sienese manner, here softening the linear character of the Paris style. The brilliant blues and reds are typically French, but some subtle half-tones are reminiscent of Lombard colouring. This picture is the product of a refined and artistic civilization, the heir of traditions which had already become secularized. These same characteristics, used in a different way, are found again in the *Last Communion of Saint Denis* (also in the Louvre), which is known to have been finished by Henri Bellechose in 1416. The official painter of the Duke had been Jean Malouel, a native of Gelderland, who was in Dijon in 1398; as he died in 1415, it is thought that he may have left the *Last Communion of Saint Denis* unfinished, and by analogy he has been credited with this *Pietà* (known as the *Grande Pietà Ronde*) to distinguish it from a small *Pietà* tondo in the same style, also in the Louvre. All these attributions must remain conjectural, however, for want of any conclusive documentary evidence.

The fact that we have few works by French primitives is not because of any lack of aptitude for painting, as some have suggested; it is because of the extraordinary lack of interest shown in them by the French humanists of the seventeenth and eighteenth centuries, who despised the Middle Ages and destroyed many of its 'out-dated' products.

VAN EYCK, JAN, c. 1390–1441   *Flemish School*
THE MADONNA OF CHANCELLOR ROLIN   Panel

Inventory: INV. 1271   Height 0.660 m. (26″)
                                                  Width 0.620 m. (24¹/₂″)

In the early eighteenth century this picture is mentioned as being in the
collegiate church of Autun, in Burgundy. It was confiscated during the Revolution, and selected by Alexandre Lenoir for the Louvre. It was acquired
by the museum as a work by Van Eyck, and was exhibited there in 1805.

The solemnity with which the Virgin presents the Christ Child to the
donor is reminiscent of early representations of the Adoration of the Magi.
Here she is seen as the Queen of Heaven; the Romanesque *loggia*, with its
sculptured capitals depicting Old Testament subjects and scenes from the
Christmas cycle, is the Temple of Jerusalem; the little garden beyond is
the *hortus conclusus*, symbol of Mary's purity, and the town seen in the
distance, with the range of snow-capped mountains in the background, is
the Heavenly Jerusalem.

Van Eyck's picture may be full of symbolic meaning, but it is expressed
through the minute representation of outward appearances. The identity of
the town has been the subject of much discussion; Bruges, Lyons, Liège,
Geneva, London, Maestricht, Brussels, Autun, Marmande, Le Réole, Prague,
and Tarbes have all been suggested in turn. According to a recent theory,
strongly supported with topographical arguments by M. Jean Lejeune, it is
a faithful representation of Liège, but there are some fairly serious objections
to this identification.

The donor is traditionally held to be Nicolas Rolin, Chancellor of Burgundy (1376?–1462), a personage of considerable importance at the court
of Duke Philip the Good. The picture must therefore be later than 1425,
when Van Eyck entered the Duke's household; it is usually believed to date
from about 1436, on the evidence of the Chancellor's apparent age and also
because it has certain affinities of style with the Van der Paele altarpiece,
which bears that date.

In spite of a certain amount of repainting, and some premature crackling
of the surface, particularly on the Virgin's face and cloak, the picture has
come down to us in exceptionally good condition, a fact which contributes
to its high quality. It is very rare for a work of this period to have survived
with all its subtleties and refinements, its glazes and its delicate transitions
of tone, so well preserved.

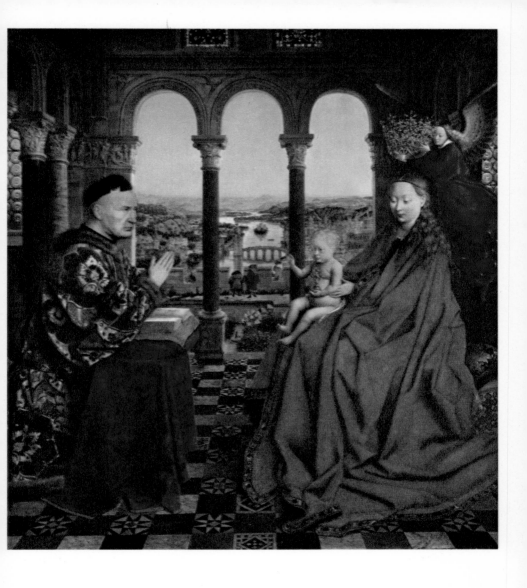

VAN DER WEYDEN, ROGIER, c. 1400–1464 *Flemish School*
SAINT MARY MAGDALEN (The Braque Triptych) Panel

Inventory: R. F. 2063 Height 0.410 m. (16¹/₄")
Width 0.344 m. (13¹/₂")

The armorial bearings on the back indicate that this portable triptych was the property of Jehan Braque and his wife Catherine de Brabant, of Tournai, who were married in about 1450–1451. Jehan Braque died soon afterwards, in 1452; his young widow, who did not marry again till 1461, must have commissioned this triptych in his memory. When she died, in 1497, she left it to his grandson, Jehan Villain. Later, some time before 1586, Villain's heirs presented the 'fort exquis tableau en paincture' to Jerome de Brabant, in order to restore the painting to the family whose arms it bore. In 1845 the picture turned up in England, in the possession of a London artist named Evans; it was purchased by the Marquis of Westminster, who bequeathed it to Lady Theodora Guest. In 1913 the Louvre bought it from Kleinberger, the dealer, for 800.000 francs.

The centre panel of the triptych represents Christ in benediction with Mary Magdalen on the right and John the Baptist on the left. On the back of the left-hand shutter is a death's-head on a broken piece of brick, with the Braque coat-of-arms; on the back of the right wing is a cross. Both the obverse and reverse of the triptych bear inscriptions of a theological or moralizing nature. One is a passage from Ecclesiasticus: 'O Death, how bitter is the remembrance of thee to a man that hath peace in his possessions! To a man that is at rest, and whose ways are prosperous in all things, and that is yet able to take meat!' On the frame round the death's-head can be read the words: 'Mirez-vous si orgueilleux et avers, mon corps fu beaux ore est viande à (vers)'. The skull and these melancholy lines no doubt allude to the death of Jehan Braque. In 1854 Waagen read an inscription 'Braque et Brabant', which is now almost invisible.

The picture dates from Rogier's finest period. His visit to Italy (in 1450) inspired him with a feeling for form which later gave way to a greater degree of realism and a certain weakening of style. The dignity and spirituality of the three figures is perhaps an echo of Fra Angelico's art.

MARIA ERGO ACCEPIT LIBRAM VNGENI NARDI PISTICI PNIOSE ET VNXIT PEDES IHV

MEMLING, HANS, c. 1433–1494 *Flemish School*
MYSTICAL MARRIAGE OF SAINT CATHERINE OF ALEXANDRIA Panel

Inventory: R. F. 309
Height 0.25 m. (9⅞")
Width 0.15 m. (5⅞")

This picture was bequeathed to the Louvre in 1881 by M. Edouard Gatteaux; the other wing of the diptych of which it originally formed a part was re-united with it in 1894, when M. and Mme. Edouard André left to the museum the panel showing Jean du Cellier being presented by St John the Baptist. The panel illustrated here depicts St Catherine, in a gown of gold brocade with a red velvet bodice, seated on the left and receiving the ring from the Holy Child. The latter is held by His mother, who sits in the centre of a half-circle formed by St Agnes, St Cecilia (playing a portable organ), St Barbara, St Margaret of Antioch and St Lucy.

The same subject was also painted by Memling in a triptych dated 1479 in the Hôpital Saint Jean, Bruges. A certain awkwardness of drawing, particularly the over-long arm of St Catherine, suggests that our picture is an earlier work; it still shows traces, moreover, of Dirck Bouts' influence. Memling favoured the theme of the 'Virgo inter virgines' (with or without St Catherine); he may have borrowed it from the northern Low Countries, where it was a speciality of the painter known as the 'Master of the *Virgo inter Virgines*'. Here the theme is combined with another derived from Memling's native German Rhineland: that of the *hortus conclusus*. Mary and the virgins are in fact gathered in the open air to assist at the mystical marriage; they are in a meadow, in the middle of which an enclosure bounded by a hedge of roses can clearly be seen behind the group.

The châteaux of the Middle Ages used to have a walled garden where fruit trees and medicinal herbs were grown, as well as a few ornamental plants. During the Italian Renaissance, this enclosed garden survived under the name *giardino segreto*. When the Virgin became identified with the Spouse of the Song of Songs, the epithet *hortus conclusus* was applied to her; and this enclosed garden, the symbol of her purity, was made in the pattern of the feudal garden.

Thanks to Memling, Flemish art, which had been realist in the case of Van Eyck and austere with Rogier van der Weyden, but always virile, now acquired a certain femininity. The artist subscribed to the courtly tradition, which had a secular origin during the eleventh and twelfth centuries, but was sublimated to the cult of the Blessed Virgin from the thirteenth cencury onwards.

FOUQUET, JEAN, d. between 1477 and 1481   *French School*
PORTRAIT OF CHARLES VII, KING OF FRANCE   Panel

Inventory: INV. 9106   Height 0.86 m. (34″)
       Width 0.72 m. (28½″)

In the eighteenth century this picture was in the Sainte Chapelle at Bourges, which was built by the Duc de Berry, and whose destruction was authorized by letters patent of Louis XV in 1757. These letters refer to 'le tableau et portrait de Charles VII l'un des rois nos prédécesseurs étant en la dite Sainte Chapelle, lequel nous voulons être transporté et placé en notre cabinet des tableaux du Louvre'. The portrait must have been moved during the Revolution, because under Louis Philippe it was bought for the museum at Versailles, as an 'ouvrage grec', for the sum of 450 francs.

This is a secular portrait, and not a donor picture. It is still in the original frame, on which the following inscription appears: 'le très victorieux roi de France Charles septièsme de ce nom'. This inscription suggests that the portrait may have been executed either after the truce of Arras in 1444, which gave France time to recuperate, or after 1450, the date of the Treaty of Formigny which ratified France's victory. By the latter date, Fouquet had already visited Italy; he must have done so before 1447, since he painted the portrait of Pope Eugene IV who died in that year. Since the Charles VII portrait is still entirely Gothic in spirit and shows not the slightest trace of Renaissance influence, it was most probably painted in about 1444.

A water-colour copy (now in the Bibliothèque Nationale) which Gaignières made of this portrait when it was still in the Sainte Chapelle at Bourges revealed that in his time it was without the clumsy brown checkwork on the green background of the painting which was visible up to 1939. At this date the objectionable addition was removed, though it was not possible to eradicate every trace of it.

THE MASTER OF MOULINS, c. 1490   *French School*
SAINT MARY MAGDALEN AND A DONOR   Panel

Inventory: R. F. 1521   Height 0.53 m. (21″)
                                           Width 0.40 m. (19³/₄″)

This picture was formerly in the Somzée collection in Brussels, and was bought from the London dealer Agnew in 1904 for 125.000 francs. It must be the left wing of a triptych of which the centre panel and the right wing have not survived.

It was once thought to be a work of the Flemish school, but is now attributed to the unknown master who painted the large triptych of the Virgin in Moulins cathedral, commissioned about 1498–1499 by Duke Pierre II of Bourbon and his wife Anne of Beaujeu. About ten other paintings have been grouped with this triptych; certain analogies between the facial types and details of costume in these paintings and in the *Virtues* on the tomb of the Dukes of Britanny at Nantes, by Jean Perréal, have led to the supposition that this artist could perhaps be the Master of Moulins. Perréal played an important part in the life of Charles VIII's court and that of Louis XII; in 1487 he was in the service of the Sire de Beaujeu, who became Duke of Bourbon in 1488.

This identification remains hypothetical, however. It has not yet been possible to discover the status of the lady represented as the donor.

The picture is even finer in quality than the portraits in the Moulins triptych. By the ivory complexion of the Saint and the more rosy one of the donor, the artist has subtly suggested that they belong to two different worlds.

The empty look in the donor's somewhat prominent eyes, her inexpressive face with its coarse features, are in marked contrast with the Magdalen's profound expression and the intelligence and nobility of her features. This ideal type created by the artist corresponds with the type of Virgin with which he was familiar, but is perhaps inspired by someone he knew. The same contrast can be seen in the hands of the two women. There is no life or spirituality in the stiff, joined hands of the donor, which reveal a petty soul; but the exquisite right hand of Mary Magdalen, immaculate, supple and sensitive, vibrates like an angel's wing. Yet at the same time it is full of humanity, and combines the qualities of gentleness and firmness found in those rare women who are the guiding spirit of their homes. Such a combination of realism and the ideal is only to be found in French art.

SCHOOL OF AVIGNON, MID FIFTEENTH CENTURY *French School*
PIETÀ   Panel

Inventory: R. F. 1569   Height 1.62 m. (63³/₄")
                                                 Width 2.18 m. (85³/₄")

This painting, formerly in the Charterhouse of Villeneuve-les-Avignon, was very nearly burnt in 1793, being considered merely a religious emblem of no use either to the citizens or to the Republic. It was saved by a priest, and in 1801 it was in the parish church, where its beauty was later noticed by Degas. It remained there till 1872, and was then removed by Revoil, the architect in charge of Historical Monuments, and placed in the Hospice (now a museum) with other works from the Charterhouse. It remained the property of the vestry, however. Its existence was made more generally known during an exhibition of French primitive painting organized by Henri Bouchot in 1904; it was then bought from the municipality by the Société des Amis du Louvre for 100.000 francs, and presented to the museum in 1905.

The nobility of its style, and the sublime sense of sacrifice which it expresses, make this picture one of the supreme manifestations of Christian art, in addition to being a masterpiece of painting. The panels on which it is painted have become warped with age, but this only serves to increase the effect of intense suffering which it conveys. Out of respect for this great work of art, no restoration work has been carried out either to the support or to the painted surface, once it was ascertained that no further deterioration was taking place.

For nearly fifty years, historians have tried in vain to identify the artist. After some uncertainty at first, when it was believed to be possibly of Spanish origin, it is now universally attributed to the School of Avignon. It is thought to have been painted in the third quarter of the fifteenth century, possible by Enguerrand Quarton. The Charterhouse of Villeneuve commissioned a *Coronation of the Virgin* from this artist in 1453. This painting is now in the Hospice there, and is very close in style to the *Pietà*.

It has recently been suggested by Jean and Hélène Adhémar that the donor was neither a Carthusian nor even a canon, but a layman, and that the building in the background was inspired by Hagia Sophia, Constantinople.

106

FRA ANGELICO (GUIDO DI PIETRO DA VECCHIA; *Italian School* in religion *FRA GIOVANNI DA FIESOLE*), d. 1455
CORONATION OF THE VIRGIN   Panel

Inventory: INV. 314   Height 2.13 m. (84")
                                                             Width 2.11 m. (83¼")

The predella is in six parts, and represents scenes from the legend of St Dominic, grouped round a painting of the dead Christ with the Virgin and St John. (Pages 283–284)

This work comes from the church of San Domenico at Fiesole; Vasari saw it there, and described it in glowing terms. It was deposited in the Accademia along with other works from the suppressed religious houses; there it was seen by Vivant-Denon in 1811, and chosen for the Musée Napoléon, of which he was director. It arrived there in 1812, and was exhibited in 1814. The Florentine commission of 1815 left it in the possession of the Louvre.

Historians have disagreed over the question of when Fra Angelico painted this picture; it is extremely difficult to establish a chronology for his work. The suggested dates range from 1425 to 1439; around 1435 seems to be the most likely period. Opinions also differ over the extent to which his pupils were responsible for its execution – a problem which crops up in connection with almost all Fra Angelico's work. The quality of the painting is excellent, but the last two panels of the predella are definitely weaker than the rest. The latest hypothesis is that of Mr. J. Pope-Hennessy, who suggests that the work was finished by Domenico Veneziano. His argument does not rest on any difference of quality, but on what seems to him to be a difference of style between the upper part (Fra Angelico) on the one hand, and the lower part and the predella (Veneziano) on the other. However, the dissimilarity of architectural styles could be accounted for at this date by the survival of a tradition; Fra Angelico could have kept to the Gothic style (because of its religious significance) for the Coronation dais, and used the Renaissance style elsewhere, as Jean Fouquet did in the *Heures d'Etienne Chevalier*. The use of two or more different viewpoints is also quite common in Renaissance painting. Finally the more vivid tonality apparent in the right-hand part of the picture is due to the fact that the surface in that area is more worn.

SASSETTA (STEFANO DI GIOVANNI), 1392–1450   *Italian School*
VIRGIN AND CHILD ADORED BY ANGELS   **Panel**

Inventory: R. F. 1956. 11   Height 2.05   m. (79″)
                                                   Width 1.195 m. (47″)

This Madonna, together with a St John the Evangelist and a St Anthony
of Padua, was bought by the Louvre in 1956 from a collection at Bordeaux,
for the sum of 50.000.000 francs – partly with the accumulated interest from
a Canadian endowment.

I discovered the three pictures at Bordeaux in 1950; they were at that
time attributed to Fra Angelico. I immediately identified them as part of
the large polyptych by the Sienese artist Stefano di Giovanni (Sassetta),
painted between 1437 and 1444 for the church of the monastery of San
Francesco at Borgo San Sepolcro, in the Marches. It is surprising that they
should have escaped the researches of such critics as Berenson and John
Pope-Hennessy, who had made a close study of this altarpiece. An examination of the documents established that these pictures were certainly
mentioned during the nineteenth century, but modern critics had dismissed
this evidence as unreliable. In 1823 Romagnoli saw a Madonna and four
saints and a *St Francis in Ecstasy* from the Borgo San Sepolcro altarpiece,
in the possession of Don Pietro Angelucci, parish priest of Monte Contieri;
the same panels, assembled as two triptychs, were again seen in about
1855–1860 by Cavalcaselle, in the Lombardi collection in Florence. One
of these 'triptychs', showing St John the Baptist and the Blessed Ranieri
Rasini on either side of St Francis in Ecstasy, was later bought by Bernard
Berenson, and the three panels are now in his villa *I Tatti*, at Settignano
near Florence. The other group of three was acquired in 1901–1902 by a
private collection in Bordeaux, as a work by Fra Angelico. Since I was
negotiating the purchase of these three pictures for the Louvre, I could not
announce my discovery myself; it was published by Enzo Carli.

The Borgo San Sepolcro polyptych, one of the most important works of
the early Renaissance in Italy, was also one of the three finest masterpieces
of Sienese art – the other two being Duccio's *Maestà* and Simone Martini's
Annunciation. It had the unusual feature of being painted on both sides. On
the reverse were the *St Francis in Ecstasy* and eight scenes from the legend
of St Francis (the most famous of which is at Chantilly); on the obverse
was the Madonna with four saints. The two saints in the Louvre were not
on either side of the Madonna, according to Enzo Carli's reconstruction, but
were both to her left.

UCCELLO (PAOLO DI DONO), 1397–147
Inventory: M. I. 469. Panel. Heigh

This picture is part of a painting in three panels, representing the Battle
of San Romano, which used to be in the Palazzo Medici in Florence; the
work is mentioned in 1498 in an inventory of Lorenzo il Magnifico. Vasari
describes them in 1568, in one of the editions of his *Vite;* in 1598, they
again occur in an inventory of the palace. The Palazzo Medici was sold to

THE BATTLE OF SAN ROMANO. *Italian School*
1.80 m. (71″). Width 3.16 m. (125¹/₂″)

Gabriele Riccardi in 1655, and the pictures were transferred to the Medici furniture store, where they were re-discovered in 1784. Two panels were sold in the nineteenth century; the National Gallery, London, acquired one of them in 1857, and the other came to the Louvre with the Campana collection in 1864. The third remained in Florence, and is now in the Uffizi.

PISANELLO (ANTONIO DI PUCCIO PISANO), c. 1380–1455

A PRINCESS OF THE HOUSE OF ESTE

Italian School
Panel

Inventory: INV. 1422 A

Height 0.43 m. (17″)
Width 0.30 m. (11³/₄″)

This picture first came to light in 1860 in a sale, when it was bought by the German Consul Felix Bamberg. In 1893 the Louvre acquired it from M. Cyrus Picard for 30.000 francs.

The identity of the sitter remains a mystery. The only solid basis for hypothesis is the embroidery on her sleeve, representing the two-handled vase of the Este family (which is also found on the reverse of the medal which Pisanello designed for Lionello d'Este). Attempts have therefore been made to connect the portrait with various princesses of this family; Pisanello was one of the artists employed by them, and stayed on several occasions in Ferrara, where he decorated a room in the Palazzo Schifanoia. Marguerite of Gonzaga (d. 1439) is one possibility; she was the wife of Lionello, and the picture might have been painted at the time of their marriage in 1433. One is even tempted to identify this fresh and modest young face as Genevra d'Este, because of the sprig of juniper on the sleeve – though this may simply be an emblem of happiness and not a pun on her name. She was the unfortunate wife of the redoubtable Sigismondo Pandolfo Malatesta, who subjected Romagna to fire and the sword, and whose shameless *affaire* with Isotta degli Atti was the scandal of the age; it was he who commissioned Alberti to build the Tempio Malatestiano at Rimini. He had his wife poisoned in 1440, when she was only twenty-two. It has also been suggested that the lady may be a Gonzaga princess – Beatrice, or Margaret, or the learned Cecilia, whom Pisanello also depicted on a medal.

In 1958 this picture was included in the exhibition 'From Altichiero to Pisanello' at Verona. Comparing the *Princess of the House of Este* with the *Portrait of Lionello d'Este* from Bergamo, which is painted in a freer style, M. Alfred Frankfurter expressed the opinion that the former, executed with greater finish and precision, was a copy after a lost original. But one could reverse the relationship and compare the *Lionello* unfavourably with the *Princess*. The *St Eustace* in London, a certain attribution, is painted in exactly the same manner as the *Princess;* I went to London immediately after the Verona exhibition and was able to verify this. Moreover, the most recent writers on Pisanello – Mme. Maria Fossi Todorow and M. Raffaello Brenzoni – have no doubts whatever about the Louvre picture.

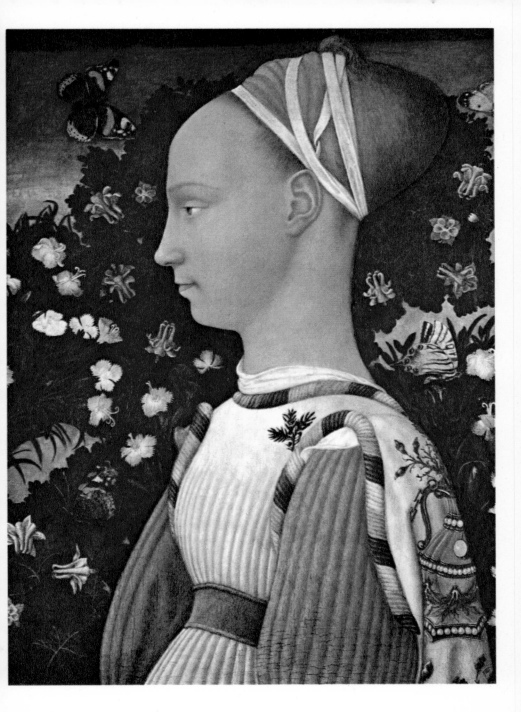

Inventory: M. I. 693   Height 0.35 m. (13³/₄")
                                               Width 0.38 m. (15")

At the bottom of the picture is the inscription: '1475. Antonellus Messa-
neus me pinxit'.

The painting was bought at the Pourtalès-Gorgier sale in 1865, for 113.500
francs.

A dozen of Antonello's portraits have come down to us, of which this is
certainly the finest; in fact, together with the *Virgin of the Annunciation* in
Palermo, it is his masterpiece.

This is one of the most striking Quattrocento portraits we possess. Few
works express so strongly the proud commanding spirit characteristic of
the early Renaissance. The clenched jaws and stern expression, the iron will
and penetrating intelligence revealed in the face of the sitter, and the scar
on his upper lip suggest that he may have been a military leader; hence the
nickname 'Il Condottiere'.

The picture belongs to the final stage of Antonello's career. It must have
been painted in Venice; he was there in 1475, and in March 1476 he had
not yet left the city since he was then working in San Cassiano. From his
contact with northern artists in Sicily – among them, no doubt, Petrus
Christus – he acquired the Flemish technique of painting in oil. The *Crucifixion* in Antwerp, also painted in 1475, shows how closely he was then
studying Flemish painting. The fluid style of the *Condottiere* is usually said
to be due to the influence of Giovanni Bellini; in fact, never again was
Antonello to approach so near to both the spirit and the technique of Jan
van Eyck, which enabled him to suggest in a most striking fashion the
transparency of the skin and to hint at the warmth of the flesh. But he is
entirely Italian in his way of analysing the structure of the face and using
it to convey a sense of monumentality and of suppressed energy.

The work is still on its original panel of poplar wood, and is in exceptionally good condition; only two or three worm holes have been plugged. But
the background, the cap and the clothing have darkened so that the face
stands out dramatically against the surrounding obscurity.

An old copy of this picture has been mentioned in the Willcott collection
at Westport.

116

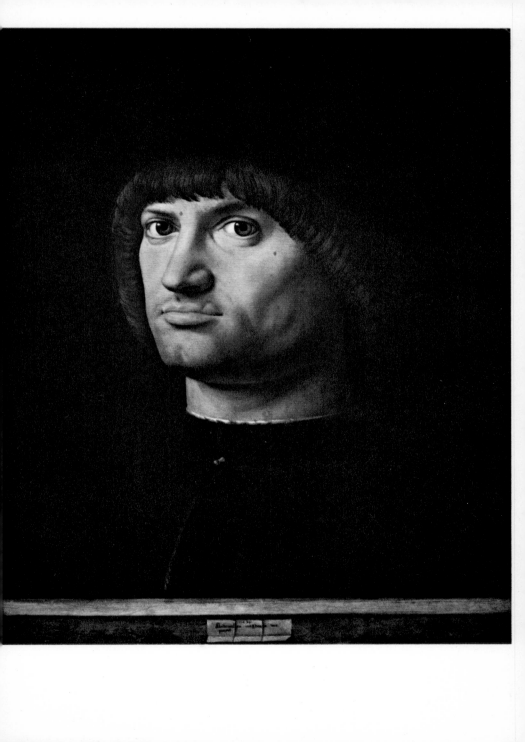

MANTEGNA, ANDREA, 1431–1506   *Italian School*
OUR LADY OF VICTORY   Canvas

Inventory: INV. 369   Height 2.80 m. (110¼")
                                                       Width 1.66 m. (69½")

    This painting was commissioned by Francesco Gonzaga to commemorate
the Battle of Fornova; on 6 June 1496, the anniversary of the battle, it was
placed in the chapel of Santa Maria della Vittoria – also the work of Mantegna, according to Vasari. The picture was brought to the Louvre in 1797.
    In 1942 L. Ozzola discovered a full-sized cartoon of this picture, done
in outline. Opinions are divided as to whether it is a 'modello' sent by
Mantegna to the Marquis of Gonzaga for his approval, or a tracing made
from the finished painting, perhaps even in 1797 when it was taken to
Paris. I saw this cartoon in 1958, and agree with M. Paccagnini, Director
of the art galleries at Mantua, who believes it to be a modern work.
    In 1494 King Charles VIII of France, who had conquered the kingdom
of Naples, found that a league was being formed against him which threatened to interrupt his lines of communication with France. The army of the
league, led by Francesco Gonzaga, took up its position at Fornova, on the
Taro; the French army abandoned its baggage, which contained all the
treasure accumulated in Italy, and in spite of its inferior numbers managed
to defeat the enemy, killing a great many Italians (6 July, 1495). Francesco
Gonzaga vowed to build a church to the Madonna if he escaped with his
life; he was reproached with having let the French army pass, and he called
the church 'Our Lady of Victory' to throw people off the scent. It was
built on the site of a house once occupied by a Jew, who had been accused
of removing an image of the Virgin from its façade.
    The Marquis is represented at the feet of the Virgin, clad in his armour;
it was originally intended to depict his wife, Isabella d'Este, opposite him,
but for some unknown reason Saint Elizabeth was substituted for her. Behind
them are two patrons of Mantua, Saint Andrew and Saint Longinus. The
branch of coral suspended above the Virgin was believed by the Italians
to be a protection against 'diabolica varia monstra'.

Inventory: INV. 368   Height 0.67 m. (26^1/$_2$")
Width 0.93 m. (36^3/$_4$")

This panel is the central part of the predella of a large altarpiece painted between 1457 and 1459 by Mantegna for the high altar of San Zeno, Verona; it was commissioned by Gregorio Correr, the abbot of that monastery. It was brought to the Louvre in 1798 and put on exhibition immediately. In 1806 two of the predella panels (the *Mount of Olives* and the *Resurrection*) were sent to the museum of Tours. In 1815 the central panel and the two wings were taken back to Italy and exhibited in the city museum at Verona; after 1918 they were returned to the church of San Zeno, where they still remain – though they are not very easy to see. The commission of 1815 charged with reclaiming the works of art taken from the Veneto left the predella panels in the possession of the Louvre and the museum of Tours.

The *Crucifixion* was in the middle of the predella, exactly in the centre. Mantegna was striving after an effect of steep perspective such as he had already achieved in the Eremitani chapel at Padua. The figures in the foreground, cut by the frame, increase the effect of recession; the vanishing lines of the ground are curved inwards and, as it were, contracted. The artist's feeling for nature is revealed by the minuteness with which he has represented every detail of the landscape. The accurate delineation of the Roman soldier's equipment is evidence of an attitude to antiquity unknown in Florence at that period. Florentine artists sought to understand and emulate the aesthetic quality of antique sculpture and architecture, but cared little for historical exactitude, which Mantegna on the other hand pursued with the passionate devotion of an archaeologist. In fact, the Veneto was from the fourteenth century onwards the chief Italian centre for the traffic in *anticaglie;* Venetian towns possessed *cabinets d'antiquités* long before these were found in Florence.

BOTTICELLI (SANDRO FILIPEPI), c. 1445–1510 *Italian School*
ALLEGORY Fresco

Inventory: INV. R. F. 321   Height 2.12 m. (83½″)
                                                                            Width 2.84 m. (11³/₄″)

This fresco and its companion (INV. 322, page 285) were discovered in 1873 under a layer of paint in a villa occupied by Doctor Pietro Lemmi at Chiasso Macerelli, just outside Florence. Both paintings were removed from the wall, suffering some damage in the process, and were bought for the Louvre in 1882, through the mediation of Charles Ephrusi, for 46.517 francs.

The paintings were on the external wall of a loggia, separated by the opening; a third fresco was also discovered, but in a ruinous condition. Their attribution to Botticelli was accepted without hesitation.

The Villa Lemmi was at the foot of the hill at Careggi on which stood one of the houses of Cosimo de' Medici. It belonged to the Tornabuoni family, which had friendly relations with the Medicis between 1469 and 1541. It has therefore been supposed that these frescoes may have been painted to commemorate the marriage of Lorenzo Tornabuoni and Giovanna degli Albizzi, which was the occasion for magnificent festivities. One of the paintings might possibly depict Giovanna being welcomed by Venus, who leads her towards the Three Graces – or perhaps they are Virtues; while the other could be Minerva (or possibly Venus again) leading Lorenzo to a gathering of the Liberal Arts, who are seated in a semicircle at the edge of a wood and presided over by Rhetoric. The historical hypothesis remains problematical, and the interpretation of the allegories obscure; the meaning of the pictures is certainly linked with the cycle of Platonic ideas which was a subject of speculation for the humanist scholars of the time. Marsilio Ficino taught that Love was the 'teacher of the Arts', a most suitable allegory for a marriage; as for Lorenzo Tornabuoni, who paid for his loyalty to the Medici family by dying on the scaffold (4 August 1497), he had been the pupil of Angelo Poliziano, who had dedicated a poem to him.

Thieme, however (1897–1898), pointed out that, though the man certainly has the features of Lorenzo Tornabuoni, the young girl cannot be Giovanna degli Albizzi, whose face is familiar to us through the medal by Niccolo Fiorentino, the *Visitation* by Ghirlandaio in Santa Maria Novella, and a portrait by the same artist in the Pierpont Morgan Library, New York. The young woman in the Louvre picture resembles the one who follows Giovanna in the *Visitation*. M. Salvini (1958) concurs with these remarks.

122

CARPACCIO (VITTORE SCARPAZO), c. 1460–1525   *Italian School*
THE SERMON OF SAINT STEPHEN   Canvas

Inventory: INV. 181   Height 1.52 m. (60″)
                                              Width 1.95 m. (77″)

This picture was one of five scenes representing the life of Saint Stephen, painted between 1511 and 1514 for the Scuola dei Lanieri, Santo Stefano, Venice. The series was broken up in 1806, when the religious houses were suppressed. Two panels went to the Brera, Milan; in 1812 Vivant-Denon exchanged some of the northern paintings in the Louvre for Italian works in the Brera, and one of these panels was transferred under this arrangement. The second (*St Stephen disputing with the Doctors*) remained in the Brera. The *Consecration of St Stephen* was in the Kaiser-Friedrich-Museum, Berlin. The *Stoning of St Stephen*, signed and dated 1520, is in the Stuttgart Museum. The fifth picture, the *Judgment of St Stephen,* is lost; but it is known through a copy and some drawings.

The Sermon of Saint Stephen the deacon, represented in the Louvre painting, took place in Jerusalem. This gave Carpaccio an excuse for filling his canvas with picturesque oriental costumes and architecture. Jerusalem in the early days of Christianity is here based on Constantinople – a fantastic and imaginary Constantinople full of Turkish, antique, Byzantine and Italian elements. Carpaccio refers with pride, in a letter to the Marquis of Mantua, to a view of Jerusalem which he had painted. In the background, to the left, can be seen the mosque of Omar, and on the hill the church of the Holy Sepulchre; but in the middle distance is an exact reproduction of the Arch of Trajan at Ancona, which was later to inspire Palladio's *Arco delle Scalette* at Vicenza.

It has been thought that the artist was invited to Constantinople by the Turks after Gentile Bellini's visit there in 1479. But his ready imagination could very well have been prompted by drawings brought back by other painters. As for Oriental costumes, there were plenty of these to be seen every day in the port of Venice.

The legend of St Stephen is the third and last of the cycles painted by Carpaccio. The artist, now an old man, was assisted by Francesco Bissolo, a pupil of Giovanni Bellini. It is at this period that he shows himself most sensitive to the quality of the light in his pictures.

124

LEONARDO DA VINCI, 1452–1519   *Italian School*
THE VIRGIN OF THE ROCKS   Canvas

Inventory: INV. 777   Height 1.99 m. (78¹/₂")
Width 1.22 m. (48")

The earliest known reference to this painting is in 1625, when Cassiano del Pozzo mentions it as being in the château of Fontainebleau. It was also described in 1642 by Père Dan in his *Trésors et merveilles de Fontainebleau*. Another version of approximately the same size (1.89 m × 1.20 m.) is in the National Gallery, London; it was bought from Lord Suffolk in 1880. Its pedigree can be traced back to its removal from the church of the hospital of Santa Catarina alla Ruota, Milan, who sold it to Gavin Hamilton in 1789. This picture had two wings (not by Leonardo), representing angels; these were also bought by the National Gallery, and come from the same church. The painting is unfinished.

In a contract dated 25 April 1483, the confraternity of the Conception at San Francesco Grande, Milan, commissioned Leonardo da Vinci and the brothers Evangelista and Giovanni da Predis to paint three pictures (a Virgin with angels); these were to be fitted into a carved wooden frame ordered from Giacomo del Maino in 1480, which Leonardo and the da Predis brothers were to polychrome. Between 1483 and 1506 various disputes arose, which were settled by a new agreement drawn up in 1506. Lomazzo mentions the picture as being at San Francesco Grande in 1586; it was transferred to Santa Catarina alla Ruota at the end of the eighteenth century.

The Louvre version is entirely by Leonardo's hand, and far superior in quality to the London picture, which is thought to have been executed mostly by the da Predis brothers, over a design prepared by Leonardo. The Louvre picture is still in his Florentine manner, and certainly earlier than the London one, which is clearly based on it. It has been suggested that a substitution of the paintings took place, carried out by Leonardo himself. In the Louvre picture the presence of the infant St John the Baptist, patron of Florence, who is pointed out by the angel, and the root of *Iris Florentina* to the left, seem to indicate that the work was commissioned for a Florentine church. Perhaps Leonardo took the unfinished painting to Milan at the end of 1482, and completed it in that town; then he may have made a replica for the confraternity of the Conception at San Francesco Grande, leaving out the more direct allusions to Florence (in particular the iris and the finger of the angel pointing to St John the Baptist, who seems to be the principal figure in the Paris version).

126

LEONARDO DA VINCI, 1452–1519   *Italian School*
MONA LISA (LA GIOCONDA)   Panel

Inventory: INV. 779   Height 0.97 m. (38¹/₄")
                                           Width 0.53 m. (21")

According to Vasari, this picture is a portrait of Mona or Monna (short for Madonna) Lisa, who was born in Florence in 1479 and in 1495 married the Marquis del Giocondo, a Florentine of some standing–hence the painting's other name, 'La Gioconda'. This identification, however, has sometimes been questioned.

Leonardo took the picture with him from Florence to Milan, and later to France. It must have been this portrait which was seen at Cloux, near Amboise, on 10 October 1517 by the Cardinal of Aragon and his secretary, Antonio de Beatis. There is a slight difficulty here, however, because Beatis says that the portrait had been painted at the wish of Giuliano de' Medici. Historians have attempted to solve this problem by suggesting that Monna del Giocondo had been Giuliano's mistress.

The painting was probably acquired by Francis I from Leonardo himself, or after his death from his executor Melzi. It is recorded as being at Fontainebleau by Vasari (1550), Lomazzo (1590), Peiresc, and Cassiano del Pozzo (1625). The latter relates that when the Duke of Buckingham came to the French court to seek the hand of Henrietta of France for Charles I, he made it known that the king was most anxious to own this painting; but the courtiers of Louis XIII prevented him from giving the picture to the English king. It was put on exhibition in the Musée Napoléon in 1804; before that, in 1800, Bonaparte had it in his room in the Tuileries.

It was stolen from the Salle Carrée on 21 August 1911 by Vicenzo Perrugia, an Italian workman. In 1913 it was found in Florence, exhibited at the Uffizi, then in Rome and Milan, and brought back to Paris on 31 December in the same year.

Vasari relates that Leonardo worked on it for four years without being able to finish it; yet the picture gives the impression of being completely realized. The dates suggested for it vary between 1503 and 1513, the most widely accepted being 1503–1506.

Taking a living model as his point of departure, Leonardo has expressed in an ideal form the concept of balanced and integrated humanity. The smile stands for the movement of life, and the mystery of the soul. The misty blue mountains, towering above the plain and its winding river, symbolize the universe.

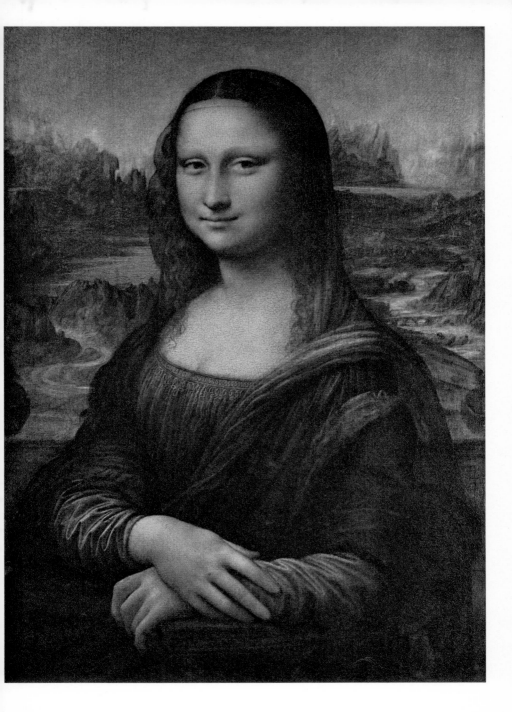

LEONARDO DA VINCI, 1452–1519
VIRGIN AND CHILD WITH SAINT ANNE

Italian School
Panel

Inventory: INV. 776

Height 1.685 m. (66¼")
Width 1.30 m. (51¼")

This picture was seen in Leonardo's studio in the château of Cloux, near Amboise, by the Cardinal of Aragon and his secretary Antonio de Beatis, in October 1517. Paolo Giovio, in his life of Leonardo, mentions it in 1529 as being in Francis I's study at Fontainebleau. There is no reason for doubting this contemporary evidence; the picture must therefore have left the royal collection, probably as a gift, at some unknown date, because Richelieu bought it at Casal in Piedmont in 1629. In 1636 it was presented to Louis XIII together with the Palais Cardinal (now the Palais Royal).

The Royal Academy in London owns a cartoon by Leonardo of the same subject, but differing in important respects from the Louvre painting. We know from a letter that in 1501 Leonardo made another cartoon, which is now lost. The picture was commissioned by the Servites, in Florence. It is unfinished; perhaps it was abandoned because of the artist's sudden interest in mathematics, and his engagement as engineer in the service of Cesare Borgia. He must have worked on it again in Milan, round about 1508 to 1512, but still did not bring it to completion. Another hand seems to have finished the lamb, which he had perhaps only sketched in; the landscape, Saint Anne, the Virgin and the Christ Child are the work of Leonardo himself. The paint is applied thinly; it is limpid and transparent, so that in some places the underlying sketch is visible. This has become apparent since the very dark varnish was lightened and some overpainting removed in 1953.

The theme of the Christ Child on the knee of the Virgin, who is herself seated on Saint Anne's lap, is fairly rare, but examples of it can be found from the Middle Ages onwards—the stream of life flowing through three generations. Leonardo must have chosen this unusual theme for symbolic reasons, which have been variously interpreted. Sigmund Freud made out the shape of a vulture in the Virgin's garment, and suggested a psycho-analytical explanation—since as a child Leonardo dreamt that he had been attacked in his cradle by a vulture.

130

RAPHAEL (RAFFAELLO SANZIO) 1483–1520   *Italian School*
SAINT GEORGE AND THE DRAGON   Panel

Inventory: INV. 609   Height 0.32 m. (12¹/₂″)
                                            Width 0.27 m. (10³/₄″)

This picture and the little *Saint Michael,* also in the Louvre, are a pair; in the Mazarin collection they were joined together, forming a diptych, and bound in leather. Louis XIV acquired them from Mazarin's heirs in 1661.

The *Saint George* has sometimes been ascribed to the artist's Roman period, because of the fact that the horse resembles one of the horses of Monte Cavallo (the Quirinal). However, Raphael could easily have known this particular horse from a drawing of it, done by one of Leonardo's pupils. To judge by the still somewhat naïve and Peruginesque style of the painting, it is really one of Raphael's early works, dating from about 1502. He did another painting of the same subject a little later (National Gallery, Washington), and towards the end of his life he painted a large *Saint Michael* which is also in the Louvre (page 281).

Lomazzo, in his *Trattato della Pittura* (1584), mentions a *Saint George* by Raphael, commissioned by the Duke of Urbino, which was painted on a little chess-board *(tavoliere);* according to the old catalogues the little *Saint Michael,* if not the *Saint George* as well, had a draught-board on the back which is now covered over. Examination by means of X-rays and infra-red rays has not confirmed this statement. In the text referred to above, Lomazzo seems to have confused various pictures of the same subject. If we can rely to some extent upon his late and somewhat muddled testimony, it is possible that the two little pictures in the Louvre were painted for the Duke of Urbino.

The Uffizi has a pen-and-wash cartoon for the *Saint George.*

In spite of the presence of a not very frightening carnival dragon, the *Saint George* creates an impression of grace and charm, with its fresh colouring, the limpid atmosphere of the landscape, its youthful, elegant character, and the poetic figure of the princess in the pink gown, who seems about to vanish like an apparition. The *Saint Michael,* conceived in an atmosphere of fantasy so unusual in Italian art, suggests that Raphael may have seen a picture by Jerome Bosch; after all, Michelangelo did a painted version of Schongauer's engraving, the *Temptation of Saint Anthony.*

In 1860, Degas did a drawing of the *Saint George* in a notebook. It is in the Bibliothèque Nationale (carnet 327 réserve fo 25).

RAPHAEL *(RAFFAELLO SANZIO)* 1483–1520   *Italian School*
MADONNA (LA BELLE JARDINIÈRE)   Panel

Inventory: INV. 602   Height 1.22 m. (48″)
     Width 0.80 m. (31¹/₂″)
Signed: Raffaello Urb. MDVII   (Rounded at the top)

This picture figures in the inventory drawn up by Le Brun, Keeper of the King's Pictures, in 1683. As there is no earlier reference to it, it is presumed to have been acquired by Francis I. As it is dated 1507, it cannot be the Virgin painted for Filippo Segardi, which Raphael left unfinished when he went to Rome in the summer of 1508.

The name by which the picture is known was bestowed upon it because the Virgin is out-of-doors in a country setting; it is already referred to as 'La Jardinière' in the eighteenth century (Mariette, *Abecedario*).

During his Florentine period (1504–1508) Raphael painted about a dozen Madonnas. It has been thought that this preoccupation with the theme of maternity and childhood arose from the fact that Raphael's mother died when he was only eight.

A cartoon which Raphael prepared for this picture is now at Holkham Hall, in the Earl of Leicester's collection. A number of preparatory drawings and early copies are in existence. Delacroix copied the figure of the Christ Child (Robaut 24), and the composition inspired this *Madonna of the Sacred Heart* (Robaut 26).

The unusual character of the town on the right of the picture has never been pointed out; it is entirely gothic in style, with its tall spires, its paired windows surmounted by an *oculus,* the high buildings with pitched roofs and the pepper-pot tower. There are other instances of this in Raphael's work (the *Dream of the Knight* in the National Gallery, London, the *St George,* the Madonna in the Kaiser-Friedrich-Museum, Berlin, and the *Canigiani Madonna* in the Alte Pinakothek, Munich). Raphael may have seen urban landscapes of a gothic nature in Lombardy; the snowy hill-tops in the little *Conestabile Madonna* in the Hermitage seem to prove that he had seen the Alps. In some of his pictures, however, the buildings in these towns are so very northern that their presence can only be explained as an imitation of the Flemish primitives. The little *St Michael* is another example of Raphael's imitation of the gothic (see previous item). No doubt he was attracted by the transparency of the technique in Flemish paintings, and the purity of their sentiments. His work was completely transformed when he went to Rome, and he lost his taste for the gothic and for Flemish art.

RAPHAEL (RAFFAELLO SANZIO) 1483–1520   *Italian School*
PORTRAIT OF BALTHASAR CASTIGLIONE   Canvas

Inventory: INV. 611   Height 0.82 m. (32¹/₄")
                                                Width 0.67 m. (26¹/₂")

This picture was in the Luca van Uffelen sale at Amsterdam, 9 April 1639; Rembrandt made a sketch of it there (now in the Albertina, Vienna) and made a note in the margin that it came from Italy and was valued at 3.500 florins. It became the property of the Spaniard, Alfonso Lopez, adviser in Amsterdam to the King of Spain; he sold it to Mazarin, and Louis XIV bought it from the latter's heirs in 1661.

Raphael painted two portraits of his friend Balthasar Castiglione. Pietro Bembo refers to one of them in a letter dated April 1516; it was then nearly finished. According to a letter from Paulucci of Ferrara to Count Alfonso d'Este (12 September 1519), Castiglione subsequently sat for another portrait by Raphael. Antonio Bella Negrini, in his *Elogi dei personaggi della famiglia Castigliona* (Mantua, 1606), mentions two portraits of Balthasar by Raphael in the possession of that family.

Balthasar Castiglione, whom Charles V called 'uno de los mejores caballeros del mundo', was a diplomat who lived at the courts of several Italian princes, including that of Guidobaldo da Montefeltro, whom he considered a perfect example of 'il cortegiano'. In his work of that name, which forms a pendant to Machiavelli's *Il Principe* (rather as an angel can be said to form a pendant with a devil), Castiglione uses the word *cortegiano* not in the sense it has since acquired, but as signifying 'a man of the court'. The ideal he defends in this book is that of a harmonious way of life, governed by reason and by love in the Platonic sense. This ideal is also that of Raphael, as he has expressed it in the *Stanza della Segnatura*.

This portrait reveals Raphael's admiration for Leonardo da Vinci. He has painted Castiglione in the attitude of *La Gioconda,* a pose he also used in the case of *Maddalena Strozzi* (Borghese Gallery), *Maddalena Doni* (Pitti Palace), and the portrait of a woman in the Uffizi. The same painting also inspired a drawing which is now in the Cabinet des Dessins in the Louvre.

We know from the inventory made after Rubens' death (1640) that this artist had copied the Castiglione portrait (No. 78). No trace of the copy, however, has survived. Matisse also made a copy, which is today in the Musée de Bagnols-sur-Cèze.

CORREGGIO (ANTONIO ALLEGRI), 1494–1534   *Italian School*
THE MYSTICAL MARRIAGE OF SAINT CATHERINE   Panel

Inventory: INV. 41   Height 1.05 m. (41¼")
Width 1.02 m. (40¼")

The history of this picture can be traced right back to the beginning. Vasari mentions it as being in the house of a Modenese doctor, Francesco Grillenzoni; in 1582 Cardinal Luigi d'Este bought it, and presented it to Catarina Nobili Sforza, Countess of Santa Fiora and grand-niece of Pope Julius III. It was still in her possession in 1595. In 1614 it was in Rome, the property of Cardinal Sforza of Santa Fiora, who had no doubt inherited it. It was subsequently owned by Scipione Borghese, and then by Cardinal Antonio Barberini; the latter gave it to Mazarin in about 1650. Louis XIV bought it from Mazarin's heirs in 1661, for 15.000 *livres.*

Correggio first depicted this subject in a small composition of which several versions exist; that in the Naples museum is most likely to be the original one, though its attribution is not certain. The Louvre painting dates from about 1520; it is related to a group of Madonnas in which Correggio expressed his ideal of femininity – graceful, and with a touch of coquetry. The group includes the *Madonna suckling the Child* in Budapest, the *Madonna with the Basket* in the National Gallery, London, the *Madonna adoring the Child* in the Uffizi, and the *Madonna with St Sebastian* in Dresden. In all these works, painted at the same period (just after 1520), there is a 'loving' quality which gives a feeling of intimacy to the pictures of a mother and child. Perhaps they reflect the artist's own conjugal happiness; in 1520 he married a young orphan girl named Girolama Merlina, whose delicate and graceful beauty had charmed him. In all the pictures the Child is of the same type; perhaps the model was Correggio's son Pomponio, baptised 3 September 1521.

In 1958 the varnish which covered the painting was lightened to some extent, revealing its almost miraculous state of preservation. The only damage is to the arch of the saint's eyebrow. With its poplar-wood panel intact, it is one of the best preserved works of the Italian Renaissance.

A number of replicas of this painting have been made, many of which still survive; it has often been a source of inspiration to artists. In the nineteenth century it was copied by Ricard, and several times by Fantin-Latour.

138

GIORGIONE (GIORGIO BARBARELLI?), 1477?–1510   *Italian School*
CONCERT CHAMPÊTRE   Canvas

Inventory: INV. 71   Height 1.10 m. (43¹/₄")
                                             Width 1.38 m. (54¹/₄")

The earliest reference to this picture is in 1627 when, along with the other Gonzaga paintings in Mantua, it became the property of King Charles I. At some unknown date it was acquired by Everhard Jabach, a banker living in Paris, who may have obtained it from the Earl of Arundel. It finally passed into Louis XIV's collection.

The painting may perhaps have been bought by Isabella d'Este, which would explain its presence in the Gonzaga collection. We know that in 1510, when she heard of Giorgione's death, she wrote to Taddeo Albano of Venice asking him to obtain for her a painting of a 'Notte' (probably a Nativity) which she thought was amongst the artist's possessions. Taddeo Albano replied that nothing of that kind was to be found amongst the property he had left. So perhaps she then bought the *Concert Champêtre*.

In the seventeenth century the picture was enlarged by the addition of a fairly wide strip at the top edge and another at the left side. These strips are now hidden by the frame. Some additions were made during the seventeenth century to the foliage at the left.

The painting figures in old inventories as a work by Giorgione; Waagen, in 1839, was the first to question this attribution, believing it to be by Palma Vecchio. Since then, historians have expressed varying opinions. Contemporary critics are divided into those who uphold the original attribution to Giorgione and those who believe it was painted by the young Titian under Giorgione's influence. In 1955 it was possible to study this picture alongside other paintings by Giorgione, at the exhibition of his work in the Palace of the Doges; but the problem is still unsolved. The opinion of the majority is in favour of Giorgione's authorship; the Titianesque characteristics are sometimes explained (by Pallucchini, for example, and Giorgio Castelfranco) by the hypothesis that Titian finished the painting. This is not impossible, since Giorgione died young, and left behind half-finished works which were completed by Palma or Titian. X-rays reveal an alteration in the position of the nude woman on the left – possibly evidence in favour of this theory.

The subject of the painting, the intimate fusion of figures and landscape in the warm summer light, and the harmony of colouring, make this picture one of the most complete expressions of Venetian art.

TITIAN (TIZIANO VECELLIO), 1477–1576   *Italian School*
Young Woman at her Toilet   Canvas

Inventory: INV. 755   Height 0.96 m. (38")
                                               Width 0.76 m. (30")

This picture was acquired with the Gonzaga paintings from Mantua by
Charles I in 1627. Later it was bought by the banker Everhard Jabach, and
from him it passed into Louis XIV's collection. It is mentioned in the
inventory of Le Brun, Keeper of the King's Pictures, in 1683.

In Charles I's collection the painting was known as 'Titian's Mistress'.
Various attempts have been made to identify the two sitters, and the names
suggested include Alfonso d'Este and Laura di Dianti, Francesco Covos and
Cornelia, Federigo Gonzaga and Isabella Boschetti, Alfonso di Ferrara,
Marquis del Guasto and Maria of Aragon. It has also been claimed that
the couple represent the artist and his mistress Violante. Some of these iden-
tifications are impossible for chronological reasons, and all are now rejected.

The picture is usually dated about 1515, and belongs to the 'Giorgiones-
que' group of paintings by Titian, together with the *Flora* in the Uffizi, and
the *Sacred and Profane Love* in the Borghese Gallery. The rounded oval of
the woman's face, her shining eyes, the Venetian blonde of her hair with its
auburn lights, and her pearly shoulders, all go to make this picture the very
incarnation of the Venetian ideal of feminine beauty, opulent and sensual.

The Louvre picture is most closely related to the Uffizi *Flora*, but the
latter is in better condition. The former, which is described in Bailly's inventory of 1709 as having been enlarged, has suffered a certain amount of
damage and undergone several restorations. It was transferred to a new
canvas in 1751; damp caused it to flake, and in 1818 it was re-fixed. For
this reason, and because of the darkness of the background, only a very
cautious cleaning-off of the varnish was possible; enough was done, however, to reveal the colours and tonal relationships of the picture. Previously,
the blue dress had appeared green, and the hair was lost against the linen
chemise.

The existence of numerous copies testify to the picture's fame; even the
Royal collection possessed one (mentioned there in 1709). The most famous,
once thought to be an original, was in the collection of the Regent, the Duke
of Orleans, and had belonged to Queen Christina of Sweden.

TINTORETTO (JACOPO ROBUSTI), 1512–1594. PARADISE. *Italian School*

Ridolfi mentions this picture as being in the possession of the Bevilacqua family in Venice, where Goethe saw it shortly before it was removed in 1799 by the French commissioners to be sent to the Louvre.

It is believed to be the design produced by Tintoretto in the competition held in 1579 for the decoration of the Great Council Chamber after the fire in the Doge's Palace in 1577. His rivals were Paolo Veronese (whose

Inventory: INV. 572.   Canvas.   Height 1.43 m. (57¼″).   Width 0.76 m. (30″)

design is in the Museum at Lille) and Francesco Bassano (sketch in the
Hermitage, Leningrad). The commission was awarded jointly to Veronese
and Bassano; but when the former died in 1588 the work had apparently
not yet begun. Bassano, for his part, fell a victim to neurasthenia, and
committed suicide in 1592. The work was then entrusted to Tintoretto, who
carried it out with the collaboration of Palma Giovane.

145

TITIAN (TIZIANO VECELLIO), 1477–1576   *Italian School*
CHRIST CROWNED WITH THORNS

Inventory: INV. 748   Height 3.03 m. (119¹/₄″)
Signed: Titianus F   Width 1.80 m. (70¹/₂″)

This painting was formerly the altarpiece in the Santa Corona chapel in Santa Maria delle Grazie, Milan. It was sent to Paris in 1797, and exhibited in the Louvre from 1798 onwards.

Vasari and Ridolfi both mention it as being in Santa Maria delle Grazie. It was probably painted in about 1542, when the chapel was being decorated with frescoes by Gaudenzio Ferrari.

Professor Suida has pointed out that this is, for Titian, an unusually mannerist work. The literal imitation of the antique is itself a mannerist characteristic; it is seen in the bust of Tiberius, and also in the attitude of Christ, reminiscent of the Laocoon, in details of the crouching soldier's military equipment, and the breeches of the soldier on the left—a garment worn by barbarians in antiquity. The monumentality and the sense of movement in the composition, the emphatic drawing, and the exaggeration of the muscles are all mannerist features which Titian could have borrowed from Giulio Romano's frescoes at Mantua.

Thirty years or so later, Titian again made use of most of the elements of this composition in a picture now at Munich. He omitted the greater part of the antique details, and sought to express pathos not through naturalism, but by means of the nocturnal atmosphere which bathes the figures in a dramatic *chiaroscuro*.

The Ospedale Maggiore in Milan has a very good contemporary copy, showing only the figures, without the upper part. There is also a copy in the Accademia in Venice. A drawing in pen and bistre wash, attributed to Gian Domenico Tiepolo and sold in Paris (Georges Petit), 30 May 1921, is evidently based on an engraving of the picture; it shows various figures in the same attitudes, but reversed.

Included in the Comte de Pourtalès' sale, 1 April 1865 (No. 119), was a little painting on paper (0.54 m. × 0.32 m.), described as 'the first precious sketch of the magnificent picture (by Titian) in the Louvre'. I saw this picture a few years ago, and believe it to be a study made after the picture at the end of the seventeenth century.

VERONESE (PAOLO CALIARI), 1528–1588   *Italian School*
THE MARRIAGE AT CANA (DETAIL)   Canvas

Inventory: INV. 142   Height 6.66 m. (262¼")
    Width 9.90 m. (354¼")

This picture was ordered from Veronese by the Benedictines of San Giorgio, Venice, to decorate their refectory (built by Palladio). It was delivered on 8 September 1563, and installed at the end of the refectory in the same year. It was chosen for the Louvre by the French commission on 11 September 1797 and was exhibited in the Salon Carré in 1801. In 1815 the Austrian commissioners agreed to exchange it for Le Brun's *Feast in the House of Simon*. It remained on exhibition in the Salon Carré till 1951, when it was transferred to what had formerly been Napoleon III's Salle des Etats. Other large works of the Venetian school were also put on exhibition in the same room.

There are 132 figures in this huge painting (page 293). It was completed in a year, when the artist was 34. He received 324 ducats for it, plus the cost of his food and a cask of wine.

The Frenchman, Salomon de Brosse, and Zanotti, the author of *Della pittura veneziana* (1771), speak of a tradition preserved in an old manuscript which could still be seen in the monastery of San Giorgio in the eighteenth century. According to this tradition, the feast here represented was an ideal banquet in which some of the great Renaissance princes were depicted as taking part. At the table, the newly-married pair are supposed to be Alfonso of Avalos, Marquis del Vasto (Charles V's governor in the Milanais), and Eleanor of Austria, the Emperor's sister, who married Francis I after Pavia. Leaning towards the bride and groom are Francis I and Mary of England, sister of Henry VIII; the man with the turban, next to them, is Suleiman the Magnificent, the Turkish Sultan. Next comes Vittoria Colonna, Michelangelo's patroness; and after her the Emperor Charles V. The central figures in the foreground can be identified from their known portraits. The man on the right, standing, and drinking a toast, is presumed to be Veronese's brother Benedetto; the orchestra is made up of artists, with Titian holding the contrabass, Veronese himself playing the viola, Tintoretto the violin, and Jacopo Bassano the flute. The bearded man leaning towards Veronese and also playing the viola could be Palladio, architect of the refectory of San Giorgio.

In this large decorative canvas Veronese has abandoned classical perspective, with its single vanishing point, to make use of multifocal perspective.

148

VERONESE (PAOLO CALIARI), 1528–1588   *Italian School*
THE PILGRIMS OF EMMAUS   Canvas

Inventory: INV. 146   Height 2.41 m. (95″)
                                                       Width   4.15 m. (163½″)

It is not known how this picture originated, or in what circumstances it was painted. It formed part of Richelieu's collection in the Palais Cardinal, and together with this palace (now the Palais Royal) it was left to the King in 1642. It was moved to Fontainebleau, then to the Tuileries, and finally to Versailles, where it hung in the Salon de Mars, in the *grands appartements,* as a companion to *Alexander and Darius* by Le Brun.

This picture is intensely alive and animated, and shows how little the artist cared for religious scruples; his encounter with the Inquisition is well known. The donor's large family literally invades the composition, mingling on equal terms with the characters of the Gospel.

The signature may not be original. The style of the painting is characteristic of the period 1560–1563, when the *Marriage at Cana* was also executed.

Inventory: INV. 1444   Height 0.710 m. (28″)
                                                  Width 0.680 m. (27″)
Signed on the roll of parchment, resting on the book: 'Quinten Matsys, Schilder 1514'.

This is one of the best-known works of the Flemish school. It was bought for the Musée Napoléon in Paris, in 1806, for 1.800 francs. Its history can be traced, with a few gaps, back to the seventeenth century; it is believed to have belonged to Rubens. The high reputation it enjoyed can be measured by the frequent praise bestowed upon it, and the numerous copies made of it.

It is painted in a somewhat archaic style, reminiscent of the fifteenth century, and of Van Eyck's detailed naturalism. It is, in fact, known that there formerly existed a work by Jan van Eyck dated 1440, which represented 'a merchant at his accounts, with an assistant, the figures half-length'. It is believed that Matsys must have followed Van Eyck very closely in painting this merchant, evidently a jeweller, counting his gold with his wife at his side. She is turning the pages of a Book of Hours, and seems to have paused, as if fascinated by the precious metal, at a page on which can be made out a picture of the Virgin. An inscription on the original frame—fortunately recorded before the frame was lost—gave evidence of the moralizing intention of the work; it was a passage from Leviticus (XIX. 36): 'Satura justa et aequa sint pondera' (Just balances, just weights . . . shall ye have). This picture has been the source of many currents of inspiration. Matsys himself made use of the same setting for his portraits of Erasmus and Aegidius in 1517. The theme, popularized by a variant painted by Marinus van Reymerswael, gave rise to a whole section of sixteenth-century genre painting. Finally, this painting constitutes a link between the artistic vision of Jan van Eyck and that of Vermeer in the seventeenth century.

The convex mirror in the foreground is a device already used by Van Eyck to show a concentrated image of the fourth side of a room, where the painter is standing (*Arnolfini and his Wife*, the National Gallery, London). Here the fourth side has a window, and the mirror thus provides an opening on to the outside world.

MABUSE (JAN GOSSAERT)   *Flemish School*
c. 1478 – d. between 1533 and 1536
THE CARONDELET DIPTYCH   Panel

Inventory: INV. 1442 and 1443   Height 0.430 m. (17")
                                            Width 0.270 m. (10³/₄")

Signed at the bottom of the right wing: 'JOHANNES MELBODIE
PINGEBAT', and dated at the bottom of the left wing: 'FAIT L'AN 1517'.
On the frames: various inscriptions referring to the Virgin or indicating the
donor.

Carondelet is represented, half-length, praying before the Virgin; on the
back of the portrait is his coat-of-arms, and on the back of the Virgin is
a *trompe-l'oeil* skull, with a pious inscription and the date.

Carondelet was born at Dôle in 1469, and died at Malines on 8 February,
1545; he was the son of the Chancellor Carondelet. He was a church digni-
tary, holding various offices and benefices, and played a political rôle in the
Low Countries. Having entered the church, he acquired various important
posts. From 1497 he was a member of the Grand Conseil pour les affaires
de Justice. In 1517 he went to Spain with Charles V, and returned with
him to the Low Countries in 1519. In 1531 he became President of the Privy
Council. In addition, he acquired numerous ecclesiastical dignities; in 1493
he was Archbishop of Palermo and Primate of Sicily. He was a scholar and
a humanist, and a friend of Erasmus, who dedicated his *Saint Hilaire* to
him; evidently he had a liking for having his portrait done, since there are
two others of him by Mabuse, another by Van Orley, and one by Vermeyen.

This work dates from Mabuse's mature period; it shows his preoccupation
with the sculpted form which he acquired through contact with Michelangelo
and antique statues in Rome in 1508. In this year he accompanied Philip
of Burgundy, natural son of Philip the Good and Admiral of the fleet, who
was sent as a private ambassador to Philip II. According to M. Edouard
Michel, the artist based this painting on some antique bust – Euripides,
Socrates, or Julius Caesar. The artist was torn between the Flemish tendency
towards naturalism and Italian idealization, as can be seen in his portrayal
of the Virgin (page 294). For this reason the donor portrait is superior to
the other wing, both in truth to life and in pictorial quality; it is, moreover,
in a better state of preservation. The finest piece of painting is the skull on
the back – an illusionistic still life reminiscent of surrealist works of the
modern school.

154

DÜRER, ALBRECHT, 1471–1528   *German School*
PORTRAIT OF THE ARTIST   Parchment pasted on canvas

Inventory: R. F. 2382   Height 0.565 m. (22¼/")
Dated 1493   Width 0.445 m. (17½")

Former Felix collection (Leipzig), Leopold Goldschmidt (Paris). Bought in 1922 from the sequestrator Nicolas de Villeroy, for the sum of 300.000 francs.

The date, and the plant in the artist's hand, seem to suggest that this is a betrothal portrait *(Brautporträt)*. Dürer has in fact depicted himself in the act of offering a flowering spray identified by botanists as *eryngium amethystinum*; its German name is 'Mannestreue', meaning conjugal fidelity. This umbelliferous plant is used in medicine, and is regarded as an aphrodisiac. In 1493, Dürer was 22 years old; he had completed his apprenticeship with Wolgemuth, begun in 1486, and had started his tour as a journeyman, which was to last four years. In 1492 it had taken him to Colmar, the home of Schongauer; but he was too late to meet this artist, the object of his youthful admiration, who had died before he arrived there. He was back in Nuremberg in 1494, after Whitsun. 'Hans Frey (one of the senior citizens) negotiated with my father', writes Dürer, 'and gave me his daughter Agnes, with a dowry of 200 florins; and we were married on the Monday before the feast of St Margaret.' The portrait was originally painted on vellum (it was later transferred to canvas); for this reason, Thausing believes that it was sent by Dürer to support his suit.

Goethe saw a copy of this portrait in the museum at Leipzig, and wrote of it: 'I thought Albrecht Dürer's self-portrait, dated 1493, to be of inestimable value'.

The artist was temperamentally inclined to philosophical doubts. He often analysed his own face in drawn or painted effigies – sometimes idealizing it, sometimes not. Here he seems to have seen himself as in a mirror, with the rather sallow skin which some have ascribed to his Hungarian ancestry, others to some liver complaint. The lines written beside the date in this picture reveal the philosophical and Christian intention of the work:

Myn sach die gat
Als es oben schtat.

In others words: My affairs follow the course allotted to them on high. Marriage has in part determined his destiny; the Bridegroom puts his future life in the hands of God.

Inventory: INV. 1345   Height 0.42 m. (18¹/₂″)
                                    Width 0.32 m. (12¹/₂″)

This picture was bought by Louis XIV from Everhard Jabach, the Cologne banker, whose seal appears on the back of it. It is included in Charles Le Brun's inventory of the King's pictures, drawn up in 1683. As well as Jabach's stamp, the picture also bears two of Charles I's seals on the back, and a label proving that it belonged to that monarch; it appears in the first list of his pictures, compiled in about 1624. Together with an unidentified Titian, it was given by the king to the Duc de Liancourt, who had presented him with a John the Baptist by Leonardo, brought to the Louvre by Louis XIV. The Erasmus portrait is also recorded as having been in the Earl of Arundel's collection.

Holbein seems to have been the Dutch humanist's favourite painter; he did several portraits of Erasmus. The earliest seems to be the one belonging to the Earl of Radnor, at Longford Castle (a copy of which is in the Louvre); this shows the scholar turned three-quarters from the spectator, half-length, his hands resting on a book. The Louvre painting, in which he is seen in profile, shows him at the same age, writing the first lines of his *Commentary on St Mark's Gospel,* which dates from 1523. The writing is almost illegible in the Louvre picture, but they can be read on a smaller copy in the Museum at Basle, usually thought to be also by Holbein, but of inferior quality. In the little round portrait at Basle, done ten years or so later, the scholar seems to have aged to an extraordinary degree. There is another early copy in the monastery of St Florian in Austria.

Based on representations of St Jerome, the portrait of a scholar writing or meditating in his study is a subject frequently depicted during the Renaissance. Erasmus often sat for artists; Quentin Matsys painted him when he was younger, and Albrecht Dürer, in a drawing in the Louvre and also in an engraving, showed him with his eyes lowered, looking at his book, as in the Louvre Holbein.

The Louvre portrait has the greatest intensity. It shows the humanist when he was about 56, his age beginning to tell on him. The hand pressed so firmly on the writing desk is knotted with gout. The expression on his face is attentive, but the trace of an ironical smile betrays the deliberation and scepticism of the rationalist – qualities which Erasmus never lost, even in the midst of the impassioned theological quarrels of his time.

HOLBEIN, HANS, 1497–1543   *German School*
PORTRAIT OF NICOLAUS KRATZER

Inventory: INV. 1343   Height 0.83 m. (32¹/₂″)
Dated: 1528   Width 0.67 m. (26¹/₂″)

This work is first mentioned by the artist-historian Karel van Mander; it was then in London in the collection of Andries de Loo, who died in 1590. It appeared subsequently in the gallery of the Earl of Arundel, after which it travelled to Paris, with other works by Holbein, and became part of the collection of Everhard Jabach, the banker. It was amongst the pictures which the latter sold to Louis XIV in 1671.

The portrait is a half-length, showing the sitter turned three-quarters to the right. In his left hand he holds a pair of dividers, in his right a polyhedron of boxwood, with graduated circles engraved on its different faces. On the table are scissors, set-squares, a hammer, a pair of dividers; on the wall behind him and in a niche are various mathematical instruments. A paper on the table bears the inscription: 'Imago ad vivam effigiem expressa Nicolai Kratzer monacensis q. bauarg (bavarus) erat quadregessimu . . . annu tpre (tempore) illo gplebat (complebat). 1528.'

This is one of the few surviving portraits from Holbein's first English period. Nicolas Kratzer (1487–1550), a native of Munich, was King Henry VIII's astronomer and 'deviser of the King's horologes'. He had already settled in London in 1520; he was a friend of Holbein and of Thomas More and was one of the tutors to the latter's daughters; he taught them astronomy. The Latin inscriptions on Holbein's famous drawing of the More family (Museum of Basle) are said to be in his hand, and also those on a drawing by the same artist of the clock offered by Sir Anthony Denny to Henry VIII (British Museum), which Kratzer had no doubt invented.

Holbein's hand has been recognized in an ornamental initial in the *Canones Horoptri*, a short astronomical treatise written by Kratzer; the manuscript of this work is in the Bodleian Library, Oxford.

Karel van Mander relates an amusing anecdote in connection with this portrait. Nicolas Kratzer, who was of German origin, had never managed to learn English. One day, in jest or otherwise, the king asked him how it came about that he did not speak it better. 'Forgive me, Sire,' replied Kratzer, 'but how much English can one possibly learn in only thirty years?'

An early copy of this painting was made for Sir Walter Cope, and has been in his family for more than 300 years.

CRANACH, LUCAS, THE ELDER, 1472–1553   *German School*
PORTRAIT OF A YOUNG GIRL   Panel

Inventory: R. F. 1767   Height 0.39 m. (15¹/₂″)
Signed with the bat-winged dragon   Width 0.25 m. (10″)

Bought in 1910 from M. Rosenberg for 5.500 francs.

The Lutheran Museum at Wittenberg has a late copy of this picture, which according to a local tradition represents Luther's daughter, Magdalena. In 1932, however, Friedländer and Rosenberg expressed the opinion that this could not be the case, because the child was born in 1529, and in their view this picture could not be dated later than the 1520's, for stylistic reasons. But in 1933 M. Edouard Michel pointed out that there existed an engraving of the portrait, bearing the inscription 'Magdalena D. Mart. Lutheri ex Cathar de Borha Filia. Nata An 1529, mortua die 20 Sept A 1542. Aetatis suae 14.' This print is a plate from Junker's book *Vita D. Martini Lutheri,* published in Frankfurt in 1699.

The age of the child at her death corresponds with that of the subject of this portrait; it must have been painted shortly before she died, because it certainly seems to have been done from life, not from memory. This would fix the date of its execution as 1541–1542. Unlike Friedländer and Rosenberg, M. Michel does not find this date incompatible with its style; he compares it with figures very similar in execution and drawing in the *Virgin and Child with St John* in Berlin (No. 559), later than 1537, and also the *Unterberger Madonna* at Innsbrück, 'ascribed by Flechsig to the final period of the artist's work'.

In 1942 Hans Posse, who does not seem to have known Michel's article, also dated the picture in about 1520, and therefore considered that it could not be Magdalena Luther. Nevertheless it remains a tempting hypothesis, which one is reluctant to discard. After all, the chronological argument is itself based on a hypothesis, and one should bear in mind that it is difficult to compare this picture with others, because of its unusual colour harmony –black on black.

The possibility is not ruled out, therefore, that this is a picture of the reformer's daughter, who died young. The premature sadness of the child's face lends support to the identification; the combination of blacks also has a funereal character.

The painting is one of the artist's most graceful works; he has renounced the charms of colour, and it owes everything to an incomparable elegance of line.

162

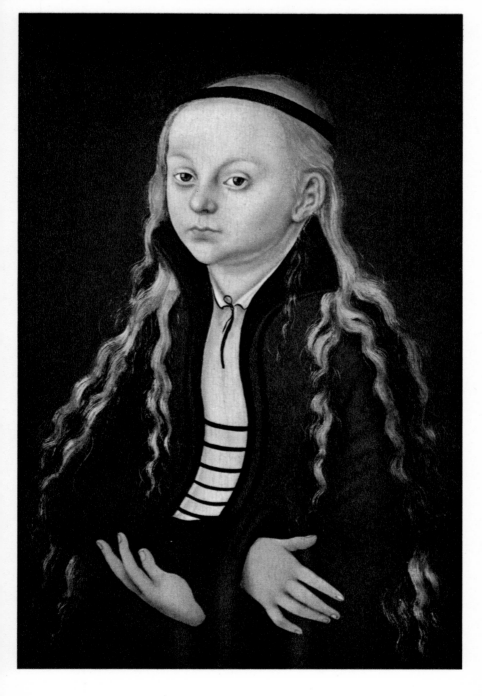

CLOUET, FRANÇOIS, 1515–1572   *French School*

ELIZABETH OF AUSTRIA, QUEEN OF FRANCE   Panel

Inventory: INV. 3254   Height 0.36 m. (14¹/₄")
                    Width 0.27 m. (10³/₄")

In 1755 this picture was in the King's Cabinet des Ordres; it had probably been placed there by Pierre Clérambault, Keeper of the royal collection, who must have removed it from amongst the Gaignières property before the latter was sold. During the Revolution it was sent to the Dépôt established in the convent of the Petits Augustins, converted into the Musée des Monuments Français. In 1817 it was transferred to the Louvre.

A replica of the painting dated 1571, in the museum at Chantilly, makes it possible to date this portrait of Elizabeth of Austria (1554–1592), daughter of Maximilian II, Emperor of Austria, and of Maria of Austria, who married Charles IX on 27 November 1570.

The Print Room in the Bibliothèque Nationale has a drawing for the portrait, bearing the same date.

The attribution to Clouet has sometimes been doubted, but the outstanding quality of the work, the limpid flesh tones, and the rich finish of the costume make it reasonably certain that the painting is by him.

There is something a little sad in the queen's expression. Her life was not happy; she loved the king passionately, but his feeling for her was simply an affectionate regard, and a genuine appreciation of her good qualities. His heart belonged to Marie Touchet.

Brantôme has left an appealing description of this princess: 'She was very beautiful, with a complexion as fair and fine as any lady in her court; and had a most pleasant manner. She was also wise, virtuous and kind, and never harmed or offended a single soul, nor uttered the slightest harsh word. She was of a serious disposition, moreover, and spoke but little, and then always in her native Spanish'. After the king's death in 1574, she did not wish to marry again, and retired to Vienna, where she founded a convent of Poor Clares. She died there, aged 38, on 22 June 1592.

The painting is executed with great finish, but is not highly detailed; the skilful use of transparent glazes serves to show up the delicate complexion so much admired by Brantôme. The work stands out by reason of its excellent condition.

As with all royal portraits, a number of replicas exist, contemporary or later; some are faithful copies, others introduce variants.

SCHOOL OF FONTAINEBLEAU, c. 1550   *French School*
DIANA THE HUNTRESS   Canvas

Inventory: INV. 445   Height 1.92 m. (75³/₄")
                                          Width 1.33 m. (52¹/₂")

This picture was bought at the Lebreton sale in 1840 for 226 francs. It was first sent to Fontainebleau. A smaller copy was ordered for Versailles from Hippolyte Flandrin, and cost more than the original (400 francs).

At the time of its purchase, the painting was taken to be an allegorical portrait of Diane de Poitiers, Duchesse de Valentinois, Henri II's mistress. This identification was subsequently abandoned, but has lately been taken up again. Père Dan, author of *Trésors des Merveilles de la maison royale de Fontainebleau*, written in 1642, records in the Pavillon des Reines Mères (no longer standing) 'a portrait from life of Madame Gabrielle Destré, Duchesse de Beaufort, as Diana'. He says it is the work of Ambroise Dubois, who was a contemporary of Gabrielle d'Estrées. The face of the Louvre *Diana*, however, is not that of Gabrielle. In the catalogue of the exhibition *The Triumph of Mannerism* (Amsterdam, 1955), M. Charles Sterling returns to the earlier identification of the model as Diane de Poitiers, after comparing the face with known portraits of this royal favourite.

The character of Diana played an important part in poetry and painting in the reign of Henri II, not only because of Diane de Poitiers but also because of the passionate attachment of the French kings to the pleasures of hunting. The general pose of this striding Diana was probably inspired by an antique marble (a copy of a fourth-century work) brought back from Italy by Francis I, and now in the Louvre (No. 589). Louis XIV had a bronze replica made of it for the Jardin des Buis (now the Jardin de Diane) at Fontainebleau. The style created at Fontainebleau by Rosso and Primaticcio has also left its mark on this painting; the lengthened proportions recall Primaticcio, and the modelling of the bust is reminiscent of figures by Rosso. The style is much closer to work done in 1550–1560 than to the group known as the 'second school of Fontainebleau', at the end of the sixteenth century; which excludes the possibility of attributing it to Ambroise Dubois. In fact, the picture calls to mind sculpture rather than painting – in particular the work of Jean Goujon. The head, with its blue eyes and blond hair, is very beautiful and very individual, in spite of the mythological idealization. The canvas has been slightly enlarged on the left.

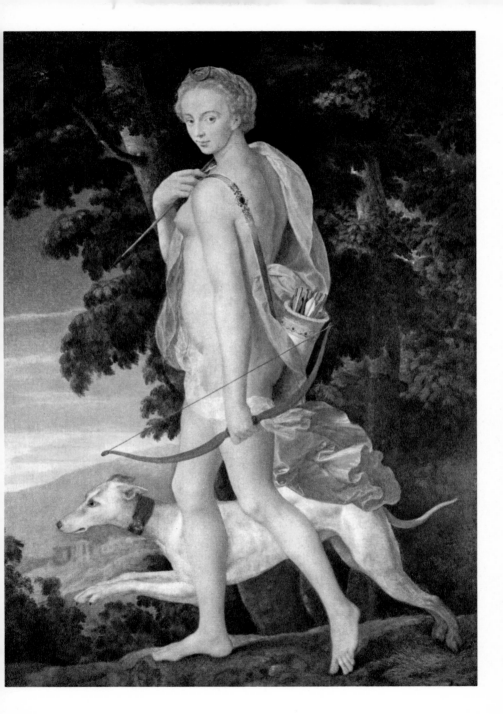

Inventory: R. F. 730   Height 0.180 m. (7¹/₄″)
Signed on bottom left: BRUEGEL MDLXVIII   Width 0.215 m. (8¹/₂″)

This little picture is the only work by Brueghel in the Louvre. It was the gift of Paul Mantz, art critic and honorary Director-General of Beaux-Arts, in 1892. Little is known of its previous history.

Attempts have been made to interpret the picture of five cripples and a beggar-woman as an allusion to a historical event; the badger's tails, or foxes' tails, on their clothes might refer to the Gueux, a rebel party formed against the government of Philip II and Granvelle; but these also occur in the *Combat between Carnival and Lent* in Vienna, dated 1559. Still, the beggars are not quite ordinary beggars; they wear carnival headgear representing various classes of society: a cardboard crown (the king), a paper shako (the soldier?), a beret (the bourgeois), a cap (the peasant) and a mitre (the bishop). The work clearly has some satirical meaning which has so far eluded us; perhaps physical imperfections are meant to symbolize moral decrepitude, which can affect all men irrespective of class.

There is a drawing of a street scene by Martin van Cleve in the Print Room at Munich which is evidently inspired by this picture; it reproduces several of the figures – the cripple with the shako, and the one with the mitre and the foxes' tails. But the mitre in the drawing is real, and not made of paper.

On the back of the painting are two inscriptions which seem to date from the sixteenth century; they record the admiration of two art lovers. One is in Flemish, and in a very fragmentary state; one can make out the word 'ruepelen' (cripples) and a sentence which means 'may your fortunes prosper' – probably the thanks of a cripple receiving alms.

The other inscription is in Latin, and can be roughly translated as follows:
Nature possesses nothing which our art lacks.
So great is the grace given to the painter;
Here Nature, translated into painted images and seen in her cripples,
Is astounded to see that Brueghel is her equal.

EL GRECO (DOMENICOS THEOTOCOPOULOS)   *Spanish School*
1548–1614
A SAINTLY KING (?)   Canvas

Inventory: R. F. 1507   Height 1.17 m. (46″)
                                              Width 0.95 m. (37¹/₂″)

Formerly in the château of Chenonceaux. Passed into the Manzi collection
in about 1875, then into the possession of M. Glaenzer, from whom it was
bought in 1903 for 70.000 francs.

Most historians agree that the picture was painted shortly before 1600;
M. Camon Azmar, however, (El Greco's most recent historian) does not
believe it was painted before that date. There is, in fact, a good deal of
uncertainty concerning the subject. The painting obviously represents a king,
since all the royal attributes are present—crown, sceptre with fleur-de-lys,
and 'main de justice'; he wears modern armour, except for the fact that the
forearms are bare—probably to suggest that he belongs to a heroic past. The
column in the background no doubt symbolises the might of the warrior.

In 1903, when the picture entered the Louvre, the *New York Herald*
published it as representing Ferdinand V, 'the Catholic', king of Castile and
Aragon, conqueror of Granada, who drove the Moors from Spain. Other
writers have identified it as St Louis, king of France, or as Ferdinand III,
the saintly king of Castile and Léon, famous for his victories over the
Moors; he forced them to withdraw to the south of Spain, depriving them
of Cordova and Seville, and was canonized in 1671. Camon Azmar regards
it as a secular portrait representing a victorious king of Spain—a Visigothic
king, one of the sovereigns already mentioned, or Alfonso VI of Castile and
Léon, the conqueror of Toledo in 1085.

There is an inferior replica of this picture, without the page, in Madrid;
Camon Azmar attributes this to Jorge Manuel Theotocopouli, El Greco's
son. It contains a variant which would be of interest were it not for the
late date of the painting: a view of Toledo evidently inspired by that of
El Greco now in the Metropolitan Museum.

An X-ray photograph recently made in the Louvre laboratories shows
that the head of the page was at first painted more realistically, and subsequently idealized; the eyes were originally shown wide open, then El Greco
lowered the eyelids to make the boy more subsidiary to the main figure.

The predominantly glaucous tone of the picture and the curiously melancholy expression of the warrior king (no doubt some swashbuckling epic
hero), contribute to the quality of strangeness in this work.

170

CARAVAGGIO, MICHELANGELO DA   *Italian School*
(MICHELANGELO AMERIGHI), 1573–1610
THE DEATH OF THE VIRGIN   Canvas

Inventory: INV. 54   Height 3.69 m. (145¹/₂")
                                              Width 2.45 m. (96¹/₂)

This picture was painted in 1605–1606 for the chapel of Laerte Cherubini,
the jurist, in Santa Maria della Scala, the church of the Discalced Carmelites
in Trastevere, Rome; it scandalized the good fathers, and had to be removed.
It was bought by Vincenzo Gonzaga for what in those days was a very high
price – 280 gold ducats, plus 20 by way of commission to the agent. On
28 April 1607, it was taken to Mantua. Charles I bought it with the Gonzaga
collection in 1627; in 1649 the Commonwealth government sold it to Everhard Jabach, the banker, from whom it was acquired by Louis XIV.

Ecclesiastical circles accused Caravaggio of having made the Virgin a
commonplace type of woman. Some claimed that he had modelled her on
a swollen corpse fished up out of the Tiber; others went so far as to say that
his model had been a courtesan from the Ortacci quarter. These accusations
were unjust, because he seems to have used the same model who sat for the
Madonna dei Palefrenieri – a poor but respectable woman named Lena.
Artistic circles hailed the work with great enthusiasm; such an unusual masterpiece was coveted by many when it appeared on the market, and the Duke
of Mantua acquired it through the intervention of Rubens, who was at that
time in his service. The details of this purchase are shown from three letters
written by Giovanni Magno, the Duke's agent in Rome, to Cheppio, coun-
sellor at the Mantuan court. Yielding to the unanimous demand of the artists
of Rome, Giovanni Magno had to make the picture available for public
admiration, and exhibited it from 7 to 14 April 1607. Rubens himself
took charge of the making of the packing-case for its journey to Mantua.
Caravaggio, uneasy on account of the brawl in which he had been involved
the previous year, was no longer in Rome at that time.

Untouched as we now are by all the passions it aroused, we are free to
admire what the artists of the time saw in it – a monument of human pathos,
which attains an antique grandeur. The reason for Caravaggio's troubles
with the Roman clergy, however, can well be understood; in striking this
note of evangelical simplicity, he was foreshadowing the Protestant art of
Rembrandt. The representation of the Blessed Virgin as a woman of humble
class, and not as the Queen of Heaven, had been demanded a century earlier
by another reformer who was also ahead of his time – Savonarola.

CARAVAGGIO, MICHELANGELO DA *Italian School*
(MICHELANGELO AMERIGHI), 1573–1610
THE FORTUNE TELLER Canvas

Inventory: INV. 55 Height 0.99 m. (39″)
Width 1.31 m. (51¹/₂″)

This painting was mentioned by Mancini in about 1620, as being in the collection of a Roman gentleman named Alessandro Vitrice. Scanelli saw it in 1657 in the collection of Prince Camillo Pamfili; Bellori also remarks that it was in the Palazzo Pamfili, beside the *Flight into Egypt* and the *Magdalen*. M. de Chanteloup, in his *Journal de Voyage du Cavalier Bernin en France*, relates that Prince Camillo Pamfili gave it to Louis XIV in 1665.

It was already famous in the seventeenth century, referred to and praised by the critics of the period—Mancini, Baglione and Bellori. A slightly different and rather heavy version is in the Capitoline Museum in Rome; this is usually considered a studio work, and has sometimes been ascribed to Saraceni. It does not, however, correspond with Bellori's very detailed description, which exactly fits the Louvre version.

Prince Pamfili's gift was not greatly appreciated at the court of Louis XIV, if Chanteloup's comments are any guide: 'Caravaggio's *Cingara* is a poor work, lacking in wit and invention'. All the same, the king shortly after-wards bought the *Death of the Virgin* by the same artist; but the court only admired 'noble' subjects and had no time for 'genre' scenes.

This painting is one of Caravaggio's earliest works; it must date from about 1588–1589. Before the dramatic inspiration of his maturity, Cara-vaggio's researches were directed towards elegance in the slightly languorous, not to say equivocal, grace of adolescents, and the minutely naturalistic representation of flowers and fruit.

Later, Bellori related that the work had been a kind of act of defiance; the artist had apparently claimed that he wanted to draw his subjects from everyday life, and not from the imitation of the antique, and had called in from the street a passing gipsy, to paint a picture of her. Mancini (1619) reports that the price received for it was very low—only 8 *écus*.

The subject, a young man of good family being made game of by a gipsy, became one of the most popular themes of the *tenebrosi* in the seventeenth century.

Before the picture was sent to the *Mostra del Caravaggio* in Milan in the summer of 1951, the thick layer of dark varnish was lightened and it was possible to confirm that it was the original work.

174

CARRACCI, ANNIBALE, 1560–1609.   FISHING SCENE.   *Italian School*

The picture and its companion, *Hunting Scene* (page 299), were given to Louis XIV by Prince Camillo Pamfili in 1665. They were included in Le Brun's inventory in 1683; and in November 1695 they were in the apartments of the King's younger brother. It was no doubt for this purpose that they were given two sumptuous gilt frames, each with attributes suited to the

Inventory: INV. 210. Canvas. Height 1.36 m. (53¹/₂"). Width 2.53 m. (99¹/₂")

subject of the painting – among the finest examples of the art of frame-making in the time of Louis XIV. In 1955, when the varnish was being cleaned, the nineteenth-century gilding covering the original gilding was removed.

These landscapes date from Carracci's Bolognese period, before 1695.

RIBERA, JOSÉ, 1588–1656   *Spanish School*
THE CLUB-FOOTED BOY   Canvas

Inventory: M. I. 893   Height 1.64 m. (64¹/₂")
                                             Width 0.92 m. (36¹/₄")
Signed in the lower right hand corner: Jusepe de Ribera español f 1642

   Part of the La Caze bequest, in 1869.
   This young vagabond is standing silhouetted against the landscape, carrying his crutch with the proud air of an hidalgo bearing arms. His smile seems
to be making game of his own infirmity; he is also careful to inform us, by
means of the scrap of writing he holds, that he is dumb as well as crippled,
because he appeals to the charity of the passer-by with a card on which is
the inscription: 'Da mihi elemosinam propter amorem Dei'.
   This is one of the painter's last works, and one of the most bitter. The
contrast of light and shade gave him pleasure; he studied the composition of
the Renaissance painters in Italy, and perhaps also the work of Flemish
artists, but in spite of all that he clung to the profoundly Spanish tradition
of realism, even after having spent nearly all his life in Naples.
   Moved by a Christian awareness of human weakness, Spanish artists often
painted pictures of beggars, cripples and idiots. This is a derivation of the
taste for scenes of low life in art, instituted by Caravaggio; Ribera was, in
Naples, its most fervent adherent.
   In this work, however, Ribera abandons Caravaggio's magical chiaroscuro;
he had employed it to give dramatic intensity to his genre subjects, but the
constant and indiscriminate use he made of it gave many of his works a
contrived air. The direct realism of the *Club-Footed Boy* is far more
moving; its profound psychological penetration recalls Velasquez. The
striking effect is increased by the low viewpoint; the figure towers above the
spectator, who is imagined to be at ground level, and is silhouetted against
the sky like a Mantegna hero. In this same sky, and what little of the
ground is visible behind the figure, Ribera shows the mastery of landscape
which he only very rarely had an occasion to display – in the scenes from
the *Story of Jacob* in the Hermitage, for example.
   The boy is reminiscent of the *Drunken Silenus* in the gallery at Naples,
dated 1626. The face, with its strong cast shadows, is harshly lit by direct
sunlight. This spectacular presentation makes a direct appeal to the sensi-
bilities of the spectator.

ZURBARAN, FRANCISCO DE, 1598–1664   *Spanish School*
SAINT APOLLONIA   Canvas

Inventory: M. I. 724   Height 1.13 m. (44¹/₂")
                                              Width 0.66 m. (26")

At the Alcazar, Seville, in 1810; sale of Marshal Soult, Duke of Dalmatia (Paris, 10 May 1852, No. 32), where it fetched 1.200 francs. Bought by the Louvre at his son's sale (Paris, 17 April 1867, No. 5).

This picture was perhaps part of the high altar of San José in the church of the Discalced Fathers of Mercy in Seville, together with a *Saint Joseph Crowned by Christ* and a *God the Father* now in the Museum at Seville, and possibly a *Saint Lucy* in the Museum at Chartres, believed to be a companion piece to the Louvre picture; this last must be a studio work, however.

The painting can be grouped with the pictures for the altar in the transept of the church of San José in Seville, dated 1636; it belongs to Zurbaran's most balanced period, when he produced his greatest masterpieces.

Renaissance artists had clothed their saints in classical draperies. Adopting to a certain extent the attitude of the Middle Ages, certain seventeenth-century painters such as Georges de La Tour, Zurbaran, and Caravaggio dressed them in the contemporary fashion; the natural mediators between God and the faithful are thus seen in a kind of mystical familiarity. There is something closer to the true mystical state in this realism than in the imaginative art of El Greco. The latter expresses aspiration towards the supernatural rather than the possession of it; it has been said to recall Cervantes rather than St Teresa of Avila or St John of the Cross. Once they have passed through the early trials of their ascetic vocation, mystics are profoundly aware of the unity of creation, the work of God; they see it as sanctified in its simple, unadorned truth. Heavenly beings do not appear to them as supernatural creatures, but as familiar realities, intimately connected with their lives. Only the worldly, those who have never experienced spiritual ecstasy, look upon the supernatural in a theatrical way, as an apparition. Zurbaran, the 'painter of monks', along with Martinez Montánes, the sculptor of carved altarpieces, is the artist who best reflects the state of mind expressed by St Teresa of Avila and St John of the Cross.

Saint Apollonia was the patroness of dentists, hence the attribute she carries: a pair of pincers holding a tooth.

S.POLO
NIA.

VELASQUEZ, DIEGO, 1599–1660   *Spanish School*
PORTRAIT OF MARIANNA OF AUSTRIA, QUEEN OF SPAIN   Canvas

Inventory: R. F. 1941–31   .   Height 2.09 m. (82¼")
                                              Width 1.25 m. (49¼")

This picture was saved from the fire at the Alcazar, and is mentioned in inventories in 1772 and 1774. In 1816 it was moved from the Palacio del Buen Retiro to the Academia San Fernando, then in 1827 to the Prado. In 1941 it was included in an exchange of works of art arranged between the museums of Madrid and the Louvre.

Marianna was the daughter of Ferdinand III, Emperor of Germany, and of Maria, sister of Philip IV of Spain; she was born in Vienna in 1634. She was to have married the Infante Balthasar Carlos, but he died prematurely and his uncle, a widower, took her as his second wife. The marriage took place in 1649. The queen died in Madrid in 1669.

Velasquez was absent at the time of the marriage; he painted the portrait after his return, in the middle of the year 1651. The court of Vienna wanted the picture; the king therefore ordered a replica from Velasquez, who carried it out himself without recourse to the sitter. It was so successful that the king could not bear to part with this new masterpiece, which was sent to the Escorial. However, a copy was actually despatched to the Emperor on 23 February 1653; it is now in the Kunsthistorisches Museum, Vienna (Cat. 621 A). This last is inferior in quality to the two others, and shows similarities with the style of Mazo.

There are therefore two copies of this work by Velasquez himself. The one still in the Prado (Cat. No. 1191) is more finished; the subsequent addition of a large drapery at the top explains its greater dimensions (2.31×1.31 m. – 91"×51½"). The Louvre version is more lightly handled, almost in the manner of a sketch. Opinion is divided over the question of which of the two is the finer and, more especially, which was painted first. At the moment historians incline to the view that the portrait done from life is the one in the Prado, and the copy originally intended for Vienna is the one in the Louvre. F. J. Sanchez Cantón, however, Assistant Director of the Prado, believes that the Louvre version was painted first.

LE NAIN, LOUIS, 1593?–1648   *French School*
THE RETURN FROM HAY-MAKING (LA CHARRETTE)   Canvas

Inventory: R. F. 258   Height 0.56 m. (22″)
Signed: Le Nain fecit 1641   Width 0.72 m. (28¹/₄″)

Bequeathed to the Louvre in 1879 by the Vicomte Philippe de Saint Albin.

Some critics (Sir Robert Witt amongst others) have thought that two of the Le Nain brothers collaborated on this picture; according to M. Isarlo, it is possibly the joint work of Louis and Antoine. M. Paul Jamot, however, believed it to be entirely by Louis, and attributed several paintings of figures out of doors to the same artist; in particular, the *Halte du Cavalier*, Victoria and Albert Museum, London, the *Famille de la Laitière* (Hermitage), the *Landscape with Figures* (Wadsworth Atheneum, Washington), and the *Landscape with Figures* in the National Gallery, Washington.

Italian painters endowed their peasants with a kind of rascally romanticism; Flemish and Dutch artists represented them as primitive creatures entirely at the mercy of their grosser instincts. Louis Le Nain, however, has invested his scenes of peasant life with a sober dignity of gesture, expression and attitude; the taciturn character of these country folk is very far removed from the outbursts of noisy merriment, the drinking-bouts and horseplay of the rustics in Flemish paintings; here indeed is the common stock of a people whose thinkers and writers turn naturally to moral reflections and philosophical meditation.

The appreciative handling of the impasto in this outstanding work is a foreshadowing of Chardin, and the subtle variation of greys in an almost monochrome atmosphere looks forward to Corot.

As M. Paul Jamot has remarked, Le Nain's paintings never actually depict 'peasant life', but a moment of arrested action. This is definitely the case in *La Charette*; children are playing in a farmyard while a mother sits holding a child, who has fallen asleep and slumps heavily in her arms. All these children, one of whom is playing the flute, are singularly grave; they are fixed in their attitudes, as if posing for portraits.

Though unobtrusive, the landscape here really contains the figures, and shows a great awareness of atmosphere. 'There is nothing here', says Paul Jamot, 'resembling either the work of the Flemish landscape painters, faithful to their native tradition, or the pleasant conventions brought back from Italy by other artists. This is an entirely new and unstudied truth to nature, which, in spite of some awkwardness, charms us with its modesty.'

LE NAIN, LOUIS, 1593?–1648
REPAS DE PAYSANS

French School
Canvas

Inventory: M. I. 1088
Signed: Le Nain fecit ano 1642

Height 0.97 m. (38¼")
Width 1.22 m. (48")

La Caze bequest, 1869.

The task of distinguishing the respective styles of the three brothers signing themselves 'Le Nain' was carried out about thirty years ago by Monsieur Paul Jamot, then Keeper of Paintings in the Louvre; this signature is found on a number of pictures. Recently discovered documents and paintings have caused some confusion among the critics, and seem to have invalidated Paul Jamot's hypotheses; they show that the three brothers did in fact produce their work collectively. This is supported, incidentally, by the fact that they never used any other form of signature but 'Le Nain', as a kind of studio stamp. It explains the existence of complex pictures where brilliant passages of painting are to be found alongside mediocre areas executed by assistants or pupils. But there are also others of a high level where the brothers worked alone or with each other, without help from outsiders; and the present picture is one of these. It is an element in the reconstruction of the œuvre of Louis, the most gifted of the three.

The Louvre has two *Peasant Families;* one of them (R. F. 2081) strikes a note of profound intimacy, a warmth of spirit, like the atmosphere of a domestic festivity. This one, however, is more austere and virile; in 1950 M. Landry, senator and Mayor of Calvi, suggested that this gathering of peasants, solemnly drinking as if they had just completed an agreement, was painted on the occasion of the annual payment of rent.

The general harmony of greys and browns is in keeping with the spirit of austerity reigning in French painting in the time of Louis XIII. Unlike the Flemings, who made their scenes of rustic life an occasion for depicting the unleashing of the coarsest sensual instincts, Louis Le Nain saw in the peasant soul a profound gravity, even solemnity; the expression of a life of toil whose hard realities have bestowed on it a sense of its own dignity. The spirit of the 'honnête homme', the symbol of the seventeenth century, permeates these peasants, silently sipping their wine. The paint quality is flowing and rich, with touches of impasto used not simply for effect, as in the work of Frans Hals, but giving proof of a sensitive brush, searching out the modelling with attention and feeling.

Several early copies give evidence of the esteem in which the painting was held.

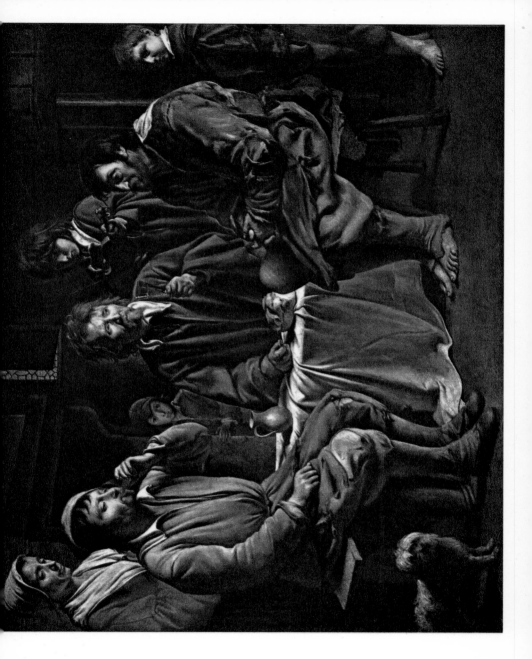

BAUGIN (Paris, c. 1630)   *French School*
LE DESSERT DE GAUFRETTES   Panel

Inventory: R. F. 1954–23   Height 0.52 m. (20^1/$_2$″)
Signed on the right: BAUGIN   Width 0.40 m. (15^3/$_4$″)

Acquired by the Louvre in 1954 from the antiquary Georges Gairac, for 5 million francs.

The existence of this painter was revealed in 1934, at the exhibition 'Peintres de la Réalité' in the Orangerie in Paris, by two pictures signed simply 'Baugin': *Still Life with Chessboard*, or the *Five Senses*, now also in the Louvre, and *Still Life with Candle*, from the Spada Gallery, Rome. The picture illustrated here, also signed, is the third member of this group of still life paintings; it was also brought to light in an exhibition at the Orangerie – the 1952 exhibition of 'La Nature Morte'. M. Michel Faré has recently analysed the inscription on the *Still Life* in the Galleria Spada, and finds reason to believe that 'Baugin' may be the same person as Lubin Baugin (1610–1663), a Parisian artist who imitated the work of Parmigianino and Guido Reni. This hypothesis had already been put forward by M. George Isarlo, but was not accepted by M. Charles Sterling; there are, however, strong arguments in its favour. In my view, the fact that the religious painting of Lubin Baugin, a rather insipid form of classicism, is very different in style from these still life pictures, does not rule out the possibility that both groups could be the work of the same man. It is not unusual to find an excellent still life artist putting up a poor performance when it comes to figures – Sanchez Cotán, for example, a Spanish painter of the same period. Lubin Baugin's religious pictures have a spirit of formal stylisation not unlike that of the Baugin still lifes. The exhibition of the 'Cabinet de l'Amateur', at the Orangerie, Paris, in 1955–1956 included a large still life depicting, in the Flemish manner, a collection of eatables, and signed 'Baugin'. If this is the same artist, the painting must belong to a different period of his life. The three pictures previously known are all closely linked by common characteristics; the soberness of the composition and the austere style of the painting evoke an aspect of French art in the reign of Louis XII which has been attributed to Jansenist influence. The philosophical speculations of our own time no doubt help us to appreciate these denuded still lifes, where isolated objects take on a kind of ghostly reality.

188

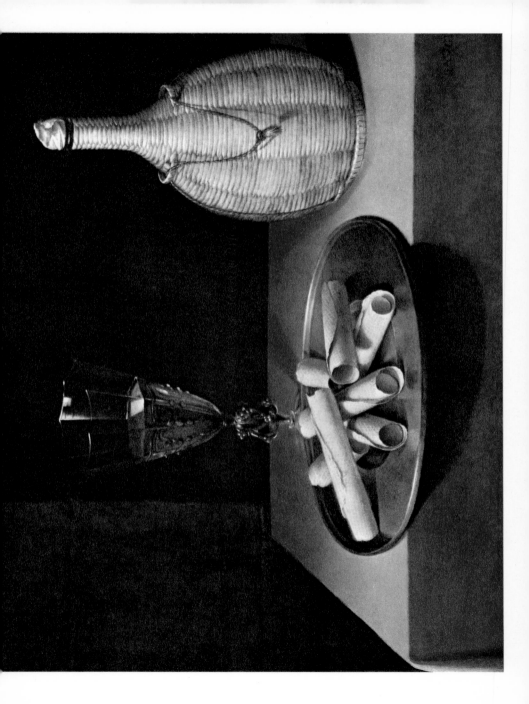

CHAMPAIGNE, PHILIPPE DE, 1602–1674   *French School*
PORTRAIT OF A MAN   Canvas

Inventory: INV. 1145   Height 0.91 m. (35³/₄″)
Signed and dated: Ph. Champaigne F. A. 1650   Width 0.72 m. (28¹/₄″)

Bought at the Saint Martin sale in 1806, for 3.780 francs.

The sitter was formerly identified as Robert Arnauld, of Andilly, the eldest of the twenty children of the lawyer Antoine Arnauld, who retired from the world and withdrew to Port-Royal when he was nearly sixty.

One is indeed tempted to see this convinced Jansenist in the noble and austere face here depicted, whose expression seems to reflect an intense preoccupation with the problems of spiritual life. However, comparison with the engraved portrait by Edelinck proves that such an identification is not possible. Nor does the date support the theory that the portrait might represent Arnauld de Luzancy, Robert Arnauld's second son; he would have been 27 in 1650, and the man shown here is older.

As the mannerist portraitists such as Antonio Moro or Bronzino had done earlier, Philippe de Champaigne concentrates on the two elements which express the sitter's character—the face and the hand. Rarely has the work of this artist reached such a high standard of execution; the work is absolutely intact, with all its original glazes. The lightening of the varnish has revealed its full quality; a tiny sample of the varnish has been left on the upper part of the window frame, at the right, and shows how much it was disfigured.

Philippe de Champaigne's strict objectivity betrays his Flemish descent; like Van Eyck, he faithfully portrays the features of his sitter in all their physical reality. But in the cool tones of this picture he turns away from Rubens, whom he imitated in his early work, and comes closer to a more truly French colour harmony. The black garment has kept all its qualities of transparency, which is very rare in old paintings. This is one of those highly individual portraits which express a whole race, a civilization, the state of mind of a people in a particular period, and outside of time.

It is characteristic of the intelligence of Baron Vivant-Denon that he should have purchased this picture in 1806, when the popularity of the 'Davidian' style of painting was at its height. But although its realism differs essentially from the idealized portraits of David, the profound honesty with which it is painted is not so far removed from the art of the painter of the *Horaces*.

190

LA TOUR, GEORGES DE, 1593–1652   *French School*
Saint Mary Magdalen with a Candle   Canvas

Inventory: INV. RF 1949–11   Height 1.28 m. (50½")
Signed: G. de La Tour fec.   Width 0.94 m. (37")

Formerly in the Terff collection. Bought in 1949 from the Administration des Douanes.

In the somewhat uncertain chronology of George de La Tour's work, this picture has been allotted a date some time between 1630 and 1635, by analogy with the *Saint Mary Magdalen with a Mirror* (Fabius Collection, Paris), which has been dated between 1635 and 1645. There is an engraving after the latter painting by J. Le Clerc.

During the seventeenth century, great devotion was shown to Mary Magdalen in all Catholic countries. She was the perfect lover of Christ, her beauty made yet more appealing by reason of her repentance, which had a special attraction for a period so passionately interested in problems of mysticism, quietism and asceticism. The theme of the repentance of sinners and of trials sent by God is illustrated in such subjects as the Repentance of St Peter, Mary Magdalen and Job. A number of written works give evidence of the cult of the Magdalen – one by Cardinal Bérulle, for example, published in 1627 – and this cult was the more widespread since Provence possessed two great sanctuaries dedicated to her: the grotto of La Sainte Baume, and the Saintes Maries de la Mer. M. Pariset, to whom we are indebted for a detailed study of the picture, has suggested that Georges de La Tour took a gipsy as his model; there were many in Lorraine in the seventeenth century.

This picture and the one in the Fabius collection seem to have been inspired by several themes popular with Italian or Dutch artists – the repentant Magdalen, Melancholy and Vanity. The artist has given it a feeling of philosophical meditation in keeping with the spirit of the time; the saint's body is enveloped in mysterious darkness, and her pensive face illumined only by the candle. The bare limbs increase the impression of destitution; on the table are some books and a candle and, on a wooden cross, a blood-stained scourge – a reminder of the more violent side of the Magdalen's penitence.

POUSSIN, NICOLAS, 1594–1665   *French School*
ORPHEUS AND EURYDICE   Canvas

Inventory: INV. 7307   Height 1.20 m. (47")
        Width 2.00 m. (78³/₄")

This picture was engraved and dedicated to Louis XIV by Etienne Baudet, together with three others representing a *Scene of Terror, Polyphemus and Galatea,* and *Diogenes.* It appears in the inventory of Bailly, Keeper of Pictures at Versailles in 1709–1710. Louis XIV acquired it in 1685 from the painter Branjon.

It has been thought that this may be the picture which Félibien mentions as having been painted for the king's architect Le Brun, between 1655 and 1660; but there is no proof to support this identification. Moreover, as M. Charles Sterling has pointed out, it belongs stylistically to an earlier period than that indicated by Félibien, which is the period of Poussin's old age. The rigorous composition, the solidity of the structures, the firmness of handling and the brilliant disposition of areas of light and dark in the sky, are more characteristic of his work between 1648 and 1650, when he painted the Louvre *Diogenes,* the Hermitage *Polyphemus* and *Hercules and Cacus,* the *Landscape with St Matthew* in the Berlin Museum and the *Landscape with St John on Patmos* in the Art Institute of Chicago.

In all his work, Poussin celebrates the alliance between man and nature which is the expression of classicism. To man, who makes history, nature lends her air of eternity. Here, in the peace of an afternoon, Orpheus sings to his cythara while the nymphs bathe; but already the serpent is about to bite Euridyce and despatch her to the Underworld. The landscape echoes the mood of the drama, and in the castle in the background a fire is breaking out, darkening the sky with its smoke.

Poussin places the story of Orpheus in the Roman Campagna; he borrows several elements from the Eternal City, such as the Torre delle Milizie, and a tower based on the Castel Sant' Angelo as it looked when it was the Mausoleum of Hadrian. Dense smoke pours from a fire which devastates the former, and darkens a sky already overcast with sombre clouds. The fall of the light divides the landscape diagonally into bright and dark areas – a division clearly seen on the Torre delle Milizie.

Many of Poussin's pictures have darkened, chiefly as a result of a red underpainting which has begun to show through the colours. The *Orpheus,* however, is free of this; it has kept its original transparency even in the darker passages, and the whole painting is particularly well preserved.

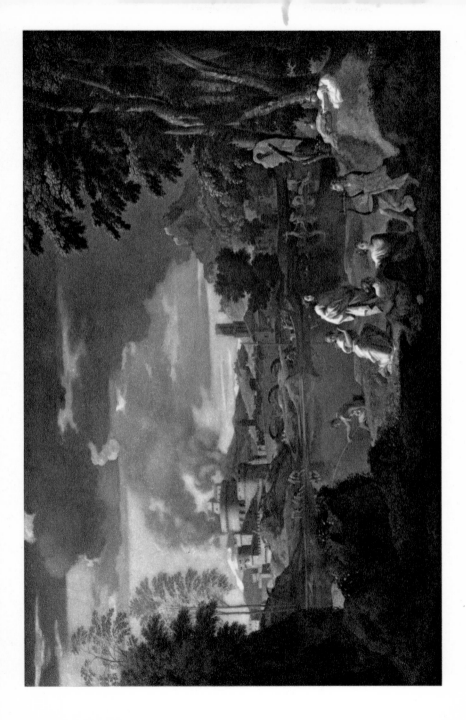

POUSSIN, NICOLAS, 1594–1665   *French School*
THE INSPIRATION OF THE POET   Canvas

Inventory: R. F. 1774   Height 1.84 m. (72¹/₂")
                                                Width 2.14 m. (84¹/₄")

This picture seems to be the one which was in the Mazarin collection in 1653. It was sold for £105 at the Bryan sale in London, in 1798 (No. 36). In 1837 it was in the Thomas Hope Collection, and then at Deepdene, in Surrey, where it was bought by Trotti. It was acquired by the Louvre in 1911 for 130.000 francs, out of the Audéoud legacy.

Apollo, accompanied by infant Cupids and by one of the Muses, is about to crown a poet who is writing under his inspiration. It is not known to what the painting alludes, nor what is its exact subject; perhaps the latter was always indefinite, because the picture appears in Mazarin's inventory of 1653 as 'Apollo with a Muse and a Poet crowned with Laurels'. Its warm colouring reveals the Titianesque strain in Poussin's work; it must have been painted at the end of his first Roman period, in about 1636 to 1638. Several other paintings of this period are related to this picture: the *Inspiration of Anacreon*, in Dulwich Gallery (of which there is also a version in Hanover), *Parnassus*, in the Prado, Madrid, and the frontispiece drawn by Poussin and engraved by Claude Mellan for an edition of Virgil published by the Imprimerie Royale in 1641–1642.

Paul Jamot put forward the hypothesis that the model for the Muse, often recognizable in other works of this period by Poussin, may have been Anna Dughet, whom he married on 9 August 1630 at San Lorenzo in Lucina.

There is a replica of this work, of slightly different dimensions (2.04 m. × 1.84 m.) which the painter Louis David obtained for Sébastien Erard at the beginning of the nineteenth century.

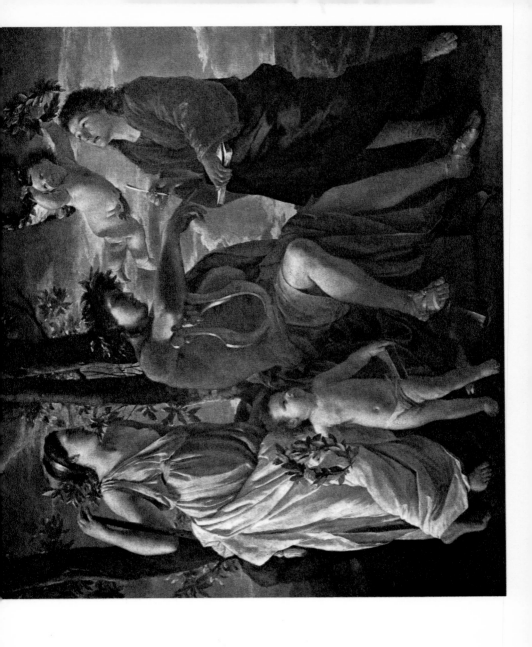

CLAUDE LORRAIN (CLAUDE GELLÉE), 1600–1682 *French School*
VILLAGE FÊTE
Canvas

Inventory: INV. 4714

Signed and dated: Claude inv. Romae 1639

Height 1.03 m. (40¹/₂″)

Width 1.35 m. (53¹/₄″)

Given to Louis XIV in 1693, together with its companion piece, *A Sea Port* (Inventory: INV. 4715), by the architect and gardener Le Nôtre.

There are several versions of this painting; two are reproduced in the *Liber Veritatis* (in the British Museum), a kind of register in which Claude recorded and drew the pictures he painted and sold. The earlier of these two (no. 13 in the *Liber Veritatis*) was painted in 1637 for Urban VIII, with a companion piece, a *Sea Port*; it next passed into the possession of the Barberini family, and was sold in 1798. It is now in England, in the collection of Lord Yarborough. The Louvre version, dated 1639, differs from the other in several respects; it is reproduced as no. 39 in the *Liber Veritatis*, and also had a companion piece—*A Sea Port at Sunset*. Another version used to be in the Stroganoff Collection, St Petersburg; according to an engraving of 1742, it was done in 1669, towards the end of the artist's life. The theme of *dolce far niente*, the tranquil repose beneath majestic classical trees, the rustic dances to the music of flutes, have often charmed Claude Lorrain; it is a reminiscence of the Golden Age, whose naïve virtues are supposed to survive in country folk.

This picture, painted fairly early in Claude's career, reveals the influence of Flemish art. The composition, with a group of trees in the centre, and openings on either side through which the light appears, was often used by Flemish landscape painters from the time of Brueghel; Paul and Matthew Bril frequently employed it, and Claude continued in their tradition in Rome. In accordance with classic sixteenth-century procedure, the bridge harmoniously unites the middle and far distances. Through the opening on the right can be seen a city bathed in a golden mist, more characteristic of the Roman Campagna than of the north. Following the usual practice of studios in the Low Countries, Claude often employed other artists to paint the little figures in his pictures; but this does not seem to have been the case here, to judge by the unity of conception between figures and landscape.

RUBENS, SIR PETER PAUL, 1577–1640   *Flemish School*
THE JOYS OF THE REGENCY (Galerie Médicis)   Canvas

Inventory: INV. 1783   Height 3.94 m. (155″)
       Width 2.95 m. (116¼″)

In the spring of 1625 the 21 canvases of the *Vie de la Reine Marie de Médicis* were installed in the Palais du Luxembourg, on the first floor in the west wing of the Cour d'Honneur. They were taken down and rolled up in 1781–1782, when the palace became an appanage of the Count of Provence. In 1803 they were put back in the east gallery of the Luxembourg, the quarters of the Sénat Conservateur; in 1816 they were exhibited in the Grande Galerie of the Louvre, but were removed between 1828 and 1838, to be used as cartoons for Gobelins tapestries. In 1900 they were put up, incorrectly, in a room which had been intended under the Empire to serve as a Salle des Etats, and which the architect Redon had re-decorated with rich stucco work. They were re-arranged in their original order in 1953.

In 1620 Marie de Médicis, having become reconciled with her son at Brissac, turned her attention to her palace in Paris, the Luxembourg, and its decoration, begun in 1613. Towards the end of 1621 she summoned Rubens to consider this question; he had worked for her sister, the Duchess of Mantua, and had perhaps also been recommended to her by the Baron de Vicq, Paris ambassador of the Low Countries. Rubens was in Paris in January 1622, and remained there the greater part of February. He arranged with the Queen to do two galleries, one in her honour and one in honour of Henri IV. She decided to begin with her own gallery. Rubens corresponded with Peiresc and the Abbé de Saint-Ambroise, who asked him to submit the sketches for the design. On 3 November 1622 Rubens had received the measurements for the three largest pictures in the gallery. On 9 May 1623 the Queen asked him to come to Paris to install the pictures; he brought the first nine on 29 May. The gallery was inaugurated on the occasion of the marriage of Henrietta of France and Charles I, King of England, which took place on 8 May 1625; the last pictures were delivered in February 1625.

The *Joys of the Regency* was hastily painted in Paris to replace the picture of *Marie de Médicis leaving Paris*, a subject which did not please the Queen. On 13 May 1625 Rubens related this to Peiresc. Here is ample proof of Rubens' genius of improvisation; perhaps the rapidity of execution of this particular work is responsible for its outstanding quality in an *ensemble* remarkable for its unity.

200

Inventory: INV. 1795   Height 1.13 m. (44¹/₂")
     Width 0.82 m. (32¹/₄")

La Live de Jully sale, 1769 (20.000 *livres*); bought by Dujeu; at the Randon de Boisset sale (1777) it was withdrawn at 10.000 *livres*, and handed over to the dealer Lebrun for 18.000 *livres*. At the Comte de Vaudreuil's sale (1785) it was bought for Louis XVI's collection for 20.000 *livres*.

Isabella Brandt, Rubens' first wife, died in 1626. The artist remained a widower for several years, then on 6 December 1630, at the age of 53, he married Hélène Fourment, a relative of his late wife. She bore him five children, one posthumously; and until his death in 1640 he constantly recorded his young wife's blond loveliness – in portraits (one, the *Fur Wrap* in Vienna, shows her semi-nude), in *scènes galantes*, and indirectly in subjects from the scriptures, the lives of saints, or mythology. Hélène's beauty corresponded to an ideal conception which he had formed in his youth, and which he represented in figures of saints well before his second wife was born.

Hélène Fourment is shown here in a pose similar to that of the Munich portrait, where she has her son François on her lap. In this picture her eldest child Claire Jeanne (born 18 January 1632) stands in front of her, and she is holding François, who was born 12 July 1633. To the right, scarcely visible, is a baby's hand, holding on to the chair; this must be Isabelle Claire, born 3 May 1637. From the apparent age of the children, the picture seems to have been painted in about 1636–1637.

The painting is in a perfect state of preservation. In certain areas it has hardly been carried further than the sketch stage – especially at the top and bottom of the right-hand side, where the ground is scarcely covered. No doubt this is why it was covered with disfiguring layers of thick brown varnish in the nineteenth century. These were removed in 1952, revealing the pearly quality of the painting; an earlier varnish left untouched by the cleaning lends a golden warmth to the picture's tonality.

RUBENS, SIR PETER PAUL, 1577–1640   *Flemish School*
TOURNAMENT NEAR A CASTLE   Panel

Inventory: INV. 1798   Height 0.73 m. (28³/₄″)
                                                Width 1.08 m. (42¹/₂″)

Mentioned in an inventory made after Rubens' death (No. 104): 'Une pièce d'une Jouste dans un paysage.' Acquired by Louis XV in 1742 for 4000 *livres*, from the estate of Amédée de Savoie, Prince de Carignan, when it was described as 'La Maison de Rubens avec un carrousel'.

After Rubens' marriage with Hélène Fourment (1630) his art became more personal; the large rhetorical baroque works gave way to more intimate and revealing pictures of his family, and paintings of landscapes. With only ten years of life left to him, he grew more sensitive to the beauty of the natural world. In 1635 he bought a château *(Steen)* at Elewyt, near Malines – a pleasant country retreat built in the previous century, and with none of the air of a feudal castle. This château still exists. Here he passed the last five years of his life, painting the magic of light, mostly at sunset – the hour he loved best. His imagination played freely about the scenes which moved him; the Elewyt countryside became a setting for scenes of rustic life (Pitti, Munich, National Gallery); his country home became a mediaeval castle, with romantic encounters taking place in the vicinity (Vienna). Here he has conjured up a tournament, in fifteenth-century armour; by a strange trick of relationship which proves the persistence of certain romantic modes of expression, the appearance of the picture and the sensitive drawing of men and horses foreshadow the mediaeval evocations of Delacroix.

A little landscape sketch in the Ashmolean Museum, Oxford, is usually thought to be the first idea for this painting.

In 1824 a lunatic attacked the painting with acid. Luckily this only affected a small area in the sky; to hide the damage the picture was covered with a layer of very dark varnish, which made it extremely difficult to see, and which has fortunately been removed recently.

JORDAENS, JACOB, 1593–1678   *Flemish School*
THE FOUR EVANGELISTS   Canvas

Inventory: INV. 1404   Height 1.327 m. (52¹/₂")
                                         Width 1.180 m. (46¹/₂")

May have belonged to the Dutch painter Pieter Lastman; the inventory
of his possessions made after his death (1632) includes '4 Evangelisten van
Jac. Jordaens'.

In the eighteenth century the picture was in the collection of Joseph-
Hyacinthe François Rigaud, Comte de Vaudreuil, Grand Falconer of France
in 1780; under the Restoration he was made Governor of the Louvre, and
he died there in 1818. To liquidate his debts, however, he had to put his
collection up for sale in November 1784. The sale lasted several days; this
particular picture was bought for the kind for 4.000 *livres* on 25 November.

The traditional title of the painting has sometimes been questioned, and
the subject identified as *Christ among the Doctors*, but this hypothesis must
be rejected. Even the youngest of the evangelists is much older than Jesus
was when this incident took place. The three older evangelists are grouped
round John, who seems to be reading with rapt attention the sentences he
has been inspired to write.

Till the fifteenth century the evangelists were represented according to
traditional prototypes formed during the Gothic period. The Florentine
Renaissance sought to individualize them; in the sixteenth century they
came under the influence of Michelangelo's prophets, and artists made use
of agitated movement and expressions to convey the idea of divine inspiration. The Carracci, and still more Caravaggio, showed them not only as
apostles, but as men of the working class.

This painting, which must have been executed between 1620 and 1625,
belongs to the first–and best–period of Jordaen's artistic production. The
grouping in the *Adoration of the Shepherds* of 1618 (National Museum of
Stockholm) resembles that in the Louvre picture, and one of the Evangelists
is of the same type as one of the Stockholm shepherds. The paint is handled
vigorously, in a technique very different from that of Rubens, with very
little use of glazes; the brush works in varying degrees of impasto, the
quality of which seems to underline the physical presence of the figures. This
richness and solidity has had the effect of preserving the picture in splendid
condition; this has been fully revealed by the recent cleaning off of the
dark varnish.

Inventory: INV. 1236   Height 2.72 m. (107")
Signed on the right: A. van Dyck f.   Width 2.12 m. (83½")

Belonged to the Comtesse de Verrue in the eighteenth century, then to the Marquis de Lassay. Afterwards in the Comte de la Guiche's collection, which was sold in 1771; then in the collection of Crozat, Baron de Thiers (1772). The Comtesse du Barry, who claimed Stuart connections, bought it next, and took it to Louveciennes; she did not keep it long, however, because in 1775 it was acquired by the Crown of France for the considerable sum of 24.000 *livres*.

Van Dyck came to the English court in 1632, and had an immediate success with Charles I, who knighted him. He became 'principalle Paynter in Ordinary to their Majesties at St James's', and from 17 October 1633 he received an annual pension of £ 200. He painted a great many portraits of the King and the royal family; the Louvre picture is included in a statement for 'Sa Magtie le Roy' drawn up in French by Van Dyck. Payment was made on 14 December 1638; the portrait is referred to in the statement as 'le Roi à la chasse', and whoever checked the bill has altered the price from £ 200 to £ 100.

The king is represented in informal attire, without any of the attributes of royalty; he has dismounted from his horse on his return from hunting. Only his majestic expression and proud attitude reveal him as 'the first gentleman in the kingdom'. The arrogant pose with hand on hip was from mediaeval times associated with nobility; Rigaud uses it for his portrait of Louis XIV in full regalia.

To the left of the picture, a glimpse of the sea and a sail make discreet allusion to his Britannic Majesty's maritime empire.

A number of copies of this painting are in existence.

During his stay in England, Van Dyck's style changed rapidly under the influence of fashionable society. He idealized his sitters, took pleasure in painting silken stuffs and elegant poses, and his art acquired a certain degree of conventionality. This particular portrait was painted when he first came to London, and still shows the fresh and forthright manner of his Antwerp period. It therefore has a greater quality of immediacy than any of the other portraits of Charles I.

Inventory: M. I. 926   Height 0.58 m. (22³/₄″)
         Width 0.52 m. (20¹/₂″)

Sale of M. de Marigny, Marquis de Ménars (Madame de Pompadour's brother), in 1782. In the collection of the expert Rémy, then in that of La Caze, who bequeathed it to the Louvre in 1869.

This painting is usually dated in about 1628 to 1630, during which period Hals produced the *Hille Bobbe* in Berlin, the so-called *Mulatto* at Cassel, and the *Jolly Drinker* in Amsterdam. However, in the Louvre painting the satirical intention is less pronounced. This gipsy woman is painted naturalistically, and is still simply a portrait; the broad smile on her face is not the wild laughter which transforms Hals' other genre portraits into stage characters.

The interest in low life which characterized the work of Frans Hals and his fellow artists of the school of Haarlem probably reflects the grimness of social conditions in Holland during the troubled period of the wars of independence; but it also has its place in an international aesthetic movement which originated in Roman circles early in the seventeenth century, generally described as 'Caravaggesque'. In the Low Countries, this tendency was combined with the native interest in genre painting, originating in Antwerp in the sixteenth century; its last manifestation was in English art, in the work of Hogarth, whose characters from low life derive from those of Frans Hals.

Together with Velasquez and Rembrandt, Frans Hals is the creator of the modern craft of painting. Before the seventeenth century, artists tried to conceal the method of execution; in their view, only drawing, composition and colour counted. For Frans Hals, the actual handling of the paint is the chief means of expression. The execution must be spontaneous, and the picture should appear to be dashed off with brio in a moment of inspiration. Hals abandoned the meticulous finish of the primitives and the deliberate brushwork of the classical school; he used broader brushes, in order to leave visible the movements of his hand, and one has the sensation of being present at the creation of the work. In his early period (to which this painting belongs), the exuberant movements of the brush across the canvas suggest the actuality of life itself, seized in all its explosive force; later, the conflict of strokes in such pictures as the *Régents* and the *Régentes* reveal an old man's impatience and anxiety.

REMBRANDT HARMENSZ VAN RYN, 1606–1669 *Dutch School*
SELF-PORTRAIT WITH CAP AND GOLD CHAIN

Panel

Inventory: INV. 1745
Signed and dated: Rembrandt f. 1633

Oval; Height 0.68 m. (26³/₄″)
Width 0.53 m. (20¹/₈″)

Duc de Choiseul's sale, 6 April 1772, no. 96. Confiscated in the Year II of the Revolution from the collection of the Duc de Brissac. (The identification of this portrait with the one figuring in the Comte de Vence's sale, which had belonged to Rigaud, is by no means certain.)

This was formerly believed to be a picture given by Lord Ancram to Charles I, but the latter work has been identified as another self-portrait which has just been acquired by the National Gallery of Washington. The date on the Louvre painting (1633) has often been misread as 1639.

More than any other painter, Rembrandt faithfully practised throughout his life this particular form of self-examination – the 'confessional' of the mirror; there are more than sixty self-portraits, from every stage of his life, as well as quantities of drawings and engravings. They can be divided into several categories. During the early part of his career, when he was a successful artist, he usually sees himself in a favourable light, richly dressed and with a self-satisfied air – or, occasionally, he seeks to render a particular facial expression, such as laughter, or concentration on work. In his last years, ruined and forsaken, and conscious that he was growing old, he seems to seek out remorselessly the signs of despair, uncertainty and decrepitude written on his face. The *Self-Portrait with a Linen Cap* of 1660, also in the Louvre, is of this kind.

The *Self-Portrait with Cap and Gold Chain* is one of the finest of his early self-portraits, showing him when he was young and successful. He was 27 years old when it was painted, and appreciated by his contemporaries; in 1632 he had received an important commission – to do a painting of Dr. Tulp's anatomy class – which enabled him to settle in Amsterdam. His expression is cheerful and contented; he has set an artist's velvet cap on his long hair, and decked himself with a big gold chain. Perhaps the happiness which radiates from this portrait is of a more intimate nature; on 5 July 1633, he married Saskia van Uylenburgh, a member of one of the best families of Friesland – a marriage of love which was also a very good match from the material point of view. The Louvre picture may perhaps be a betrothal portrait.

REMBRANDT HARMENSZ VAN RYN, 1606–1669   *Dutch School*
BATHSHEBA   Canvas

Inventory: M. I. 957   Height 1.42 m. (56")
Signed: Rembrandt f. 1654   Width 1.42 m. (56")

W. Young-Ottley sale, London, 25 May 1811; W. Young-Ottley sale,
London, 4 March 1837. In the possession of the dealer Peacock in London.
Marquis Maison's collection, Paris. Paul Périer sale, Paris, 16 March 1843,
No. 75. Bequeathed to the Louvre by La Caze in 1869.

This painting is connected with an unhappy period in Rembrandt's life.
In the year it was painted, Hendrickje Stoffels had to appear before the
consistory of her church, and was banished from it on being convicted of
being Rembrandt's mistress. The present picture had contributed to the
scandal; it is Hendrickje who is here represented in the nude. She was a
young peasant from Randorp, 22 years old, whom the artist had engaged
as a servant in 1649; in that year Geertghe Dircx (his son Titus' nurse),
who had also been his mistress, and with whom he had legal disputes, had
to be taken to a lunatic asylum.

Hendrickje had a modest and affectionate nature; a portrait of her in
the Louvre, painted in 1650, reveals her frank and gentle character. She
became Rembrandt's faithful companion till her death, six or seven years
before his own, and was his favourite model during this time. When this
picture was painted he was still in his fine house in the Judenbreedestraat;
he was forced by bankruptcy to leave it in 1656.

Bathsheba, painted from Hendrickje Stoffels, and *Danae* (1636) for which
his wife Saskia van Uylenborgh was the model, are his two most important
nudes – the only ones in which he was concerned with rendering the sensuality of flesh. For the Italians, nudes were a pretext for conjuring up the
impersonal ideal beauty of goddesses; Rembrandt, however, painted the
body of real woman, in all its living and breathing truth.

X-rays show that he had at first intended the head to be more upright;
the thighs had also been draped with a piece of material which he subsequently removed. The recent cleaning of the varnish has revealed the
excellent state of preservation of this work.

214

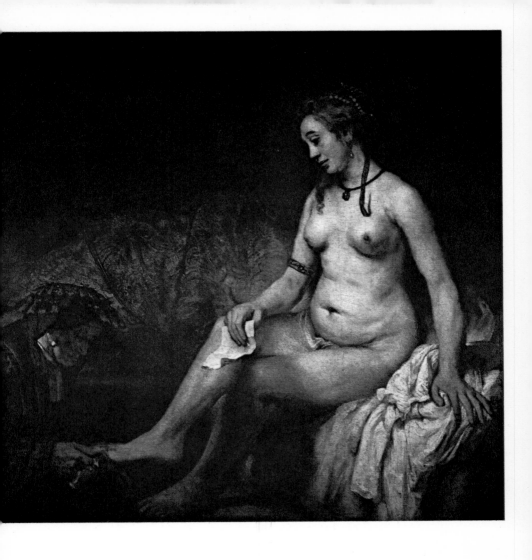

REMBRANDT HARMENSZ VAN RYN, 1606–1669   *Dutch School*
THE PILGRIMS AT EMMAUS   Panel

Inventory: INV. 1739   Height 0.68 m. (26³/₄″)
Signed: Rembrandt f. 1648   Width 0.65 m. (25¹/₂″)

Willem Six sale, Amsterdam, 12 May 1734, No. 57 (170 florins). Comte Lassay's sale, Paris, 17 May 1775; Randon de Boisset sale, Paris, 3 February 1777, No. 50. Bought at the latter sale for 10.500 *livres*.

In Rembrandt's religious painting, his protestantism reveals itself in his rejection of all the various traditions – iconographical, dogmatic, hagiographic and rhetorical – which interposed themselves between God and man in the imaginations of seventeenth-century Catholic artists.

Stripped of all historical character, both setting and costumes introduce us to a world of biblical simplicity. Rembrandt is the only Christian painter to have fully appreciated the profoundly mystical significance of this scene. Italians such as Veronese and Titian made it a pretext for worldly display; Delacroix exploited its dramatic quality; and the stupefaction of Caravaggio's disciples on recognizing Jesus conjures up an echo of coarse laughter, reminiscent of boon companions celebrating their reunion in some tavern. In Rembrandt's picture, all is silence; the action of the scene is an interior one, taking place in the heart.

The two pilgrims make only the slightest gesture; the serving boy is unaware of anything unusual. Christ's features are growing indistinct; he is becoming an apparition, and is about to disappear, remaining present only in the hearts of the two faithful disciples.

Rembrandt treated the theme of the Pilgrims at Emmaus – the expression of divine love – on several occasions. The Louvre possesses another picture of the same subject, wrongly catalogued by Bode (597) as the work of Rembrandt. In the version he painted as a young man (Musée Jacquemart-André, Paris), Rembrandt expressed in a dramatic fashion, by means of a theatrical effect of chiaroscuro, the amazement of the pilgrims when their travelling companion reveals himself to be Christ.

The Louvre picture is in excellent condition, as was revealed by the cleaning of the varnish in 1952. The amber transparency of the shadows takes on a mystical quality, enveloping the principal scene with a soft and mysterious atmosphere. Impasto is used with great restraint, and only in the central group, which gives it a stronger feeling of immediacy.

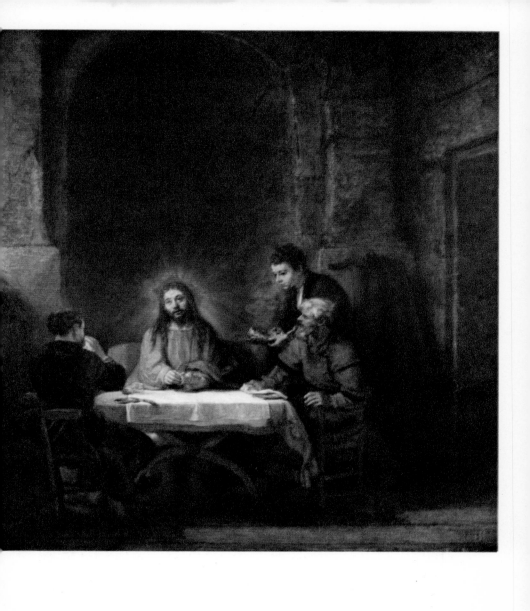

HEDA, WILLEM CLAESZ, 1594–1680/82   *Dutch School*
STILL LIFE   Canvas

Inventory: INV. 1319. Musée Napoléon   Height 0.44 m. (17¹/₄")
Signed: Heda 1637   Width 0.56 m. (22")

Developed in the course of the sixteenth century, the theme of 'The Meal'
became, in the seventeenth century, a source of inspiration for the majority
of still lifes of the Dutch School. During the first quarter of the century,
paintings still preserved the arrangement of food and objects in juxtaposition
and as if displayed on the surface of the table, viewed, as it were, from
above. After 1630, the placing of objects was determined by laws of composition; certain paintings, as for example those of De Heem, conveyed
effects of sumptuousness by the accumulation of viands and dishes, painted
in richly applied pigment. Our age is more appreciative of the few objects
portrayed by Pieter Claesz or Willem Claesz Heda, with an almost monochromatic harmony, where a subtle light gives proper value to the nuances
on an ash-grey background. The apparently simple composition is in fact
of extreme subtlety, as analysis will show. The vertical and the horizontal
in the Louvre painting are marked by the vessels and the dishes; the transparency of the glass is accentuated by the cold gleam of the silver; the
depth is indicated in two opposing directions by the knife and the over-
turned glass. The theme of this painting is the 'End of the Meal', rather
than 'The Meal' itself. All the objects and dishes collected in this extremely
sensitive atmosphere convey an impression of silence, of discreet intimacy.

The elaboration of this type of picture – the 'Meal' in a monochromatic
range of tones – is the work of two painters whose pictures are often confused, particularly because their names are not dissimilar: Pieter Claesz
and Willem Claesz Heda. Both worked in Haarlem, undoubtedly the most
important centre of Dutch art in the seventeenth century. Pieter Claesz was
the elder of the two; his work develops from the 'nature morte disposée',
where objects and food are spread out on the table, to the 'nature morte
composée', in which the artist seeks to produce an effect of rhythm by the
balancing of forms. Willem Claesz Heda had a long career, during which
his work became very repetitious. His finest paintings date from the beginning of his maturity. The Louvre picture belongs to this period of his
work; the date – 1637 – is found on several of his masterpieces.

This method of painting in subtle glazes, which seem to filter the light,
purifying it and giving a limpid quality to the paint surface, derives from
the Van Eyck tradition.

218

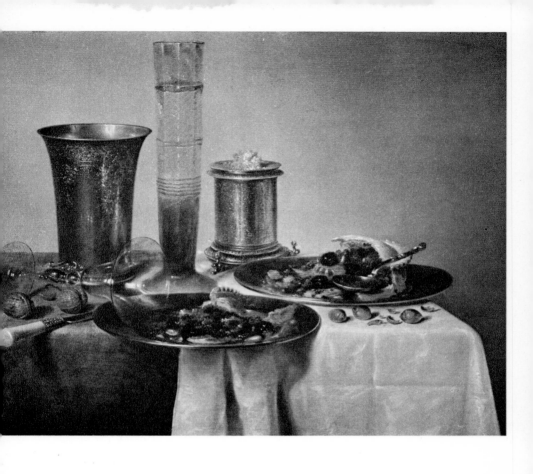

VERMEER, JAN, OF DELFT, 1632–1675   *Dutch School*

THE LACE-MAKER   Canvas

Inventory: M. I. 1448   Height 0.24 m. (9$^{1}/_{2}$")

Signed: J. V. Meer   Width 0.21 m. (8$^{1}/_{4}$")

The history of this picture can be traced with very few breaks right from the seventeenth century. On 16 March 1696 it featured at Amsterdam in an anonymous sale which included no less than 21 of Vermeer's pictures. These were sold at prices ranging from 175 florins to 17 florins; this particular picture (no. 12) only fetched 28 florins. Other sales: Jacob Crammer Simonsz, Amsterdam, 25 November 1778, no. 17. 150 florins; J. Schepens, Amsterdam, 21 January 1811, no. 5; Muilman, Amsterdam, 12 April 1813, no. 97; Anonymous, Amsterdam, 24 May 1815, 9 florins to de Gruyter; Lapeyrière, 14 April 1817, in Paris, no. 30. 501 francs; Baron van Nagell van Ampsen, La Haye, 5 September 1851, no. 40. 260 florins. Bought by the Louvre at the D. Vis Blockhysen sale in Paris, 1 April 1870, for 7.270 francs.

The style of dress, the manner of painting and the relationship with other works indicate a date around 1664 for this picture. André Malraux believes that the model who posed for the *Lace-Maker* (and for other pictures as well) was Catherine Vermeer, the artist's wife.

This painting and the *Astronomer* in Baroness E. de Rothschild's collection are the only works by Vermeer still in France.

This picture belongs to a group of small, almost square, paintings, in which a single figure is shown half-length (*Woman with a Red Hat*, Washington; *Young Girl with a Flute*, Washington). Out of this very exiguity Vermeer derives an effect of rare intimacy and of mystery. Paul Claudel has remarked on the subtlety of the composition which permeates even the lace bobbins in her hands. The recent lightening of the varnish has made it possible to appreciate the colour values of the ash-grey background. Some earlier restorer caused slight damage to the signature; otherwise the work is in very good condition.

This work has stimulated feelings of exaltation in painters of very opposite temperaments, Renoir declaring it 'the most beautiful in the world', with the *Embarkation for Cythera* by Watteau. Salvador Dali, who was commissioned by an American amateur to make a copy, produced a surrealist version of this painting.

HOBBEMA, MEINDERT, 1638–1709   *Dutch School*
THE WATER-MILL   Canvas

Inventory: M. I. 270   Height 0.80 m. (31¹/₂″)
Dated: May 1692   Width 0.65 m. (29¹/₂″)

This picture comes from the Coclers collection, Amsterdam; it was bought
by M. Rynders of Brussels in 1817, and sold to Sir George Watson Taylor
for 1.100 guineas. It was included in the latter's sale in London in 1823,
but he bought it back for 800 guineas; at his second sale at Erlestoke in
1832 the painting was bought by M. de Nieuwenhuys for 520 guineas. It
was sold with the Nieuwenhuys collection in London on 10 May 1833.
In 1854 it reappeared in Paris at the sale of Baron de Mecklenbourg; the
Louvre bought it in 1861 for 52.000 francs from one of the latter's heirs,
Baron de Witzleben.

A companion piece to this picture, the *Farm in Sunshine*, was formerly
in the collection of Leopold II, King of the Belgians; it was acquired by
M. Knoedler for 1.320.000 francs at the Ridder sale, 2 June 1924, at the
Galerie Georges Petit, Paris.

There is an intentional contrast between the sombre mass of trees in the
foreground and the clearing with its red-roofed houses on the banks of a
stream. The composition is still classical, but the spirit of the work is
romantic, and helps to explain why the English and French landscape artists
of the nineteenth century so often turned to Hobbema for inspiration.
Nature unadorned, in all its simplicity, is here painted objectively, without
any preconceived ideas; not as it was seen by the Italians, by Van Eyck or
Brueghel, but for the sake of a picturesque subject – the stream running
through a village and the footpaths by a meadow.

The companion piece to the *Water-Mill* was sold for a very large sum in
1924. His pictures were even more sought after than those of Ruisdael; this
is partly explained by the fact that they are less numerous. Hobbema was
a minor official employed in the city of Amsterdam in connection with the
duty on wines; he began by painting in his spare time, and seems to have
given it up towards the end of his life. Very little is known about this
artist, who died in extreme poverty. His painting is unpretentious, like his
life; he is the true 'portraitist' of the Dutch countryside, whereas Ruisdael
always adds some element for the sake of effect. Hobbema seems to have
had a predilection for the water-mill theme, so expressive of the monotonous
day-to-day existence of a humble life of toil. He has treated it in a dozen
paintings; but none is finer than this, one of his most famous works.

Inventory: INV. 1820   Height 0.83 m. (32³/₄″)
Signed with the monogram   Width 0.98 m. (38¹/₂″)

Acquired at the Comte de Vaudreuil's sale in 1784.

Nowadays, when we are able to distinguish the most subtle nuances in abstract pictures which would formerly have been dismissed as a boring jumble of colours and lines, the realism of Ruisdael's painting may seem a little monotonous. Yet he painted every subject that came to hand – the sea, the dunes, forests and châteaux, churches and cemeteries, towns, villages, farms, mills, fields of corn, the flat lands where he lived and the mountains which he probably never saw.

Unlike Rembrandt, he rarely painted a purely imaginary landscape; this picture, however, is one of the exceptions, and is unlike most of his work in every respect. He usually takes a low viewpoint; here he imagines himself to be on high ground, with an extensive view in front of him which seems to contain all the varying aspects of nature – mountain, river and plain, as well as château and town – as if he were trying to express a synthesis of the universal.

In spite of the broad vista presented to the spectator, who has apparently had to climb to a height in order to take it all in, the sky seems to absorb the whole of it. The wind, which moulds the cloud formations, causes an arbitrary distribution of light and shade during the fugitive instant when the clouds are pierced by a ray of sunlight. Although human elements are present (of a conventional kind, it is true), the vision creates an impression of poignant solitude; the work is of such high quality that it attains a philosophical level. The painter Fromentin, in his *Maîtres d'autrefois*, understood better than any other this spiritual range of the Haarlem painter; 'the greatest figure after Rembrandt', he said (Vermeer was still unknown). 'I imagine', he also wrote, 'that if Ruisdael had not been a Protestant, he would have belonged to Port Royal.' There is certainly an echo of Pascal in this sense of solitude in the midst of the world, experienced by a man who could seem so attached to the outer aspects of things. In the work of this artist – probably an unassuming person, who lived in poverty and died in an institution, and who can certainly never have thought of expressing 'ideas' in his canvases – there is a profound echo of the metaphysical anguish experienced by some of the great thinkers of the seventeenth century.

GUARDI, FRANCESCO, 1712–1793   *Italian School*
THE DEPARTURE OF THE BUCENTAUR FOR THE ASCENSION DAY CEREMONY
Canvas

Inventory: 2009   Height 0.67 m. (26¹/₄″)
Width 1.00 m. (39¹/₂″)

Seized from amongst Count Pestre-Senef's collection. Selected by the Museum commission, with eleven other paintings in the same series, at the Dépôt at the Hôtel de Nesles on 7 Prairial of the year V. Sent to the Museum of Toulouse, which handed it over to the Louvre, in exchange for a portrait by Ingres and another picture by Guardi, in 1952.

This work is one of a series of twelve pictures representing the 'Solenità dogali', in which the artist has faithfully copied the scenes drawn by Canaletto and engraved by Giambattista Brustolon to commemorate the festivities at the coronation of the Doge Alviso IV Mocenigo, in 1763. This has led to some confusion, and the canvases were formerly attributed to Canaletto, though their style was quite unmistakably that of Guardi. One of the pictures (No. 1330, Louvre Catalogue), bears the arms of Alviso IV Mocenigo.

Under the Empire, the series was unfortunately broken up; seven remained in the Louvre, one was sent to Brussels, two to Nantes, one to Toulouse and one to Grenoble. The return of the Toulouse painting to the Louvre, through an exchange, is the first step in an attempt to reassemble the set and display them in a special room.

Two pictures in the series represent the feast of the Bucentaur, the most sumptuous of all the Venetian festivals. It took place each year on Ascension Day, the anniversary of the setting out of Doge Pietro Orsolo's expedition, which had achieved the conquest of Dalmatia in about 1000 A. D. In a magnificent state barge, known as the Bucentaur, the Doge visited the Lido and celebrated the marriage of Venice with the Adriatic, by casting a ring into the sea. This canvas shows the Bucentaur leaving Venice; another in the series (in the Louvre) represents the Doge going to hear Mass at San Niccolò del Lido (page 305). A picture in the Museum of Copenhagen depicts the return of the Bucentaur to Venice.

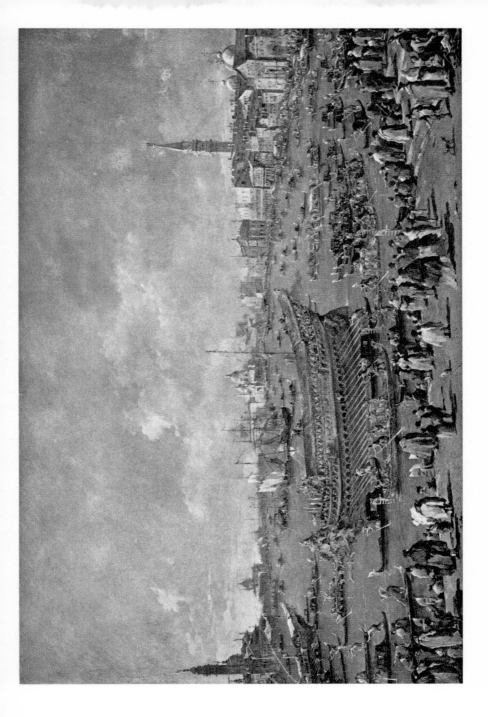

Inventory: M. I. 1121   Height 1.84 m. (72¹/₂")
Width 1.49 m. (58³/₄")

La Caze gift, 1869. According to a tradition, this picture belonged in the time of the First Empire to a dealer in pictures and engravings named Meunier; he had it for years without being able to sell it, and kept it as a sort of sign-board in front of his shop in the Cour du Carrousel, with the following inscription chalked actually on the canvas:

Que Pierrot serait content
S'il avait l'art de vous plaire.

Vivant-Denon, the director of the Musée Napoléon, bought it for 150 francs (or 300). At the Denon sale, in 1826 (No. 187), his nephew Brunet-Denon acquired it for 650 francs. In 1845 the latter sold it for 800 francs (or 1200) to the Marquis of Cypierre, who in his turn sold it to Doctor La Caze for 16.000 francs.

According to Dacier and Vuaflart, this group of Italian comedians, with the foolish Pierrot displayed in the foreground like a kind of parodied *Ecce Homo*, was perhaps conceived as a signboard for the opening of the new theatre of the Foire Saint Laurent. The *première* of the play which inaugurated it took place on 25 July 1721, a week after Watteau's death. This play was *Danae*, where Harlequin was changed into a donkey; there is in fact a donkey in the painting.

Dora Panofsky, however (1952), believes that it was a sign-board for a series of 'parades' written for the itinerant players by Thomas Simon Gueullette, Deputy Procureur du Roi at the Châtelet, and entitled *Education de Gilles*, or, '*A louer la tête d'un âne on perd sa lessive*'. These farces depict the misfortunes of Gilles, the good-hearted fool. This character was born in the seventeenth century among the fair-ground players, and became the main element in the 'parades'–short scenes performed out of doors in front of the theatre by a few actors, before the play began. Gilles adopted the costume of Pierrot, a character created by Molière in *Don Juan*. This hypothesis is more compatible with the style of the picture, since Gueullette began to write his 'parades' in 1711.

The victim of his own simplicity of heart, Gilles or Pierrot is the forerunner of the lunar pierrots of Verlaine and Laforgue, and is transformed in our own day into Charlie Chaplin.

WATTEAU, ANTOINE, 1684–1721 — French School
THE EMBARKATION FOR CYTHERA — Canvas

Inventory: INV. 8525

Height 1.28 m. (50¹/₂″)
Width 1.93 m. (76″)

This picture was Watteau's diploma piece for the Académie royale de Peinture et de Sculpture; it entered the Louvre on 4 April 1795, with the pictures belonging to the Académie, and was exhibited in 1799. It was not on exhibition in 1810, but was on view again in 1816.

Watteau's nomination was accepted by the Académie in 1712, but he had to be called to order several times, and on 9 January 1717 he was given six months to execute his reception piece. He was received on 28 August in the same year, on presentation of his picture, entitled *Pilgrimage to Cythera*.

Love is a traditional theme of French poetry since the Middle Ages. *L'Astrée* had given it distinction; in 1663, the Abbé de Tallemant in his *Voyage à l'île d'Amour* had imagined the destiny of love as a voyage to an island of blessedness. From the beginning of the eighteenth century, the idea of the departure for Cythera recurs in numerous ballets and operas, notably in *Les Trois Cousines*, a comedy by Dancourt first acted in 1700.

The handling of the paint in scumbles and glazes, thinly applied, with very little impasto, is close to that of Rubens in his final period; Watteau was able to study this style of painting in the *Kermesse*, which was then in the royal collection. Even the subject is derived from Rubens' *Jardins d'Amour*. Moreover, Watteau made a very close study of the Rubens paintings in the Médicis Gallery, when he was lodging (between 1707 and 1709) with the decorator Claude Audran III, who was the 'concierge' (director) of the Luxembourg. There are also reminiscences of Italy in this enchanted land; the general atmosphere of the painting is Venetian, and the distant mountains in their blue haze recall Leonardo's *La Gioconda* and *Saint Anne*.

Watteau made another version of it for his friend Jean de Julienne; this was bought by Frederick II. There was an opportunity of comparing the two paintings in 1950, when works from the Berlin Museum were exhibited at the Petit Palais.

The *Embarkation for Cythera* has preserved its paint quite untouched —a state rare amongst pictures—since the varnish has never been cleaned off; in the nineteenth century new layers of varnish were simply added, making it opaque and brownish in colour. In 1956 these thick coats of varnish were lightened, and the picture regained its original transparency and brightness while still retaining a layer of old varnish to protect the surface of the paint.

230

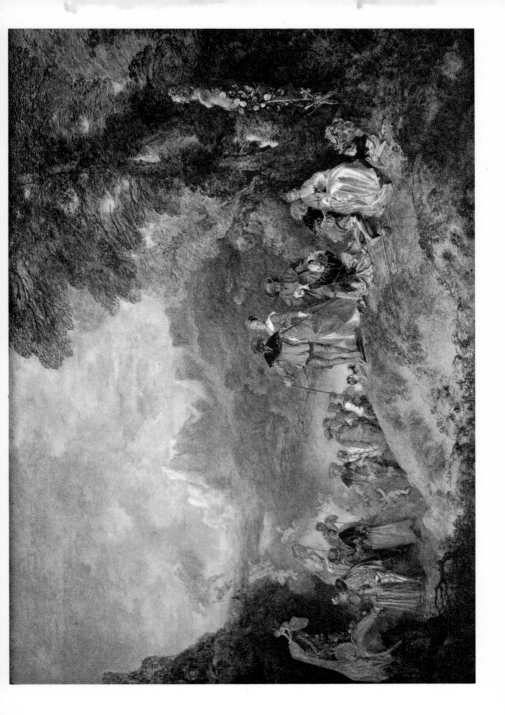

CHARDIN, JEAN-BAPTISTE SIMEON, 1699–1779   *French School*
LA POURVOYEUSE   Canvas

Inventory: M. I. 720   Height 0.470 m. (18¹/₂")
Signed and dated: Chardin 1739   Width 0.375 m. (14³/₄")

Dr. Maury's sale, 13 February 1835 (No. 15); Giroux sale, 10–12 February 1851, No. 38 (1.339 francs); bought for 4.050 francs on 11 April at M. Laperlier's sale, 11 and 13 April 1867 (No. 7).

This picture has been very popular, as can be seen from the fact that Chardin made several versions of it, and a great many copies are in existence. The earliest version is undoubtedly the one in the German Imperial collection (bought by Frederick II), signed and dated 1738, and exhibited in the Salon of 1739. A replica of the Louvre painting, signed and dated 1739, was formerly in the Lichtenstein Gallery of Austria; this has just been acquired by the National Gallery of Ottawa. A replica with variations was exhibited by Chardin in the Salon of 1769; this was in the collection of Baron Henri de Rothschild. In 1742 an engraving of the painting by Bernard Lépicié was published, with these doggerel lines:

A votre air j'estime et je pense
Ma chère enfant sans calculer
Que vous prenez sur la dépense
Ce qu'il faut pour vous habiller! ...

Fantin-Latour made a copy of the picture before 1870.

Chardin's technique as revealed in this picture (which is in good condition) belongs to a French tradition which continues into the nineteenth century with remarkably few exceptions. Apart from such artists as Fragonard and Renoir, the French usually reject the virtuosity of the transparent technique employed by the Flemish and Dutch, with its use of glazes. They work in impasto of varying thickness, which they build up gradually. Chardin learnt this craft from the Le Nain brothers, but he made it more solid by the use of thicker impasto, often increasing the 'fatness' of the pigment with an excess of greasy oil which has affected the durability of some of his works. This kind of 'modelling with paint' suggests the artisan, the painter creating his picture empirically, step by step; it also reveals a sincerely-felt emotion inspired by real objects, which is interpreted without any intellectualism.

CHARDIN, JEAN BAPTISTE SIMEON, 1699–1779 *French School*
THE RAY *Canvas*

Inventory: INV. 3197

Height 1.14 m. (45″)
Width 1.46 m. (57¹/₂″)

One of the artist's diploma pieces, on the occasion of his reception into the Académie de Peinture et de Sculpture in 1728. Passed into the Louvre with the Académie collections in 1795.

Artists who were not members of the Académie royale de Peinture et de Sculpture, and who therefore could not exhibit their work in the Salon, took part once a year in what was known as the 'Salon de la Jeunesse', held on the feast of Corpus Christi in the open air, in the Place Dauphine, and lasting two hours. On 3 June 1728 Chardin exhibited several pictures there, including the *Ray* and the *Buffet*. Some academicians who saw the work persuaded Chardin to present himself for membership of the Académie royale; on 25 September of the same year, contrary to the usual practice, Chardin was accepted and admitted on one and the same day. The Académie did not insist on a picture specially painted for the occasion, as was usually the case, but retained the *Ray* and the *Buffet* as his diploma pieces. It is related that the artist had deceived several academicians, among them Largillière and Cazes, by showing them some of his still life paintings, which they took for Flemish works. Certainly, the source of inspiration is obvious in the *Ray*, which surpasses the best work of Jan Fyt.

Cézanne made a drawing of this painting, and Matisse copied it.

The rich quality of the paint surface, which is in perfect condition, has been revealed by the recent cleaning of the varnish. The picture is exceptionally well preserved for a work by Chardin; his paintings often suffered from too heavy a use of oil with his pigment. Perhaps this one owes its good condition to the fact that it dates from his early days, when he was applying himself to improving his technique by creating a 'chef-d'œuvre' carefully executed according to the best principles of true craftsmanship. Later, he trusted too much to his inspiration, and yielded to his passion for worked-up impasto.

234

PERRONNEAU, JEAN-BAPTISTE, 1715–1783   *French School*
Portrait of Madame de Sorquainville   Canvas

Inventory: R. F. 37–8   Height 1.01 m. (40″)
Signed and dated: 1749   Width 0.81 m. (32″)

In the collection of M. David David-Weill, President of the Conseil artistique des Musées de France, who presented it to the Louvre in 1937.

Since making a colour photograph of the famous portrait of Madame de Pompadour by La Tour involved considerable technical difficulties, this picture by Perronneau has been chosen to epitomize the feminine grace of the French eighteenth century. This portrait by La Tour's rival is probably even better than the other picture as far as strictly pictorial qualities are concerned.

Posterity has for a long time accepted Diderot's view regarding the superiority of La Tour, 'machiniste merveilleux', over 'l'innocent artiste' Perronneau – the superiority of a master over his pupil. But since the retrospective exhibition of Perronneau's work in 1909, this judgment has been revised. No one questions La Tour's keen powers of observation and his realistic approach; but Perronneau's pastels are much more subtle, even though they may be of less value as psychological studies. For this reason they are more appreciated at the present time, when a painting is judged by more specifically artistic values. Unlike his rival, Perronneau sometimes used oils, always with happy results.

All the frills and furbelows, the folds in the dress, the wrinkled lace, the creases in the drapery, do more than simply make a 'picture'; they set off the refined, bony face, pale as ivory but sparkling with intelligence, of this woman, who looks as if she were posing for the artist after some illness, during a convalescence in which she was full of happiness at her recovery. Women of the previous generation had chosen to be represented as goddesses; towards 1750, they preferred to be painted in their morning *déshabillé*, but without losing any of their elegance. This air of simplicity even in the most calculated charm is an essential quality of French art; the self-possessed smile is also a characteristically French expression. It appeared on the portals of thirteenth-century French cathedrals, and again on the faces of the young saints of the fifteenth-century school of Touraine; in the eighteenth century it becomes playful in the work of Perronneau, sardonic in that of La Tour.

BOUCHER, FRANÇOIS, 1703–1770   *French School*
DIANA RESTING AFTER HER BATH   Canvas

Inventory: INV. 2712   Height 0.57 m. (22¹/₂")
Signed: 1742 Boucher   Width 0.73 m. (28³/₄")

Exhibited in the Salon, 1742. Comte de Narbonne's sale, Paris, 24 March 1850. Bought from Van Cuyck in 1852 for 3.200 francs.

This painting, and the *Leda* exhibited in the same Salon (now in Stockholm) are unquestionably François Boucher's masterpieces. As a decorative artist, Boucher had amazing facility; in this painting, done for the Salon, he wished to excel himself. It places him in the ranks of the great masters, and on looking at it one begins to realize how gifted he was, even though he did not always make full use of his talent. Renoir understood this well; he was particularly fond of the *Diana*. 'Boucher's Diana bathing', he remarked (according to Vollard), 'is the first picture which really captivated me, and I have gone on loving it all my life as one loves one's first sweetheart — although I am constantly being told that one should not like that kind of thing, and that Boucher is a mere decorator — as if that were a defect! In fact, no one has understood the female body better than Boucher — he knew just how to paint the rounded, dimpled young bottom.'

The slender nudes and the hunting theme recall the School of Fontainebleau, of which certain traditions persist in the eighteenth century. The paint surface is intact, and the old varnish, which contains no artificial colouring, gives it a slightly golden tone.

All who really love painting for its own sake, and are not swayed by changes of fashion, cannot fail to admire this miraculous picture. It is a masterpiece in the true classical manner; the technique is not too obvious, all the values are harmoniously balanced, and the elegance of the drawing and the purity of the forms outweighs the more sensual charms of colour. It calls to mind the *Grande Odalisque* of Ingres, with its combination of pale flesh tones and cool blues.

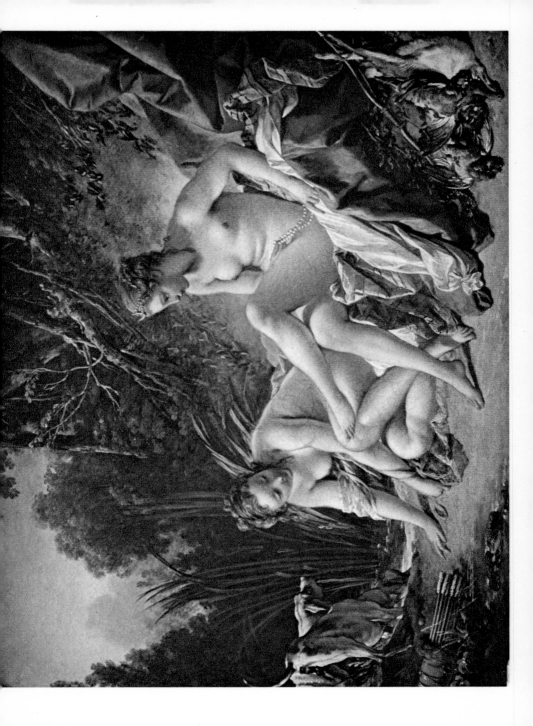

FRAGONARD, HONORÉ, 1732–1806
French School
WOMEN BATHING   Canvas

Inventory: M. I. 1055
Height 0.64 m. (25¹/₄")
Width 0.80 m. (31¹/₂")

Sale (du Barry?), 11 March 1776, no. 77
(550 *livres*); Varanchan sale, 29 December 1777, no. 12 (542 *livres*); Abbé de
Gévigney's sale, 1 December 1779, no. 594;
in the collection of L. La Caze, who
bought it in 1854 from Féral *père* for
3.000 francs. Left to the Louvre in 1869.

A display of virtuosity in the Rubens
manner seems to have been the artist's
intention, with a skilful use of scumbling
and glazes, and impasto only in the high-
lights – a triumph of luminous transparency. The swirling composition is also
reminiscent of Rubens. The pigment is
wonderfully well preserved, since the
picture was painted *alla prima* (without
interruptions in the execution), an important factor in contributing to the
durability of a work.

Fragonard must have seen a good many
paintings of this kind in the studio of his
master, Boucher; but it is still more probable that he here gives proof of the deep
impression made on him by the Nereids
in Rubens' *Débarquement de la Reine* in
the Médicis Gallery. This gallery was
a veritable school for painters in the
eighteenth century, particularly for those
who could be described as 'free painters', who did not work along the lines
laid down by the Académie de Peinture et de Sculpture, which followed the
tradition of decorative art established under Louis XIV. Perhaps it was in
order to retain his freedom of action that when he was accepted by the

Académie he never submitted a diploma piece.

This painting is sometimes thought to date from before his first visit to Italy in 1756, when his discovery of Tiepolo changed the direction of his work.

Inventory: R. F. 1580   Height 0.76 m. (30″)
                                             Width 0.62 m. (24¹/₂″)

Baron Alphonse de Rothschild bequest, 1906.

The history of this picture can be traced almost without any gaps, since its creation. It was painted in 1788, when Reynolds was at the summit of his reputation, only a few years before his death. He painted it for one of his aunts, his mother's eldest sister, Anna Maria Lady Jones; the little sitter was Francis George Hare, the nephew or adopted son of Lady Jones. When the latter died in 1829, the picture became the property of Mrs. Louisa Shipley, the sole beneficiary under her will and also Reynold's aunt; this lady left it to a cousin, Mrs. Townshend, when she died in March 1840. Mrs. Townshend presented it in 1841 to the three surviving nephews of Mrs. Shipley, Julius, Marcus and Francis Hare, the latter evidently being the subject of the portrait. Francis died in Italy in 1842, and the painting became the property of his brother Julius, Archdeacon Hare, who kept it till his death in 1855. His widow then gave it to Mrs. Augustus Hare, widow of the third brother who was Lady Jones' adopted son; she seems to have kept it till she died in 1868. There was then a lawsuit over the possession of the picture, and it became the property of M. W. H. Milligan, from whom Baron Alphonse de Rothschild bought it in 1872.

Two years after it was painted, this picture was already famous; it was engraved in colour by Richard Thew and published by Boydell in March 1790, with the title 'Infancy' and some lines of verse by Robert Burns. Two original replicas of the painting exist, one of which was in the Phillips collection at the beginning of the century; the other belongs to the Metropolitan Museum, New York.

GOYA Y LUCIENTES, FRANCISCO JOSÉ DE,   *Spanish School*
1746–1828
THE COUNTESS DEL CARPIO   Canvas

Inventory: 1942–23   Height 1.81 m. (71¹/₄″)
                                       Width 1.22 m. (48″)

Marquis del Socorro's collection, Madrid; bought from his heirs in 1913 by M. Carlos de Beistegui; in Biarritz; Carlos de Beistegui legacy in 1942; entered the Louvre in 1953.

This picture is considered to be one of Goya's finest female portraits; Beruete y Moret, Sanchez Cantón and M. A. L. Mayer all heap praises upon it. The latter regards it as the artist's finest painting of a woman; only the portrait of the Duchess of Alba or La Tirana can be compared with it.

Maria Rita Barrenechea y Morante, born in about 1700, married Count del Carpio in November 1775; she died in 1795, and perhaps it is the approach of death which stamps such anxiety on the feverish, languid face, with its great dark eyes. The slender silhouette seems to materialize like a ghost in front of the plain background; in this simple picture, free of all rhetorical devices and exercising a curious fascination by reason of this very simplicity, one finds the strange 'supernatural' quality common to all the masterpieces of Spanish painting. The sylph-like body is only the fleshly covering of a burning spirit. We know that the Countess del Carpio was a cultivated woman; she wrote some poetry which was printed at Jaen in 1783.

The pose is a curious one; the position of the feet, one at right angles to the other, suggests that she is about to perform a dance step, but this is belied by the calm and relaxed position of the crossed hands with the fan.

This picture is sometimes called the 'Marquesa de la Solana'. The Count del Carpio only inherited this title a few months before his wife's death; and this portrait is usually considered to belong to Goya's 'grey' period, just before the illness (1792) which made him deaf and gave his art a more pathetic quality.

During this 'grey' period, Goya showed himself a worthy successor of the great painter of Infantas; like many of Velasquez's finest works, this picture is a subtle harmony of greys and black, with a single note of colour – the pink ribbon rosette in the woman's hair.

Inventory: INV. 3708

Height 1.70 m. (67")
Width 2.40 m. (94½")

Louis David Sale, 17 April 1826 (No. 15); sold for 6.180 francs to Monsieur Pérignon; bought back by the State.

It was in 1800 that Madame Récamier asked David to do a portrait of her; but she was very unreliable in the matter of sittings. The fact that she had also commissioned Gérard to paint her portrait did not put the artist and his model on any better terms, and David finally lost patience. 'Madame', he is reported to have said to her one day, 'artists have their whims, as well as ladies. Allow me to satisfy mine; I intend to leave your portrait exactly as it is.'

'La belle Juliette' was then twenty-three years old; she was just at the beginning of her astonishing career as a reigning beauty. She was the daughter of a banker from Lyons. In 1793 she married a banker much older than herself. All her life, well on into middle age, she aroused passionate feelings; her last conquest was the poet Chateaubriand.

The relaxed pose in which David shows her, resting on a sofa, was a characteristic attitude. Doubtless it displayed to the best advantage the languid type of beauty which was the outcome of her somewhat lymphatic temperament. When the picture was painted, the imitation of antiquity was still practised in all its purity, without the ponderous and ostentatious quality it was to acquire under the Empire. The sofa, the stool and the lamp all point to this fashion, which affects the sitter's pose. By clothing her in a simple tunic with loosely falling folds, and showing her with bare feet which suggest the nudity of a nymph, David aimed at avoiding any accessory or garment which might unmistakably stamp the picture as belonging to his own age; he wanted to express the 'eternal feminine' in the person of this particular beauty.

According to a tradition, the accessories were painted by Ingres, who at that time was a pupil of David. In accordance with his usual method, after sketching in the pose David concentrated on the head, which is almost finished; the flowing pigment of the tunic has not yet been crystallized into its definitive form. The background and accessories are carried out in scumbles lying beneath the surface paint, which give a hidden vibration to David's work; the fact that this particular picture is unfinished reveals this quality in all its intensity.

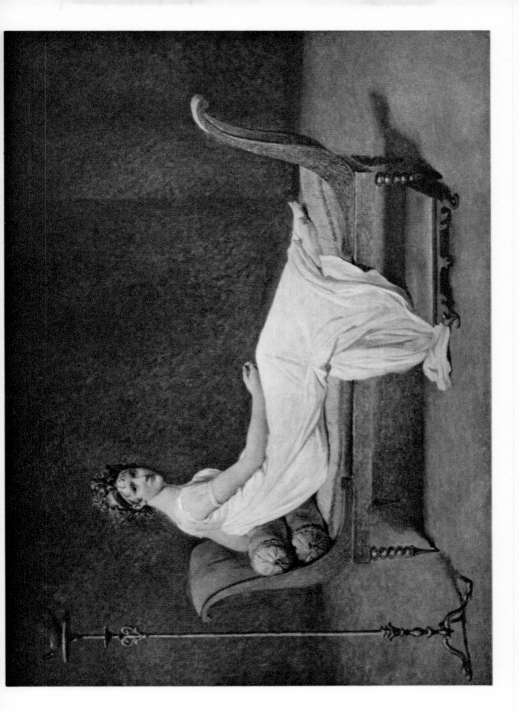

DAVID, JACQUES-LOUIS, 1748–1825   *French School*
THE CONSECRATION OF THE EMPEROR NAPOLEON I AND
THE CORONATION OF THE EMPRESS JOSEPHINE (DETAIL)   Canvas

Inventory: INV. 3699   Height 6.10 m. (240")
Signed on the right, dated on the left 1805–1807   Width 9.31 m. (360¹/₂")

David was commissioned by Napoleon to paint a large composition com-
memorating his consecration, which had taken place in Notre Dame in Paris,
on 2 December 1804. The picture (page 306) was exhibited in the Salon
Carré in the Louvre in 1808, then in the Salon of that year; it was next
placed in the Tuileries, in the Salle des Gardes. Under Louis Philippe it was
installed at Versailles in a room decorated in imitation of the Empire style,
together with David's *Distribution of the Eagles* and Gros' *Battle of Aboukir*;
in 1889 it was transferred to the Louvre, and its place at Versailles was
taken by Roll's *Marseillaise*. In 1947 this latter picture was replaced by a
replica of David's *Consecration of Napoleon*, begun by the painter in 1808
and not finished till 1822, in Brussels; this replica was bought by the Musées
de France in England, in 1946.

David seems to have derived his general composition from Rubens'
Coronation of Queen Marie de Médicis.

In accordance with David's usual method, numerous studies, both painted
and drawn, preceded the actual execution of the work. The best-known of
these is the portrait of Pius VII, now in the Louvre. The painter then made
a model, where he arranged dolls in costume.

David had originally intended to portray the event faithfully, and show
Napoleon crowning himself. The Emperor, remembering the quarrels between
the Pope and the Holy Roman Empire, placed the crown on his own head
to avoid giving a pledge of obedience of the temporal power to the Pontiff.
But he evidently felt that it would not be desirable to perpetuate this somewhat disrespectful action in paint; so David painted the coronation of Josephine by Napoleon, with the Pope blessing the Empress.

Grouped round the altar, near Napoleon, are the chief dignitaries – Cambacérès, the Lord Chancellor, Marshal Berthier, *Grand Veneur*, Talleyrand,
the Lord Chamberlain, and Lebrun, the Chief Treasurer. Madame de la
Rochefoucauld carries the Empress's train; behind her are the Emperor's
sisters, and his brothers Louis and Joseph. In front of the central stand are
some of the marshals, and in it is Marie Laetitia, Madame Mère (the Emperor's mother), who was in fact not present at the ceremony.

248

PRUDHON, PIERRE-PAUL, 1758–1823   *French School*
PORTRAIT OF THE EMPRESS JOSEPHINE   Canvas

Inventory: R. F. 270   Height 2.44 m. (96")
          Width 1.79 m. (70½")

Napoleon commissioned Prudhon to do this portrait in 1805; it hung in the château of Malmaison, where Josephine lived after her repudiation till her death in 1814. In 1815 Queen Hortense, Josephine's daughter by her first marriage with Alexandre de Beauharnais, took it to her château of Arenenberg in Switzerland, where she died in 1837. The picture passed to her son, Prince Charles-Louis-Napoleon, the future Napoleon III, and remained in the château of Arenenberg till 1843. It was allotted to the Louvre, together with six other pictures belonging personally to the Emperor, on 12 February 1879, by the Tribunal de la Seine.

Prudhon made several studies for this work, in which Josephine is shown seated in a shady corner of the park at Malmaison, in a languid attitude; she is wearing a décolletée white gown, set off by a red shawl with gold embroidery.

In 1805, Josephine was fresh from her 'triumph' at the consecration of the Emperor. Napoleon was planning to repudiate her, because of her sterility, but on the eve of the consecration she managed to force him into consolidating her position by a religious marriage ceremony. And yet there is a profound sadness in her lost expression and the tired line of her body; in spite of the Emperor's consecration, and her marriage, she was uncertain of her future and of his; and in any case her Creole temperament (she was born in Martinique in 1762) lent to her movements and attitudes a languid and melancholy charm.

This natural melancholy must have attracted the morose temperament of the artist, whose work all bears the stamp of a feeling of profound desolation, increased by his conjugal misfortunes. The pose of the sitter, characteristic of women at that period when they were resting on their 'méridiennes' or sofas, illustrates the theme of the forsaken heroine, so familiar in the novel and the elegiac poetry of the eighteenth century. But this day-dreaming conceals a deeper anguish, an unfulfilled longing for happiness such as Chateaubriand expressed in *René*, in 1802. Even the landscape, with its damp chill foliage shutting out the daylight, is in harmony with the sitter's state of mind.

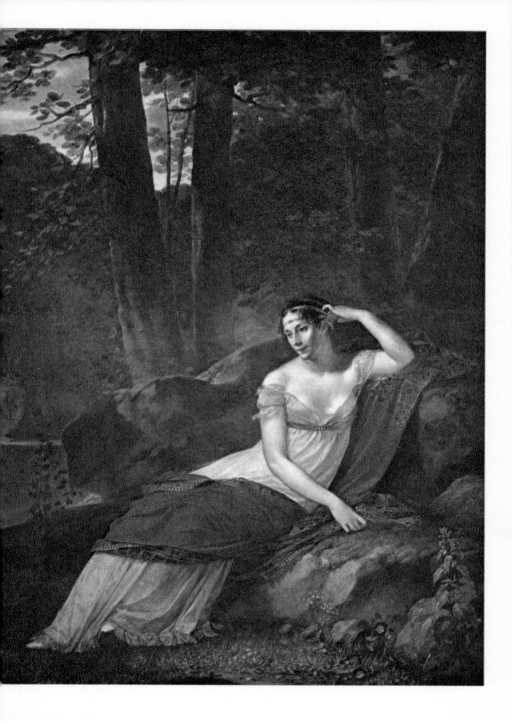

Inventory: M. I. 1446   Height 1.16 m. (45½")
                                                          Width 0.90 m. (36")

Exhibited in the Salon of 1806. Bequeathed to the State in 1870 by the widowed Madame Rivière (née Robillard), together with the portraits of Philibert Rivière and their daughter (page 309). Exhibited in the Luxembourg, then in the Louvre in 1874.

M. Rivière, who was the *maître des requêtes* of the Conseil des Etats in 1810, and who died in 1816, had his own portrait painted by Ingres, as well as those of his wife and daughter. These three portraits, which passed to the Museum in 1874, are the three finest portraits of Ingres owned by the Louvre. The portrait of M. Rivière is signed: 'Ingres, l'an XIII'; a system of dating which indicates that Ingres clung to republican habits. Mlle. Rivière was fifteen when she died in 1805; her mother died in 1848.

These three dazzling portraits, and others of the same period, prove that Ingres had achieved a personal style before his departure for Italy, in September 1806.

Although the artist had never been to Italy when he painted them, the style of these three portraits, particularly that of Madame Rivière, shows how profoundly he was affected by the art of antiquity, though in a very different way from David. As was the case in the Italian Renaissance during the fifteenth century, David's art was influenced by the masculine art of statuary, whereas Ingres sought out the more gracious aspects of antiquity among the minor arts – Greek vase paintings, intaglios and cameos, where the sinuous drawing outlines simplified tones and direct colours. In its oval frame, the portrait of Madame Rivière is not unlike a cameo, with its harmony of blue and white broken only by the cashmere shawl.

The sitter's languid pose, her kiss-curls, the inviting roundness of her body, the studied casualness of her scarf, are very unlike the austere and virile style of David's *Madame de Verninac* which is also in the Louvre and hangs not far away from *Madame Rivière*. But Ingres, who was to be Delacroix' worst enemy, remained entirely neo-classical in style; far from allowing the brush-work to be visible, as Géricault and David did later, he sought to hide every trace of his patient labour, like a true member of the classical school, in order to produce an image whose merit depended on form and colour alone, without any effects gained by brush and palette – which he would have considered vulgar.

INGRES, JEAN-AUGUSTE-DOMINIQUE, 1780–1867   *French School*
THE TURKISH BATH   Canvas

Inventory: R. F. 1934   Circular; Diameter 1.08 m. (42¹/₂″)
Signed: J. Ingres Pinxit MDCCCLXII Aetatis LXXXII

Acquired at the end of the year 1859 by Prince Napoleon, who returned it
to the artist. Bought by Khalel Bey, Turkish ambassador in Paris, for 20.000
francs. No. 34 in the Khalel Bey sale, 16–18 January 1868. Collections
Henri Say, Amédée de Broglie. Bought in 1911 by the Société des Amis du
Louvre.

As Jules Mommejà pointed out, Ingres derived the idea of these swarming
nudes in the interior of a harem from Lady Mary Wortley Montague's
letters (no. XXVI and XLII). She was the wife of the English ambassador
to the Sublime Porte; in these two letters she describes baths in the Seraglio,
which she was allowed to enter, and Ingres copied extracts from them into
his notebook (no. IX), probably in about 1817.

Several of the figures in this canvas have been taken from earlier pictures;
others are new. But as M. Hans Naef demonstrated in 1957 (in *L'Oeil*),
Ingres had not a very ready imagination, and borrowed from both French
and English prints of 'turqueries', going back to the eighteenth or even the
sixteenth centuries. Copies of these are still to be seen in the archives of his
studio in the Musée de Montauban.

This picture has existed in at least two forms. A first sketch, intended for
Comte Demidoff, was executed in 1852, but not delivered; it was probably
worked on again after this date, and at the end of 1859 it was bought by
Prince Napoleon. The appearance of this picture, which at that time was
square, is known from a photograph dated 7 October 1859. On the intervention of Princess Clotilde, scandalized by all those nudes, the Prince
returned it to Ingres; M. Reiset was entrusted with negotiating its exchange
for a portrait of the artist at the age of twenty-four (now in the Musée
Condé, Chantilly). Ingres kept the picture for several years, making various
changes in it and giving it its final circular form. He signed it in 1862,
indicating with pride that it was the work of a man of eighty-two.

GERICAULT, THEODORE, 1791–1824
French School
THE RAFT OF THE MÉDUSE   Canvas

Inventory: INV. 4884
Height 4.91 m. (193")
Width 7.16 m. (282")

For his Salon picture in 1819, Géricault chose a dramatic episode – the wreck
of the frigate *Méduse*, which had set off
with a French fleet on an expedition to
Senegal, and had been lost in July 1816.
The French admiralty was accused of
having put an incompetent officer in
charge of the expedition; he was the
Comte de Chaumareix, a former émigré
who had not commanded a vessel for
twenty-five years. The picture was an
enormous success, more on account of the
scandal than because of an interest in the
arts; but Géricault only received a gold
medal, and his picture was not bought by
the government. One wonders who it
was suggested commissioning this painter
of horror subjects to do a *Sacred Heart.*
Géricault was mortified, and decided
to exhibit his picture in England, where
a pamphlet had been published on the
wreck of the *Méduse.* He entrusted the
vast canvas to an eccentric character
named Bullock (as Lethière had done
with his *Brutus Condemning his Sons*), and it was exhibited in London from
12 June to 31 December 1820, and in Dublin from 5 February to 31 March
1821. Géricault received a third of the takings, and the operation brought
him in quite a large sum (probably 20.000 francs).

The painting was priced at 6.000 francs at the posthumous sale of the
artist's possessions. It was bought by Dedreux-Dorcy, a friend of Géricault,
for an additional five francs, and he sold it to the State for the same amount.

The most horrifying part of the shipwreck had been the drama of 149 wretches abandoned on a raft with only some casks of wine to live on, and the ensuing drunkenness and abominations. When the frigate *Argus* found the raft, after many days, she was only able to rescue fifteen survivors, of whom five died after being brought ashore. After some hesitation, Géricault chose this last episode – the sighting of the *Argus* by the survivors on the raft. With regard to the latter, he set himself to the task of carrying out an inquest as thoroughly as any examining magistrate. He rented a studio opposite the Beaujon hospital, so that he could make anatomical studies of the dying.

GERICAULT, THEODORE, 1791–1824   *French School*
THE DERBY AT EPSOM IN 1821   Canvas

Inventory: M. I. 708   Height 0.88 m. (35″)
                                     Width   1.20 m. (47″)

Elmore collection. One of six pictures belonging to the Cherubini family which were included in the Laneuville sale, Paris, 9 May 1866; sold for 6.100 francs to the picture dealer M. Couvreur, from whom it was bought by the State in June 1866 for 9.000 francs.

Géricault was always interested in horses; his early death was the result of a fall from a horse. When he was in London in 1820–1821, exhibiting his *Raft of the Méduse*, he made numerous studies both of draught-horses and thoroughbreds. On 12 February 1821 he wrote to his friend Dedreux-Dorcy that he would like to 'send all the Sacred Hearts of Jesus to the devil – a beggarly craft, at which I'll end up by dying of starvation'. (He had just been commissioned to paint a picture on this subject.) 'I am abandoning the classical buskin and the Holy Scriptures and retiring into the stables – I'll come out of them stuffed with gold.' In that year he watched the Derby at Epsom; there was a violent storm during the race, and Géricault has recorded this scene, which explains the sombre skies in the picture. Although he actually saw the race himself, he may have borrowed his composition from English sporting prints, but his debt to an engraving by James Pollard has been exaggerated. This engraving represents 'Sir Joshua beating Filho da Puta at Newmarket', with the horses in the 'Flying gallop' position. In fact, all artists saw the gallop in this way until Degas, who was the first to benefit from the revelations of photography. Even if he derived inspiration from sporting prints, however, Géricault's scene has retained nothing of their anecdotal quality; he saw with a painter's eye the brilliant shirts of the jockeys, and the shining sweaty coats of the horses against a sea of grass under a stormy sky.

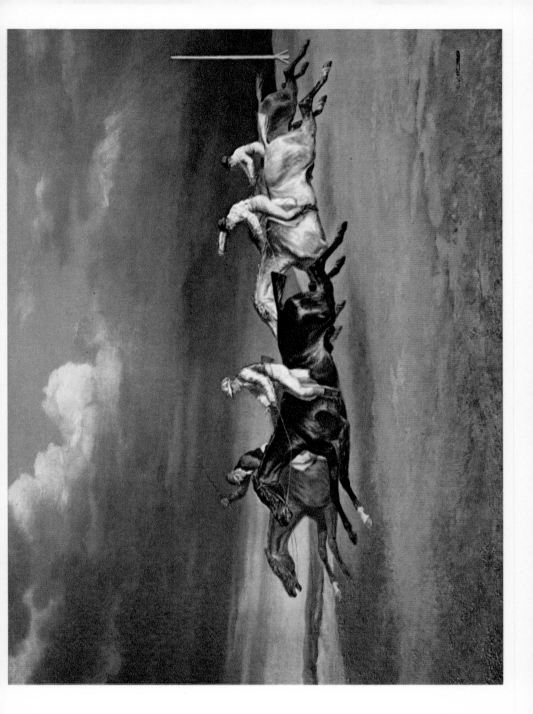

Inventory: INV. 3824   Height 1.80 m. (70¹/₂″)
Signed and dated: 1834   Width 2.29 m. (90¹/₂″)

Exhibited at the Salon of 1834, where it was bought for the Musée du Luxembourg.

The capture of Algiers in 1830 had given France the Sultan of Morocco as a neighbour. Louis Philippe's government decided to send him an ambassador extraordinary, the Comte de Mornay; the latter wished to take an official artist with him and chose Eugène Delacroix. The mission left Toulon on 11 January 1832, landed at Tangiers on the 25 January, travelled through a part of Morocco, and returned via Oran and Algiers.

During his visit to this country, Delacroix witnessed spectacles belonging to a noble and primitive way of life which provided material for his art until he died; but he had not been allowed to enter the jealously guarded harems of the Moslems. It was the chief harbour engineer at Algiers who persuaded one of the port officials, a former *reis* or owner of privateers, to allow Delacroix into his own harem.

In these few hours Delacroix did several watercolour sketches, some of which are in the Louvre. Using them as a basis, he painted a large picture on his return, and exhibited it in the 1834 salon. He wanted to show the dark tones of flesh and the subdued colours in the warm half-light of the harem.

In 1849 he painted another smaller version of the same subject, now in the Musée de Montpellier. Here the colours are softer and the atmosphere more intimate; it has a note of nostalgia absent from the 1834 Salon picture, which is still full of his first impressions, and which already foreshadows Renoir. The latter artist was well aware of this relationship; in 1872 he painted a large picture inspired by Delacroix' canvas and called *Les Parisiennes habillées en Algériennes* (Tokyo Museum). He had already done an *Odalisque*, and exhibited it in the 1870 Salon. (Chester Dale collection, New York.)

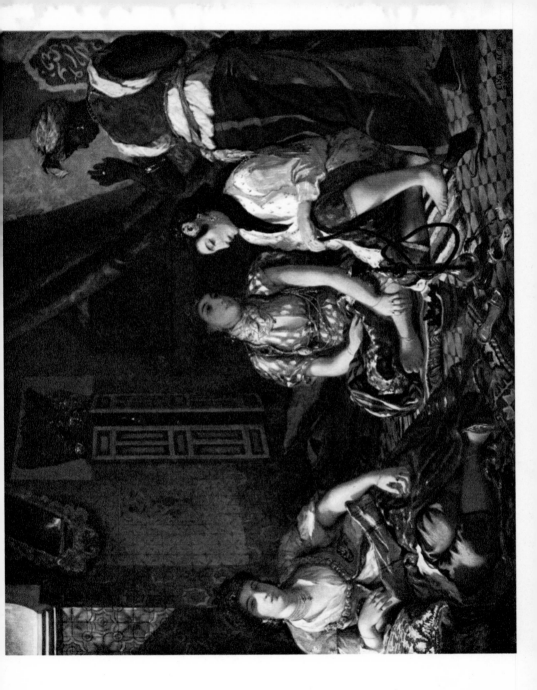

DELACROIX, EUGÈNE, 1798–1863   *French School*
THE DEATH OF SARDANAPALUS (DETAIL)   Canvas

Inventory: R. F. 2346   Height 3.95 m. (155¹/₂″)
                                          Width 4.96 m. (195″)

Exhibited at the Salon of 1827 (No. 1630); sold by Delacroix to M. Wilson in 1846; exhibited at Martinet's in 1862; Wilson sale, Paris, 31 March 1873; bought by the dealer Durand-Ruel for 96.000 francs; Duncan sale, London, 15 April 1889; bought by the dealer Haro; exhibited at Durand-Ruel's in 1878; sold by Haro to Baron Vitta. Bought from the latter by the Louvre in 1921, for 800.000 francs.

For this picture (page 308) he took his theme from a tragedy by Byron, published in 1821 and dedicated to Goethe. According to the legend, the Assyrian ruler Sardanapalus, besieged in his capital, ordered his wives, his servants and his treasures to be burnt on a pyre. Delacroix later referred to this picture as his 'massacre No. 2', the first being the *Massacres of Scio* (page 308), his picture in the 1824 Salon which shows the influence of Constable, but that of Rubens is dominant in the Sardanapalus.

Delacroix made a vigorous sketch for this picture in 1826, which he left to his friend Rivet; the Comtesse de Salvandy, née Rivet, bequeathed it to the Louvre in 1925. In 1844 he painted a smaller version; for this composition he made a number of studies in pencil, pen, wash and pastel. The fragmentary studies attributed to him are usually only copies; there are some by Andrieu in the museums at Tours and Angers.

Delacroix' work was received by the Salon in a fairly lukewarm fashion. The neo-classical school was scandalized, and even his own supporters were doubtful. However, Victor Hugo wrote to a friend 'The Sardanapalus is magnificent, and too vast to be taken in by the narrow-minded. I only regret one thing – that the painter did not show the pyre actually burning; this splendid scene would have been even finer if it had centred round a casket of flames' (3 April 1829). Delacroix had hoped to be decorated for this 'Asiatic prowess' against the Spartan pastiches of the school of David, and was bitterly disappointed. The Director of Beaux-Arts, Sosthène de La Rochefoucauld (who had encouraged Delacroix in his early days, and had had the *Massacres of Scio* bought at the 1824 Salon), is supposed to have said to him: 'If that is how you intend to paint, Monsieur, you need expect no work from me.'

DELACROIX, EUGÈNE, 1798–1863 — French School
STILL LIFE WITH LOBSTER — Canvas

Inventory: R. F. 1661

Height 0.80 m. (31¹/₂″)
Width 1.00 m. (39¹/₂″)

Painted at Beffes for General Coetlosquet. Exhibited in the Salon of 1827; in the Moreau collection; Moreau-Nélaton donation, 1906.

This painting was one of the splendid collection of works which Delacroix sent to the Salon of 1827, and which included the *Death of Sardanapalus* as well as some of his other finest pictures. On 28 September 1827, Delacroix wrote to his friend Soulier: 'I have finished the General's animal picture, and I have dug up a rococo frame for it, which I have had re-gilded and which will do for it splendidly. It has already dazzled people at a gathering of amateurs, and I think it would be amusing to see it in the Salon.'

Of all Delacroix' paintings, the *Still life with Lobster* reveals most clearly the impression made on the young artist by English painting. The background with its red-coated huntsmen is reminiscent of landscapes by Constable; the dead game in the foreground, with its incongruous lobster, rivals Jan Fyt's finest pictures.

Delacroix painted this picture when he returned from England; even before then, he was in close touch with English painters in Paris – Fielding and Bonington amongst others. But it was at the Salon of 1824 that he discovered the revolution which Constable had brought about in English painting, when he saw the three landscapes which the latter was exhibiting there. He hastily re-painted the background of the *Massacres of Scio* (page 308) along the same lines; when the state bought the picture from him for 6.000 francs (a considerable sum in those days) he lost no time in spending the money on a trip to England. This opened up a new world to him – the Parthenon marbles, the gothic style, the paintings of Lawrence and Etty, the horses (his host was the horsedealer Elmore), sailing in a yacht – a sport he was able to indulge in with an aristocratic friend of Elmore's, and the plays of Shakespeare. English painting had attracted a whole colony of French artists to London; among them Eugène Isabey, Eugène Lami, and Henri Monnier. Delacroix also renewed contact with Bonington, and worked in company with him. He was in London when he heard of the heroic death of Lord Byron, to whom he pays tribute in his Journal.

COROT, JEAN-BAPTISTE-CAMILLE, 1796–1875 French School
VIEW OF MARISSEL Canvas

Inventory: R. F. 1642 Height 0.55 m. (21⁵/₈")
Signed at bottom left Width 0.43 m. (16⁷/₈")

Painted in 1866 at Marissel, near Beauvais, and exhibited in the 1867 Salon. Sold there by Corot to M. Laurent Richard, a tailor, for 4.000 francs (Corot's letter of 30 June 1867). Moreau-Nélaton gift, 1906.

Corot became acquainted with the Beauvais region through M. Badin, the Director of the Manufacture Nationale de Tapisseries, a painter whom he had formerly known in Italy. He was at Beauvais in 1857, and visited it frequently until his death; when M. Badin left the factory one of his friends, M. Wallet of Voisinlieu, gave the artist hospitality. He explored the valley of a little stream called the Thérain, looking for riverside subjects, of which he was particularly fond. It is this stream which flows in front of the hill on which stands the village church of Marissel, near Voisinlieu.

Another smaller picture shows the same subject, seen closer up from the other side of the Thérain; it is painted in a rather freer technique, with somewhat heavy impasto; dashed off like a study, it is probably a little earlier than the Louvre picture. The latter was painted during a greater number of sessions, and is more deliberate; it is a subtle study of light, finely executed, which denotes patient observation. The light, which does not seem to have reached its full strength, is that of early morning; the trees are beginning to bear young shoots; the first hint of spring is in the air. Probably no other painter has so well expressed this uncertain moment of the changing seasons. A photograph of the same scene, taken beside Corot by M. Herbert of Beauvais, shows the slight changes the artist has made, widening the perspective leading towards the church, and omitting a wooden fence which he considered spoiled the effect. The composition is well balanced; the light colour of the sky is matched by the reflected brightness in the stream. Except for the church, the view is completely changed today.

Nothing looks simpler, more 'ordinary', than Corot's subjects. But his painting is so subtle that one can guess the month, the time of day, and even the region. The landscapes done in the neighbourhood of Beauvais have a quality of verdure and light which makes them immediately recognizable to the practised eye.

COROT, JEAN-BAPTISTE-CAMILLE, 1796–1875   *French School*
THE COLISEUM SEEN FROM THE FARNESE GARDENS ON THE PALATINE
Paper mounted on canvas

Inventory: R. F. 154   Height 0.28 m. (11″)
Signed at the bottom, on the right: Corot Mars 1826   Width 0.48 m. (19″)

Painted direct from nature in Rome, March 1826. Exhibited in the Salon of 1849. Bequeathed to the Louvre by the artist (1874).

Although he had not attended the official studios, Corot, a pupil of the neo-classical landscape painters Michallon and Jean-Victor Bertin, followed French tradition in believing that only Italy could complete the education of a landscape artist. Leaving a portrait of himself (page 310) with his parents, he left for Rome in the autumn of 1825, accompanied by Behr, a fellow-student from Bertin's studio. He found a whole group of artists studying neo-classical landscape; amongst them were Caruelle d'Aligny, from Lyons, and Edouard Bertin. He began by working in the Roman Campagna, then painted views in the city of Rome. His accuracy of vision, his sensitive freshness and, above all, his technical quality set him well above his companions, who were not slow to recognize his talent.

In March 1826, during the course of fifteen session on the top of the Palatine hill, he completed three studies: the present picture, the *Forum from the Palatine*, also in the Louvre, and the *View of the Farnese Gardens*, in the Phillips Memorial Gallery in Washington. Corot was always particularly fond of the first two pictures, recalling the most historic site in Rome; after his death, it was found that he had written on the stretcher of each of them 'pour le Muséum'. Corot always referred to the Museum of the Louvre under its original title; he wished to be represented among the immortals by these two landscapes.

When he decided in 1849 to submit to the Salon for the first time a painting done direct from nature (encouraged by the suppression of the jury), it was the *Coliseum* which he chose to send.

268

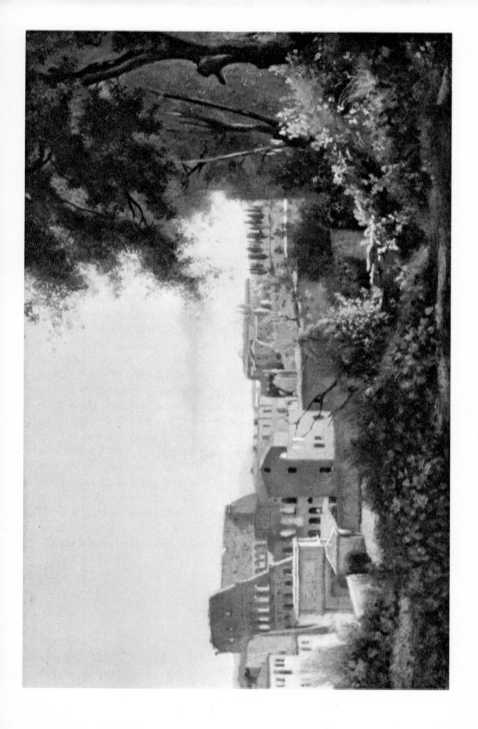

COROT, JEAN-BAPTISTE-CAMILLE, 1796–1875   *French School*
PORTRAIT OF LOUIS ROBERT AS A CHILD   Canvas

Inventory: R. F. 2601   Height 0.27 m. (10½")
Width 0.21 m. (8")

Given to the Louvre by Maurice and Christian Robert in May 1926.

Corot's life was entirely dominated by his friendships. His landscape-painting expeditions were almost always mixed up with visits to friends, during the course of the never-ending tour of France which he began anew each year. One of the homes which received him most hospitably was that of M. Robert, a magistrate of Mantes; he met him in about 1840 through Mme. Osmond, who received him in the château of Rosny, near that town. Mantes, with its old bridge and its fine Gothic church, became one of his favourite subjects. One day, for amusement, he set to work and painted a whole bathroom in M. Robert's house, in which he recorded Italian scenes for his friend.

He painted portraits of two of M. Robert's sons when they were children –Louis and Maurice. Faithful to the art to which he had dedicated his life, Corot never married; but he adored children, and no one could better express in paint their ingenuous faces, as yet unmarked by life. Other artists saw children as pretty creatures; he understood the depths of their nature. The two Robert children were painted at play; Louis in 1840, when he was three, holding a whip, and Maurice with a trumpet in 1857. These little works have something of the crystal purity of Vermeer, but with more tenderness and humanity. The child Louis did not survive, but thanks to the genius of an artist, he has achieved immortality.

After the death of Christian Robert his brother Maurice, two months before his own death, put into effect the brothers' various plans. Of the works by Corot which had belonged to their father, a proportion was set aside for the Louvre, including, with several other masterpieces, the decoration of the bathroom at Mantes, with its Italian scenes. This last, a little eighteenth-century pavilion, was destroyed during the second world war.

Inventory: R. F. 3900   Height 0.455 m. (18¹/₂″)
Signed bottom right: Th.ʳᵉ Chassériau 1841   Width 0.355 m. (14¹/₈″)

Exhibited in the Salon of 1842 (no. 62) under the title *Esther preparing to appear before Ahasuerus*. Marcotte de Quivier collection. Part of Baron Arthur Chassériau's bequest to the Louvre in 1936.

In the 1842 Salon where it was exhibited, this small picture passed almost unnoticed. For some strange reason, the lovely face was found to be lacking in charm. Louis Pesse, in the *Revue des Deux Mondes*, reproached the artist for not having given the young woman some of the beauty with which the Scriptures credit her. 'The beauty and youth of the slim, supple body is admirable,' concedes W. Ténint; 'Nothing could be better . . .; but why this long face, with haggard eyes and wild expression?'

Actually, the lengthening of the face is a mannerist trick reminiscent of Parmigianino, and often found in Chassériau's work. The heavy breasts and full lips, the vague, sleepy eyes, the slow lazy gestures, express Chassériau's languorous spirit – probably due to his Creole origin (he was born in the West Indies).

Comparing this picture with the *Suzanna bathing* and the *Marine Venus* of the 1839 Salon, also in the Louvre, one can clearly see the evolution which took place in Chassériau's work in about 1840. The *Suzanna* is still a somewhat contrived work, but the *Marine Venus* is deeply impregnated with artistic culture, more than any of Ingres' figures She has the graceful linear beauty, harmonious and flowing, of a Greek vase painting; there is nothing, even the landscape, which does not recall Greece. The *Esther* is less idealised, more voluptuous; her gloomy sensuality is reminiscent of Ingres' nudes (she has the same heavy arms as the latter, borrowed from a bourgeois standard of beauty). But another influence is also apparent here; the two slaves, one a negress, who wait on Esther recall Delacroix's harem interiors. From this period, Chassériau oscillates between these two contradictory influences, which divide his art; Delacroix' romanticism lures him away from the style of Ingres, which was his true vocation, and all too often inspires him to use heavy, vulgar colours. The present picture, however, is not yet affected by this tendency; it was painted while the career of the artist was still at the cross-roads.

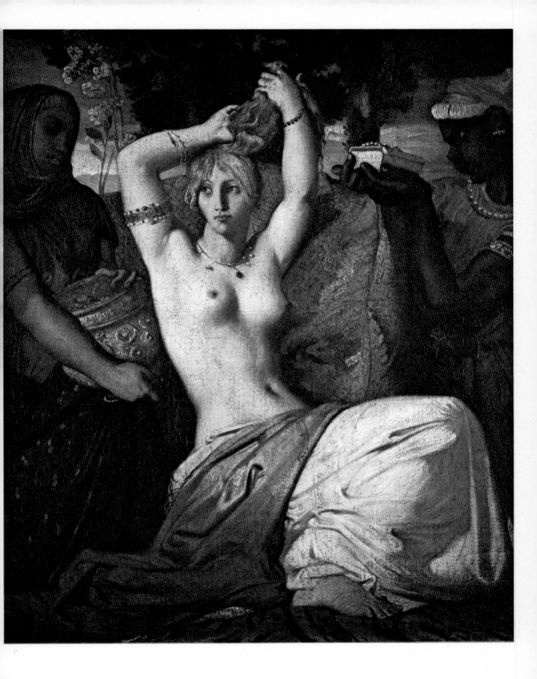

Inventory: R. F. 2630   Height 0.490 m. (19¼″)
Signed on the right: H. D.   Width 0.325 m. (12¾″)

Paul Régereau collection; Paul Bureau collection; bought by the Louvre at the Paul Bureau sale, 20 May 1927, for 701.000 francs.

Daumier lived on the Quai d'Anjou on the Ile Saint Louis, and had plenty of opportunities for observing the attitudes of the washerwomen returning from the lavoir on the Seine, as they wearily climbed the stone steps, bent beneath the weight of their bundles of washing. He was a friend of the working people, always ready to plead on their behalf; he has used these silhouettes to express the great and noble servitude of labour. Nevertheless, there is strength as well as fatigue expressed in the body of this mature woman, accompanied by her child, whom there is evidently no-one to mind at home. The summary handling of the paint avoids any suggestion of anecdote and gives a monumental quality to this little picture.

In various forms, Daumier was preoccupied with the theme of maternity (*The Market, The Soup, The Washerwoman, The Third-Class Carriage, The School*, and so on); he always shows the mother crushed by a burden of toil, and having to care for her children as well.

Daumier painted several variations of this subject, which he called *La Laveuse*. An account of a visit which the publisher Poulet-Malassis paid to his studio on the Quai d'Anjou (published by Jean Adhémar) mentions 'a washerwoman dragging a little girl along the *quais* in a high wind–with such a sad feeling about it that one feels she is taking the bundle of washing to the pawn-shop'. This does not refer to the Louvre picture, but to one in the Tate Gallery. The painting from the former Gerstenberg collection (Adhémar 115, Fuchs 72) is only a very skilful copy of the latter picture, as is also another replica in the Museum at Prague. There is also a sculptured version (apocryphal) in the Museum of Baltimore, U.S.A., of the washerwoman on the *quai* with the wind blowing out her dress. In another picture she is shown going down the steps (Fuchs 74). In the Louvre painting she is climbing them laboriously, with her child; like M. Adhémar, I think this is the picture exhibited in the 1862 Salon.

There is an almost identical replica in the Metropolitan Museum, New York, which seems to be by Daumier himself; the one in the Albright Gallery, Buffalo, is much less certain.

COURBET, GUSTAVE, 1819–1877   *French School*
THE PAINTER'S STUDIO – A REAL-LIFE ALLEGORY, 1855   Canvas

Inventory: R. F. 2257   Height 3.59 m. (141¹/₂″)
       Width 5.98 m. (236″)

Painted at Ornans, from November 1854 to March 1855. Rejected by the Salon of 1855, and included in the exhibition of his works which Courbet held in the Avenue Montaigne, in the precincts of the Exposition Universelle, inside a hut which he had built for the purpose. Exhibited at the Société des Beaux-Arts, Bordeaux, in 1865. Carried off by Durand-Ruel in February 1873, with 57 other canvases also saved from the seizure of his goods with which Courbet was threatened. Exhibited in 1873 at the Cercle Artistique of Vienne, then sent back to Ornans. At the sale held by Juliette Courbet on 9 December 1881, was bought by the dealer Haro for 21.000 francs. Included in the Courbet exhibition at the Ecole des Beaux-Arts in 1882. Withdrawn from the Haro sale on 1892 for 100.000 francs. At the sale of the elder Haro in 1897, sold to Victor Desfossés for 26.500 francs; in 1899 bought back by his widow for 60.000 francs in competition with the Louvre, who raised the bidding to 57.000 francs. Used as a painted curtain at the Hôtel Desfossés. Sold by Mme. Desfossés in 1919 to Barfazanges; sold by them to the Louvre for 900.000 francs, raised with the help of the Amis du Louvre, various art-lovers and public subscription.

276

COURBET, GUSTAVE, 1819–1877   *French School*
STREAM IN A RAVINE

Inventory: INV. R. F. 275   Height 0.90 m. (36")
Signed: G. Courbet – 65   Width 1.30 m. (51")

This picture was included in the Exposition Universelle of 1867, and was bought from the artist in the same year by the Comte de Nieuwerkerke, Director of Museum, for Napoleon III, at the price of 2.000 francs. It was part of the Emperor's personal property, and was allotted to the Louvre by the Tribunal de la Seine, along with other pictures, on 12 February 1879. In 1881 it was exhibited in the Luxembourg, with the title *Le puits noir*, which is really the name of another picture painted in 1855.

The landscape represents what is known in Franche-Comté as a *'cluse'* – a gorge through which runs a winding stream, its bed littered with rocks, between steep walls covered with wild vegetation. The stream depicted is the Loue, a capricious rivulet flowing through the village of Ornans, where Courbet was born. The artist seems to have returned to this spot several times; it can be recognised in a number of his pictures (Galerie Charpentier sale, Paris, 19 May 1950, Louvre, MNR 174, in store at the Museum of Besançon). One of these works, somewhat smaller than the present picture, exactly resembles the Louvre picture as far as the details of execution are concerned; it is dated 1866 and is in the Museum of Montpellier, to which it was given by Bruyas, Courbet's friend and patron. It is entitled *Solitude*: 'A splendid landscape, full of deepest solitude, which I have painted in the valleys of my native countryside', Courbet wrote to Bruyas, concerning this picture. 'It is perhaps the best I have ever painted; it shows the Loue walled up between vast boulders of mossy rock, with thick sunlight foliage in the background.'

Courbet loved to seek out some unspoilt corner in these lonely gorges, where the damp atmosphere conveys the impression of a strange world from which the primordial waters have only just receded. In this work, in which one senses the enthusiasm of the artist, Courbet's technique is at its peak of perfection. He has only used the brush in the background shadows; elsewhere the picture has been done with the palette knife. Courbet crushes his pigments and spreads them diagonally with his knife, thus letting underlying coats of paint show through; this creates effects of transparency and depth as rich as those obtained by means of glazes in the work of earlier artists. His splendid greens evoke the luxuriance of a semi-aquatic world where vegetation runs riot.

278

In the foregoing pages
are illustrated in colour a selection of the great masterpieces contained in
the Louvre, a fragment only of its vast treasures.
There follow in monochrome
238 reproductions of paintings that give a further taste of the incredible
richness and variety of the collection in the museum.

Bernardo Daddi The Annunciation

French School The Parement de Narbonne

Giotto St. Francis of Assisi

Italian School
St. Francis of Assisi

P. Veneziano Madonna and Child

L. Veneziano
Madonna and Child

G. da Fabriano The Presentation in the Temple

FIFTEENTH CENTURY

Attributed to Henri Bellechose
The last Communion and
the Martyrdom of St. Denis

Burgundian School
Portrait of a Lady
Margaret of York

French School Pietà of St.-Germain-des-Prés

Fouquet Juvénal des Ursins

French School Reredos of the Paris Parlement

French School Man with a Glass

Master of Moulins Child

Master of Moulins Charles Orland

School of Amiens
Priesthood of the Virgin

Master of St. Bartholomew The Descent from the Cross

School of Avignon Christ standing in the Tomb

Fra Angelico The Dream of Innocent III   SS. Peter and Paul appearing to St. Dominic   Raising of Napoleone Orsini by St.Dominic

Fra Angelico The Risen Christ   *Fra Angelico* The Death of St. Dominic

J. Bellini Madonna and Child   *Fra Angelico* Martyrdom of SS. Cosmas and Damian   *Roberti* St. Apollonia
with Lionello d'Este

Sano di Pietro Dream of St. Jerome   *Sano di Pietro* Apparition of St. Jerome and St. John the Baptist

Sano di Pietro St. Jerome and the Lion

Cosimo Tura Pietà

Baldovinetti Madonna and Child

Ghirlandaio Portrait of an old Man

Alunno da Foligno Christ Carrying His Cross

Botticelli Allegory

Botticelli Madonna and Child

285

Mantegna Parnassus

Mantegna St. Sebastian

Mantegna
Wisdom overcoming
the Vices

G. Bellini Sacra Conversazione

G. Bellini The Resurrected Christ

L. Signorelli Birth of St. John the Baptist

Cima da Conegliano Madonna and Child

R. van der Weyden The Braque Triptych

286

French School Charlotte de Roye   *French School* Jean Babou   *French School* A Musician

Corneille de Lyon Clément Marot   *Corneille de Lyon* Ch. de Cossé

Corneille de Lyon Jacques Bertaut   *F. Clouet* Pierre Quthe   *F. Pourbus* Henry IV

J. Cousin Eva Prima Pandora   *Perugino* Apollo and Marsyas   *Perugino* St. Sebastian

Perugino Combat between Love and Chastity   *Leonardo* The Annunciation

Leonardo Bacchus   *Leonardo* St. John the Baptist   *Leonardo* La Belle Ferronnière

Raphael The Madonna with the Veil

Raphael The Holy Family of Francis I

Raphael Joan of Aragon

Raphael St. Michael

Solario The Madonna with the Cushion

Boltraffio The Madonna of the Casio Family

J. di Barbari Madonna with the Fountain

S del Piombo The Visitation

289

Palma The Adoration of the Shepherds

Savoldo Portrait of a Man

Lorenzo Costa Allegory

Lorenzo Costa Mercury combating the Vices of Olympus

Andrea del Sarto Charity

Correggio Allegory of the Vices

Correggio Allegory of the Virtues

Correggio Antiope

Lorenzo Lotto St. Jerome

Titian Francis I

Titian The Pilgrims at Emmaus

Titian The Entombment

Titian Madonna and Child with SS. Stephen, Ambrose and Maurice

Titian Allegory of Alfonso d'Avalos

Titian The Man with the Glove

Titian Jupiter and Antiope (or: The Pardo Venus)

Tintoretto Susannah Bathing

Tintoretto Self-Portrait

F. Bassano The Descent from the Cross

L. Bassano The Striking of the Rock

Veronese Esther Swooning before Ahasuerus

Veronese Susannah Bathing

Veronese The Feast in the House of Simon

Veronese Portrait of Countess Nani
(La Belle Nani)

Veronese The Marriage at Cana

Veronese Destruction of Sodom

Veronese Calvary

El Greco Christ on the Cross

293

Cranach the Elder Venus   *Moro* Cardinal Granvelle's Dwarf   *Mabuse* Madonna and Child

SEVENTEENTH CENTURY

A. Le Nain Family Reunion   *M. Le Nain* The Tric-Trac Players

L. Le Nain Nativity   *L. Le Nain* A Blacksmith in his Forge   *G. de La Tour* The Adoration of the Shepherds

294

Le Valentin The Fortune-Teller

Simon Vouet Riches

G. de La Tour
St. Joseph the Carpenter

Simon Vouet
The Presentation in the Temple

Ph. de Champaigne The Echevins

Ph. de Champaigne Ex Voto de 1662

Ph. de Champaigne Richelieu

Poussin Portrait of the Artist

Poussin The Israelites gathering Manna

Poussin Ruth and Boaz

Poussin Bacchanal

Poussin The Triumph of Flora

Poussin Echo and Narcissus

Poussin The Shepherds of Arcadia

Poussin Diogenes throwing away his Bowl

Poussin The Rape of the Sabines

Claude Vignon Death of a Saintly Hermit *Le Sueur* The Death of St. Bruno *Le Sueur* The Mass of St. Martin

Le Sueur Diana, Apollo and Mercury paying homage to Love *Le Sueur* Melpomene, Erato and Polymnia

Le Sueur A Reunion of Friends

Bourdon Encampment of Soldiers and Gipsies

Claude Ulysses restores Chryseis to her Father

Claude A Sea Port at Sunset

Claude The Campo Vaccino, Rome

Claude Cleopatra disembarking at Tarsus

Baugin Still life with Chessboard

J. Linard Basket of Flowers

Tournier Christ on the Cross   *Jouvenet* The Descent from the Cross   *Mignard* Portrait of the Artist

A. Carracci Hunting Scene

Caravaggio Alof de Wignacourt

Il Gentileschi The Holy Family Resting   *Domenico Fetti* Melancholy   *Guercino* St. Benedict and St. Francis of Assisi

Domenichino St. Cecilia   *Ribera* Adoration of the Shepherds   *Zurbaran* St. Bonaventure and
the Envoys of the Emperor Paleologus

Salvator Rosa Battle Scene   *Murillo* The Miracle of St. James

Murillo The Virgin of Seville   *Murillo* The Beggar Boy   *Frans Hals* Descartes

Rembrandt Self-Portrait, bare-headed   *Rembrandt* Hendrickje Stoffels   *Rembrandt* Flayed Ox

Rembrandt Self-Portrait as an old Man

Rembrandt Holy Family   *Rembrandt* The Angel Raphael

Potter Horse in a Meadow

Claesz Still life

Terborch Young Woman entertaining a Soldier

J. van Ruisdael The Thicket

Pieter de Hooch The Card-Players

Gerard Dou The Dropsical Woman

Van der Heyden The Château of the Dukes of Burgundy

EIGHTEENTH CENTURY

Largillière Portrait of the Artist

Watteau Jupiter and Antiope

Watteau La Finette

Watteau L'Indifférent

Desportes Portrait of the Artist as a Huntsman

Nattier A Repentant Woman in the Desert

F. de Troy The Lute-Player

J.-B. Pater The Toilette

303

Quentin La Tour D'Alembert   *Quentin La Tour* Madame Pompadour   *Chardin* The Benedicite

Chardin Self-Portrait   *Chardin* Pipe and Drinking Glasses

Fragonard Imaginary Portrait   *Greuze* The Broken Pitcher   *Boucher* The Déjeuner

304

Fragonard Le Feu aux Poudres   *Fragonard* The Music Lesson

G.-B. Tiepolo The Last Supper   *Guardi* The Bucentaur

Vigée-Lebrun The Artist and her Daughter   *Goya* F. Guillemardet   *Goya* Spanish Lady

305

David The Consecration of Napoleon as Emperor

David Self-Portrait

David The Sabines

David The Horatii

David Madame de Verminac

David Madame de Sériziat

David Monsieur de Sériziat

Géricault Riderless Horse Races, Rome

Géricault Mounted Officer of the Imperial Guard

Géricault The Plaster Kiln

Gros Napoleon at Eylau

Gros Les Pestiférés de Jaffa

Girodet de Roucy Atala in the Tomb

Boilly The Arrival of the Diligence

Delacroix
The Duke of Mornay's Apartment

Delacroix Self-Portrait

Delacroix The Massacres of Scio

Delacroix Dante's Barque

Delacroix Liberty at the Barricades

Delacroix The Death of Sardanapalus

Delacroix The Battle of Taillebourg

Delacroix Entry of the Crusaders into Constantinople

Ingres La Grande Odalisque

F. Gérard The Countess Regnaud

Ingres La Source

Ingres Portrait of Madame Panckouke

Ingres La Petite Baigneuse

Ingres Portrait of M. Rivière

Ingres Portrait of Mlle. Rivière

Corot Self-Portrait

Corot Lady in Blue

Corot The Woman with the Pearl

Corot The Belfry, Douai

Corot Château Saint-Ange

Corot Saint-André-de-Morvan

Corot The Bridge at Narni

Corot Souvenir of Mortefontaine

Corot The Cathedral of Sens

Corot The Cathedral of Chartres

Corot Maurice Robert as a Child

Corot Florence from the Boboli Gardens

Corot The Château of Rosny

Corot Le Pont de Mantes

Th. Rousseau Storm Effect

Decamps The Defeat of the Cimbri

Chassériau The Two Sisters, 1843

J.-F. Millet Spring

J.-F. Millet The Angelus

Courbet Portrait of Berlioz

J.-F. Millet The Church at Gréville

Courbet The Burial at Ornans

Courbet La Roche de Dix Heures

Th. Rousseau The Oaks

Courbet The Haunt of the Deer

LIST OF ILLUSTRATIONS

Colour plates are indicated by the page number in italic

314

315

319

321

INDEX OF NAMES

327